Beauty for Ashes

Beauty for Ashes

SELECTED PROSE
& RELATED DOCUMENTS

Francis Warner

With CD
Francis Warner
musician–poet
in performance

2013

The publisher wishes to thank
the Albert and Temmy Latner Family Foundation
for a generous grant towards the publication of this book;
H. A. Latner for sponsoring the CD;
and John & Lucy Stopford for sponsoring the colour plates.

Published by
Colin Smythe Limited
Gerrards Cross, Buckinghamshire SL9 8XA

First edition, 2012.
Second edition, revised with additions, 2013.

A CIP catalogue record for this book is available
from the British Library

978-0-86140-184-1

Text prepared by Alison Wiblin
Index compiled by Susan Reynolds
Designed and typeset in Cycles by Libanus Press, Marlborough
Printed and bound in Great Britain by Apple Litho (Bristol) Limited

'. . . to comfort all that mourn . . .
to give unto them beauty for ashes'
ISAIAH 61. *vv.*2–3

For Martin Michael

In the worst bombing of the war you came,
Born on the floor, through that night's massacre,
Under a table, lullabied in flame
And noise earth-shaking, tiny voyager.
Now, at the other end of life, alone,
I sort through an old attic box and find
Your gas-mask, its red rubber dry as bone
With kite-shaped nose and goggle-eyes dirt-blind,
Its metal drum, blue, rusted, still intact
With patterned perforations underneath.
I used to fit it round your head, compact,
Secure, as you were growing infant teeth.
      In evil you were our pin-prick of light,
      Brother undimmed, our new dawn since that night.

Contents

Introduction to Lecture

May I thank the University of Cambridge, and in particular Dr Rebecca Lingwood and her colleagues at the Institute of Continuing Education at Madingley Hall, for inviting me to recall these events of some seventy years ago, through which I lived.

Their invitation has compelled me to turn round and face experiences I have spent a lifetime trying to forget.

In the process I have found that, far from being distant memories, they are immediate and clear as the first glass splinter of bomb-blast that cut my shielding hand.

May I also thank two of my colleagues: Dr John Thompson for providing the photographs by William Vandivert, war photographer in Europe for *Life* magazine 1940–45, for what for some of them is their first public showing, and David Goode for giving us this evening's piano recital in homage to musicians of the Blitz.

This lecture is dedicated to the memory of my eldest brother, David Hugh Warner, 1932–2008.

Francis Warner in 1941

Armageddon and Faith

A survivor's meditation on the Blitz, 1940–45

Cambridge University's Commemorative Lecture for the seventieth
anniversary of the Blitz. 19 February 2011 at Madingley Hall

If you stand on Epsom Downs near the racecourse, in the meadow behind
the Grand Stand, and look north you will see below you Epsom as the start
of a conurbation that reaches right up to London's Wembley Stadium, easily
recognized from this vantage point today by its huge arch.

With the exception of the arch, this is how the Nazi bombers flying in
across the Channel saw London, marking especially the Leatherhead railway
line from the South Coast that, as it comes in to Epsom, divides into two rail
arteries supplying Clapham Junction and London's Victoria and Waterloo
stations.

The London Defence Line ran through Epsom, and the last battle to
defend London was planned to be fought here. Preparations, anti-tank
defences, can still be seen in the grounds of Manor Park estate.

Epsom, then, was their first, and particularly their last target. If raiders
were still carrying bombs as they turned for home, they would jettison them
over Sutton, Ewell and finally Epsom as they saw the green countryside of
the Downs approaching. This air corridor was known as bomb alley.

The sky above Epsom Downs, therefore, was where British single-seater
Spitfires and Hurricanes defending London would try, over open ground, to
intercept the Nazi bombers – the two-seater Junkers dive-bombers, the
Heinkel III K, mark 5s, and the Dornier 215s, each with their four-man crews
and their three mobile machine-guns.

The Spitfires and the Hurricanes were faster and more manoeuvrable
than these, but they also had to contend with fighter escorts flying above
the bombers, one- and two-seat Messerschmitts, which were as swift as the

British planes, and could have up to six machine-guns, as well as a cannon firing through the airscrew hub.

The Battle of Britain lasted from 10 July to 31 October 1940, and my third birthday fell during that October. For the next five, formative years of childhood I experienced at immediate hand my country fighting all-out war. Through most of our first decade my brothers and I knew nothing else. Every day was dominated by it. Every night was pitch black, and for long stretches of time exhaustingly interrupted.

Throughout that astonishingly beautiful summer and autumn, and indeed daily from 8 August until 31 October, the Royal Air Force and the Luftwaffe could be seen by everyone, spiralling above us killing each other.

In addition, overlapping, from 7 September began the night Blitz concentrated on London for fifty-seven consecutive sunsets until the all clear sounded at four or five in the morning. Thereafter frequent heavy bombing continued all winter and spring until the following May.

The Blitz then became intermittent as other cities were bombed, with the onslaught on London intensifying in January 1943. Worse was that of January 1944. Then came the arrival of the 'doodlebugs' or V1 rockets, which were followed by the huge and terrifying V2 rockets against which there was no defence. That was during the last eleven months of the war: but in no year was Epsom spared being strafed and bombed.

Perhaps War Office statistics may evoke the ferocity, if not the experience, of five years of Blitzkrieg focused on the little Surrey town of Epsom, with the next town, Ashtead, two miles away to the south-west, and Ewell one and a half miles to the north-east; Epsom, this sitting target at the foot of the Downs that tried so hard to shield our wild cradling and uncertain childhood:

192 houses annihilated.
413 houses rendered uninhabitable.
12,234 houses damaged [including our two Vicarages].
Approx. 440 high explosive bombs dropped on Epsom,
    in addition to

Many thousands of incendiary bombs, [and]
Many thousands of personnel (or butterfly) bombs

all raining down on four square miles.

At the crest of the Downs, as you leave the racecourse and start to walk downhill from the meadow along Downs Road, you come to Epsom cemetery. In that peaceful setting is a neat set of war graves holding eleven of those young men who gave their lives defending us. Each of them was buried by my father, who was Vicar of Epsom; and there, as he wished, with my mother he lies buried near them.

With four of his sons under nine in 1940, and two brothers on active service, he cared deeply for the school-leavers and young men in their early twenties fighting in the sky, at sea like his own brothers, and on land. He sensed their loneliness as they waited, asked his parishioners to open their houses to them, and created a free 'In and Out Club' by Epsom's central clock tower for the troops (he was also Officiating Chaplain to the Armed Forces); vulnerable, many far from home – Canadians, Poles; as the war ground on, from all over the Commonwealth, later, the United States . . .

By the eve of D-Day thousands had used this meeting-place gratefully, as their letters testify. The town so seethed with khaki-dressed forces personnel that we children were unable to push our way through the middle of the road.

Suddenly, all were gone. That Tuesday morning the Headmistress told us to go home because sixty-five miles south the invasion of France had begun, and our soldiers were fighting their way up the beaches. By now, of course, we knew a number of them. Her simple words burned into our brains.

We left, spending the rest of the day by the wireless. That was 6 June 1944, the beginning of the last year of the war, of full Armageddon; four long years after the Battle of Britain in 1940.

To return to that battle.

As you leave the cemetery and turn downhill, the road eventually becomes Church Street, where Epsom's parish church, St Martin's – a powerful and defiant architectural statement in flint completed in 1908 – towers. Down the flight of steps from the West Door and across the parade ground can be seen Ye Olde King's Head pub, 26 Church Street; and a few buildings further along is number 18, the beautiful, large Queen Anne Vicarage with substantial garden behind, where – until we were bombed out – I was brought up.

Goering was under criticism for the continual loss of his raiding aircraft, and began a massive thrust to break the R.A.F. at midday on 27 September 1940, lasting through the night and on.

It was in this many-windowed brick house during this, one of the heaviest bombing raids of the war, with over one thousand enemy aircraft stacked four miles into the sky above us while we tried through unimaginable noise to sleep in the reinforced cellar underneath, that, in the shuttered and candlelit dining room above us, on a mattress on the floor so she could roll under the table if the house went down, without painkillers, my mother gave birth to my younger brother.

Puzzled about her sleeping arrangements I had asked 'Will you be all right, Mummy?' as we descended to the cellar, not understanding that she was facing the most terrifying experience of her or any woman's life. 'Yes, darling; I'll be all right. God bless you,' she said quietly.

As was appropriate her Blitz baby was named Martin, after the patron saint of our church, and Michael, as this was now Michaelmastide, and there was, in all truth, 'war in heaven'.

In the garden of the old Vicarage was a fecund and spreading mulberry tree, still there today. We enjoyed its fruit, but more important to us boys were its leaves, which we fed to our silkworms.

David, my eldest brother, was adept at spinning off their gold silk. He was in charge of all four of us, and never showed the slightest fear, however menacing destruction around us. We looked up to him, so were blithely confident all would be well. Our cause was self-evidently right, and the British always won.

But in case Hitler attacked our rocking horse, our only expensive toy, David called a Council of War on the garden steps to the cellar. He proposed we find brushes, green paint, and also some mulberry-coloured to daub spots on the green as it was summer; and together we painted the wooden horse as it rocked.

Scraping off the old paint. David, mounted, organizing

Now camouflaged, it was dragged by us under the mulberry leaves so that if the house fell we should still have our toy (we'd seen Mother burying some of the family silver in the garden), and with luck Nazi pilots might not catch sight of it, thanks to our ingenuity.

Annie, our elderly maid who lived with us, died. As the months went by it became clear that this unwieldy house was more than Mother could manage. What with the new baby, unremittingly broken nights, the never-assuaged need to feed five hungry males (we were fortunate, though, in having in the large garden an area for vegetables), and the claims on a Vicar's wife of sorrow and danger throughout the parish, the pressures began to tell on her health.

When a high explosive bomb missed our church but wiped out the buildings on the other side of Ye Olde King's Head, it was time to move. All our windows were blown out. Rubble, hot shrapnel, and grief were on our doorstep, and ash mottled everything. In addition, Nature having overlooked to supply mankind with a means of side-head sneezing, we brothers had to blow the all-pervading white-powdered dust out of each other's ears before pillow-time.

So we moved to safety – one street away; to a new Vicarage, number 13 Worple Road, just beyond the little school, Miss Chadband's Salcombe House, where I went in the mornings to learn my alphabet in a cellar full of pit props holding up the ceiling, in case . . .

This was a necessary precaution. In 1942, during my first term, Petworth Boys' School, twenty-six miles south-west, was bombed in a daylight raid, killing the Headmaster and thirty-one others, boys and staff. They are buried in a mass grave in the cemetery on the Horsham Road. A stick of eight bombs spread at the Epsom Convent School in Dorking Road causing devastation just missed the school: but during my second term, on 20 January 1943 in Catford, twelve miles north-east, on that same Cherbourg to London radio-beamed flight path over us as Petworth, Sandhurst Road School was deliberately targeted, according to eye-witnesses, by a low-flying aircraft with machine-gun and bomb, leaving thirty-one children aged from five to fifteen, and six members of staff, laid out dead on the playground. A further seven children died later in hospital.

From these facts we schoolchildren, however young, could not be shielded; nor would we forget. At Christmastide when I hear, read from the lectern, of Herod's massacre of the innocents:

Children's bodies and those of some of their teachers lie covered by tarpaulins after the bombing of Sandhurst Road School, Catford   *© Imperial War Museum*

> In Rama was there a voice heard, lamentation . . . Rachel weeping
> for her children, and would not be comforted, because they are
> not. *Matthew 2.v 18.*

my mind goes back to those school deaths each side of me in my first two
terms at school; and now to those young bones in their mass graves.

Our new Vicarage was by the bowling-green, a well-built, two-storeyed
house with a bay window each side the front door. One day I walked home
from Salcombe House School, past the bowling-green, to our new home, and
as there was no one in, and it was a perfect day, I went to the garden and sat
in the apple tree.

I looked up.

High above came a speck streaking into this vast, neck-wrenching
expanse of blue, a sun-gleamed diamond slitting open the air-mail summer
sky to leave in its track a narrow line of milk that spread, dispersed, and faded
into altostratus cloud.

Coming in at an angle from over the racecourse on Epsom Downs
flashed another. As it approached the first, I could hear above the distant
drone of their engines a new sound, like the cigarette-card I'd wedged into
the spokes of my cycle to make it clatter like a motor bike.

The two streaks of milk crossed, curdled, and continued on their way
making a giant kiss across heaven, until the first began to arch into a
white rainbow, to corkscrew, then disappear, shedding a flimsy mushroom
suspended in the sky dangling a kicking man.

By this stage I had seen many a swirling dog-fight above us – one could
not miss them – but this was the first I had watched alone. At that moment
something in my childhood understanding grew up.

My mother's sister, my Aunt Robine, now came to live with us, bringing
their mother, my grandmother. Robine took a teaching job at the Orchard
School, on the other side of town, where I followed my brothers. She
escorted us there each day through Rosebery Park, the youngest keeping
up on a scooter. She wrote in a little notebook of this time:

> I was in Epsom . . . when a German plane turned up and began

to machine-gun the road. We (the pedestrians) ran to the nearest house, and were amused to be assured by a voice with a strong American accent: 'You're safe here. This is neutral ground. It is an annex of the Embassy in London.'

Notebook, p.17.

Sometimes we had to dive into the air-raid shelter in the Park on our way to and fro, but on the whole daylight raids were few, and quite short.

But for a long time we had nightly air-raids. There were some exciting nights, as we were in 'bomb-alley' . . . However the Germans were so punctual that you could set your watch by them: which was a great help in organising bedtime.

Notebook, pp.18–19.

There, with self-effacing humour and understatement, she closes the door. What I can add is what it felt like in our second Vicarage *after* bedtime: upstairs at the tape-crossed window armed with our *Aircraft Recognition* book, peeping with my brothers through the blackout at the moon on the barrage balloons as they swayed like bloated, drunken dolphins; the banshee wailing of the siren bomber-alerts, rising and falling, up and down. The odd lack of any other noise at all.

Then the throb of bombers overhead, hundreds of them, and that feeling, that surge of relief, as our Spitfires and Hurricanes arrived (we knew their distinctive sound, when we could hear them); the distant double boom of anti-aircraft guns; the night sky scissored by sharp-etched, probing beams of searchlights: on one occasion watching with heart-stopping clarity a Junkers 87 riding down the searchlight beam to dive-bomb artillery – and our debate over which had won.

The inevitable knock at the door, and a voice telling us to get away from the window, dress quickly, and come down to the Anderson shelter or hide under the stairs.

As the shelter was at the end of the garden among the trees, we used it sparingly; but when we did, we absorbed with the night air on our cheeks a sky deafeningly full as far as the eye could glean. Close to us dull red glow of cigarettes pricked the darkness by the bowling green as fire-watchers in their round, black, tin hats trod over the rubble, marking craters, warning, going about their work.

Our lives and our nation were under threat. That awareness never left us; but we lived with it, as children do, with a stoic calm, assuming it to be normal.

Colin Perry, who was older than us – eighteen – caught our outlook and responses well:

> 10 July 1940
>
> Tonight is said to be the night for the German invasion . . . England today reminds me of David; Germany and her conquered lands of Goliath. It came to me . . . as I visualised over a map that I was a watcher miles above the earth, viewing the German invasion of this country. Britain seemed so tiny, so forlorn, that as I saw the waves of aircraft, the mass of shipping, converging upon her shores from so vast an enemy territory I could see nothing which could prevent the success of that invasion. The British were rushing hither and thither . . . bombed here, bombed there. The British air fleet seemed puny as it attempted to destroy and wreak retaliation on the enemy. I could see absolutely nothing which could stem the sadistic, degenerate, all-destroying Nazi war machine, as it descended upon those green, peace-loving shores. It was then that I remembered David slew Goliath, and God was in His Heaven, and I no longer feared. Indeed I lifted up my heart, and thanked God I was privileged to live in such momentous times.
>
> At any moment – now, as I write this – the attack may commence. We are awaiting with calm fortitude for the inevitable. Air raids, massed murder, total devastation of beautiful buildings: the unknown: and gas, too, maybe, to poison our food and pollute our water . . . We have witnessed countries torn to shreds by this

Moloch of our age. We, alone, await his onslaught, calm, confident, determined.

　　Despite all this . . . it is not the war which occupies the whole
of my inner mind, but 'the Girl in the ABC [café]' . . . She smiled
at me over the waitress's shoulder today . . . I hope she has a
pleasant voice.

Colin Perry, *Boy in the Blitz*, London (Sutton Publishing), 2000, pp.16–17, 21–22.

Beside Colin Perry, speaking for us who were children, we must set the
words of Churchill shortly before, on 18 June 1940, broadcasting to all and
each of us on the wireless.

What General Weygand called the 'Battle of France' is over. I
expect that the battle of Britain is about to begin. Upon this battle
depends the survival of Christian civilization . . . The whole fury
and might of the enemy must very soon be turned on us. Hitler
knows that he will have to break us in this island or lose the
war. If we can stand up to him, all Europe may be free and the
life of the world may move forward into broad, sun-lit uplands.
But if we fail, then the whole world, including the United States,
including all that we have known and cared for, will sink into
the abyss of a new dark age made more sinister, and perhaps
more protracted, by the lights of perverted science. Let us therefore brace ourselves to our duties and so bear ourselves that, if
the British Empire and its Commonwealth last for a thousand
years, men will still say, 'This was their finest hour'.

Charles Ede (ed.), *The War Speeches of Winston Churchill*, vol 1, London,
(Cassell) 1951, pp.206–207.

Churchill's great speech crystallized and defined our approach to the ordeal.
　　What were the feelings of those, only a year or two older than Colin Perry,
answering Churchill's call and doing their duty in the air? Here
is David Crook of 609 Squadron high above us on 27 November during
the very hours my brother Martin was struggling to come into our darkened
candlelit world:

Soon we saw a squadron of Me 110s circling over Swanage at 25,000 feet, waiting to protect their bombers on their return. We immediately turned towards the enemy fighters and started to climb above them . . . Generally we were outnumbered by anything from three to one to up to ten to one. But on this glorious occasion there were fifteen of them and twelve of us, and we made the most of it.

We were close to them now and we started to dive. I think that these moments just before the clash are the most gloriously exciting moments of life. You sit there behind a great engine that seems as vibrant and alive as you are yourself, your thumb waits expectantly on the trigger, and your eyes watch the gun sights through which in a few seconds an enemy will be flying in a veritable ball of fire.

All around you, in front and behind, there are your friends too, all eager and excited, all thundering down together into the attack! The memory of such moments . . .

Patrick Bishop, *Battle of Britain*, London (Quercus), 2009, p.362.

To us everything seemed heightened. On Sunday the collect for morning service felt as though it had been written for us that dawn:

O God, who art the author of peace and lover of concord . . .
Defend us thy humble servants in all assaults of our enemies;
that we, surely trusting in thy defence, may not fear the power
of any adversaries . . .

Even the daily psalms spoke on our behalf:

Mine enemies are daily in hand to swallow me up: for they
be many that fight against me, O thou most Highest.
Nevertheless, though I am sometime afraid: yet put I my trust in
thee.   Ps.56, vv 2–3.

Even pilots could be 'sometime afraid'. Here at Madingley we remember

the American dead in their beautiful cemetery on our hill. Raymond W. Wild
was a B-17 pilot with the 92nd Bomb Group (H) stationed down the road
in Podington, Northamptonshire, three years later, in the autumn of 1943.
He said:

> There isn't anybody that wants to get killed . . . you'd think, 'Oh
> boy, I'm not going on this, this'll kill me.' And then you'd say,
> 'What I'll do is, I'll wait a while and then I'll go on sick call and
> get out of it.' Then you'd go down to the airplane and you'd
> figure, 'Well, I'll go on sick call later.' And then you'd see every-
> body get in their planes and you'd know they were just as fright-
> ened as you were, and you'd think 'What the hell, I'll go about a
> hundred miles and find something wrong with the airplane.'
> But they had this tradition that an Eighth Air Force sortie never
> turned back from the target. So, in the end, you didn't dare turn
> back. Pride made you go.
> Philip Kaplan, *Bombers – The Aircrew Experience*, London (Arum Press),
> 2000, p.18.

This is far from the Battle of Britain Public School ethos in which from an
early age – in my case from eight – we were toughened, and we have just seen
exemplified in David Crook experiencing 'the most gloriously exciting
moments of life.'

But, we must remember, the bomber pilots, if shot down, did not fall
into an English village. Here is Churchill again two months after that speech
of his I read to you. He spoke this on 20 August 1940.

> The great air battle which has been in progress over this island
> for the last few weeks has recently attained a high intensity
> . . . All hearts go out to the fighter pilots, whose brilliant actions
> we see with our own eyes day after day; but we must never
> forget that all the time, night after night, month after month,
> our bomber squadrons travel far into Germany, find their
> targets . . . often under the heaviest fire, often with serious loss,
> with deliberate careful discrimination, and inflict shattering

blows upon the whole of the technical and war-making structure of Nazi power.

Charles Ede (ed.), *The War Speeches of Winston Churchill*, vol 1,
pp.239–241.

There was one bomber pilot I knew, and loved. His name was John Hugh
Davis. Co-pilot of a somewhat primitive Armstrong-Whitworth 'Whitley',
his first flight was with his squadron attacking the Nazi battle-cruisers
Scharnhorst and Gneisenau at Brest, where the warships were in dry-dock.
All aircraft returned safely.

He was just twenty-two when, on his second sortie over Germany, he was
shot down, caught in a fire-wall of flak. Flames began to spread through his
aircraft as it faltered into its descent. The nineteen-year-old pilot beside
John, at the controls, on reaching for his parachute from the hook behind
him and finding it missing, panicked.

'Don't worry, take mine', said John, and helped him into it, and out of
the plane.

It was now high time for John
to jump, so he picked up the fallen
parachute, which had just time to
open before he landed in a tree. It
was 15 September 1941.

For three years and eight
months John was a prisoner of war
in the Nazi camps, enduring all the
deprivations, and long marches, we
find so hard to imagine.

One morning they woke and
found all the guards had gone.
About half the camp's prisoners
left at once for the woods. He
and others remained to see what
would happen. All who left were
killed. The Allies liberated those

Warrant Officer John Hugh Davis in 1941

who remained a day or two later, and he arrived home for de-briefing on
11 May 1945.

His medals, which he never applied for, have just arrived and are in this
room, in the keeping of his only child, Penelope, whom I married. John's
granddaughter, Miranda, is in New Zealand, but here is his grandson
Benedict, who himself has just had his twenty-third birthday.

What we learned in the Vicarage was the meaning, and consequences, of
some deaths. My father spoke little of his nightly visits to the burning
bombed and dying; the moments of bereavement; his cleaning, for instance,
of a husband's brains, blown out by shrapnel, from the wall of a distraught
wife's – or rather widow's – living room. Our parents protected us from
these. I only learned of this when reading his biography. But in total war even
the youngest will have to face the fact of sudden and shocking death soon,
sometimes in oblique ways.

My mother asked us four boys to stay in this afternoon because the children of a friend of our parents, boys we knew well, were coming round at
short notice. Please would we play a long game of 'Monopoly' with
them, keep cheerful, and ask no questions.

We knew their father had recently been reported 'killed on active service', so we were only too glad to help in this way. But that was not it.

Their eldest brother, Colin, had become a Prefect at Epsom College. The
death of his father hit him hard, and he was cautioned by the Headmaster
about his recent behaviour. Colin's mother had spoken to him to say he must
grow up, take the responsibilities of the eldest man now in the family, and
cause no more complaints from the school.

Colin had tried, but once more tripped on some behavioural issue; been
called to the Headmaster's study and stripped of his Prefectship.

He had left that study, gone straight home, this morning, climbed up into
the loft and, with his chemistry set, killed himself.

This was near the end of that long, bitter war. I had encountered my first
moral crisis four years earlier when, working just outside our Vicarage in my
short trousers, doing my bit for the war effort, preparing for the coming
invasion, I was trying to lasso with a noose of cotton a fat bumble bee. My

hope was that as I held the other end of the cotton the bee would fly above my hand like a barrage balloon, so when the Nazis arrived outside our house, I should have an effective weapon: better still if I could have a fleet of several bumble bees, buzzing in an attacking ball.

Workmen were filling in holes in Worple Road. One, older, with a war wound and looking ill, dug slightly apart. He saw me at my front door and made a gesture showing he was thirsty. I went in, filled a brown tin mug with water, and took it out to him. He drank quickly. Then he smiled his thanks and, putting a red plastic disc in the mug for me, handed it back; but he never spoke.

I assumed it was one of those red discs we used at the nearest British Restaurant for cheap, off-ration meals. In my bedroom I looked at it, and to my horror saw it showed the hated swastika. You can see it because I have it here. The road worker, it dawned on me, must have been a Nazi prisoner-of-war. Guilt engulfed me. I had carried Hitler's triumph sign into our home; betrayed our country in its hour of need. I was evil. And yet . . . Was I? War was not as straightforward as I thought. I hid it in my metal badges' box for seventy years and told no one, until today.

Or rather, yesterday. Preparing for this lecture, I asked a colleague over lunch what he thought it was.

The Swastika at the bottom is self-evident. Above it are the words Gau Ost-Hannover. Gau, he told me, is an old German word, revived by the mythologizing Nazis, and here means Administrative District: so the words translate as Administrative District of East Hannover.

Above this, in large capitals in the Old German script style, are three letters:  N.S.V. These, he revealed, stand for Nationalsozialistische Volkswohlfahrt, which means National Socialist (or Nazi) People's Welfare.

Donors, when Nazis came round with their collecting boxes, were given a small souvenir gratitude-gift of negligible value. More generous donors were presented with a disc, such as this, which could be worn as a lapel badge.

And what was the National Socialist Welfare programme to which this raiding machine-gunner (he was too old to be a pilot), this wounded and thirsty prisoner-of-war had been so generous a donor? One that ran children's homes, provided assistance to pregnant mothers, and so on.

That small boy with the brown tin mug is still morally puzzled, seventy years later.

It was not only badges we collected, but also matchboxes, cigarette cards, and – when lucky – 'tin toadstools'. After a street had been strafed, most bullets had sunk into the road surface if it was soft; but if they hit the stone curb they turned into heavy blunted mushrooms. If we were out on the Downs, though, and a sudden dog-fight erupted above us, we would 'listen for snakes': hear the pitter-patter and rustle in grass of – we could never see them fall – a squirt or two landing underfoot having missed their evading target. We'd find warm bullets of both kinds – a small boy's ultimate treasure.

How, you may begin to wonder, did the young do their courting? I will show you with an example rather more successful than that of Colin Perry and his unaware girl in the A.B.C. café.

Henry Chadwick, who was reading music at Magdalene College, Cambridge, and soon to embark on his third year, had met Margaret Brownrigg – also a musician – at a Sunday tea party at St Paul's vicarage. (Bedford College, London, where she was studying, had been evacuated to Newnham College, Cambridge.) Henry was smitten.

He invited her to a Promenade Concert at the Queen's Hall, London, to hear Moiseiwitsch playing a piano concerto on 7 September 1940.

As this was in the vacation, Peggy and her brother Stewart boarded their train from Wimbledon, but on the way in to central London the sirens sounded. Raiding bombers were flying overhead in a steady stream, so the train stopped for twenty minutes and all the passengers lay on the floor to avoid bomb-blast and glass.

During the Prom the sirens sounded from 5.00–7.00 pm, and then from 8.00 pm until 5.00 am, when the weary audience emerged to see the dawn sky lit up as the London docks were on fire.

Moiseiwitsch had entertained the audience into the small hours by improvising with the orchestra a 'toy symphony', after the example of Haydn, in which those lying on the floor could participate.

Here is Henry's letter, written a few hours later:

> Somewhere in High Wycombe
> 8th September 1940

My dear Peggy,

I am so glad that you got home safely last night, even though it was such a business. I was possibly rather a fool to leave cover and to walk down to Piccadilly Circus during the raid as that part was bombed a bit. Actually I was very envious of you sleeping in the Queen's Hall as the noise was terrific and I did not get to sleep till well after the 'all clear'. There was one particular bomb which I heard whining as it fell; it must have been within 1/4 mile, – actually for a moment I imagined it was the end!

Thanks so much for coming to the concert with me. I thoroughly enjoyed listening to the music, but it was made even more so by having you and Stewart (or does he spell it Stuart?) to enjoy it with! I hope to go again on Wednesday night to the Brahms concert, if the Hall still stands [It was destroyed by a direct hit, an incendiary bomb through the roof, some months later.]; if you can take it, do come up again. I believe a lot of our camp officers are coming too – as Donald Creaton etc.

My sister and I arrived here at 5.00 [pm]. The place is packed out with people who found last night's raid too hot, and it was 10.00 [pm] before we were fixed up for bed and breakfast. However, all's well that ends well and I am now sitting on my bed deciding that 12 hours sleep might just about see me through.

'A little folding of the hands.'

Yours aye,

Henry

Henry Chadwick was indeed successful, and with their three daughters Lady Chadwick is with us here this afternoon.

With these introductory thoughts in your minds, I should now like to take you back to the beginning of my and my family's particular witness to these events; to 1936, three years before the outbreak of World War II; the year before I was born.

In my Aunt Robine's tiny notebook she wrote:

> During this time I had some interesting holidays . . . a friend and
> I had a trip in Germany, seeing Heidelburg . . . and going on the
> Rhine. This was the year the Germans walked into the Rhineland,
> and Hitler was getting into power – Police and Military hastened
> to be the first to salute each other in the street, starting 100 yards
> off to be in time. They looked absurd.   *Notebook*, p 7.

Absurd they may have looked, but war in Spain had begun in earnest, and in July 1936, while Hitler was at Bayreuth for the Wagner Festival, a messenger came with a letter from General Franco asking for his help in the Spanish Civil War. Ignoring the advice of his Government not to get involved, Hitler eventually sent his crack Condor Legion of Junkers and Heinkel bombers and Heinkel fighters to carpet-bomb – under Franco's orders and when the streets were seething with people – the defenceless market town of Guernica, the ancient capital of the Basques. Those who tried to escape to the fields were hunted from the air by the Heinkel fighters and machine-gunned. It was April 26 1937.

We know Picasso's great painting, begun a few days later on hearing the news.

What Hitler wanted was to see how civilians, and also his own pilots, would react to carpet bombing – what he was later to call 'Koventrieren': to annihilate or raze a city to the ground, a word coined after his destruction of our Coventry and its cathedral.

In this dress rehearsal of Guernica he found he need not have worried. Hitler could now make this his new weapon in his coming war.

In October 1937 I was born at Bishopthorpe, in the Vicarage, under the protecting shade of the Archbishop of York's palace. My father was Vicar of Bishopthorpe – population 900 – but, more important in retrospect, also personal chaplain to the Archbishop, a man he had long admired, William Temple. He was to remain his personal Chaplain until the end of Temple's life.

Perhaps part of the attraction of this young priest was his growing family. The Temples had no children; so William became Godfather to my brother Andrew, and Mrs Temple, Frances, was my Godmother – hence my name. He christened me on St Stephen's Day, 1937, from his wife's arms.

Temple's thinking greatly influenced my parents, both of whom, like Temple, had read 'Greats' at Oxford. On Temple's death in October 1944 my father compiled a selection from the Archbishop's writings, published as *Daily Readings from William Temple*. William, now Archbishop of Canterbury, had been for some years the moral voice of Britain. His social concern for instance led him to being one of the urgent moving spirits calling for what became after his death our National Health Service. As Britain prevaricated in the face of coming war, it was he whose clarity of moral thought complemented Churchill's fierce if lonely political clear-sightedness.

The Prime Minister, Neville Chamberlain, returned from Munich, his third personal meeting with Hitler, and told the House of Commons he had brought back with him 'peace in our time', and that it was 'peace with honour'. He now asked for cordial relations between this country and Germany. The House was ecstatic; hailed him as 'a great leader and peacemaker'.

William Temple, Archbishop of York with his godson, Andrew, the author's brother, in July 1935

Churchill rose.

> The Prime Minister desires to see cordial relations between this
> country and Germany. There is no difficulty at all in having
> cordial relations between the peoples. Our hearts go out to them.
> But they have no power . . . there can never be friendship between
> the British democracy and the Nazi power, that power which
> spurns Christian ethics, which cheers its onward course by a
> barbarous paganism, which vaunts the spirit of aggression and
> conquest, which derives strength and perverted pleasure from
> persecution, and uses, as we have seen, with pitiless brutality the
> threat of murderous force. That power cannot ever be the trusted
> friend of the British democracy.
>
> *The War Speeches*, Vol I, pp.32–33.

It was a brave speech.

William Temple's voice was equally clear in the moral sphere:

> . . . a fight for good against evil broadly speaking I think it is. I
> have said so repeatedly in the clearest language I know . . . But
> of course the main concern of the Church must be with the qual-
> ity of the people carrying on the fight. Therefore one cannot say
> only that it is a fight of good against evil but also that we have to
> make ourselves more fit to serve the good cause . . .
>
> William Temple, *Some Lambeth Letters 1942–44*, ed. F S Temple, Oxford,
> 1963, pp.25–26.

Once war came, many asked how it could be reconciled with the sixth
commandment. Temple wrote from Lambeth Palace:

> There is no record that our Lord ever said 'Thou shalt not kill'.
> The Mosaic sixth commandment is more accurately represented
> by the Prayer Book than by the Bible version, for the word in the
> Hebrew does not refer to killing of any kind but definitely to
> 'Murder', that is to say killing for personal advantage or the satis-
> faction of personal passion . . .

I am quite sure that it is our duty at present to fight the war through and win it, and if we are to fight then of course we must do so effectively; but it is quite possible to fight without malice, indeed the malice is much more likely to be found among folk at home than in the Fighting Forces.

W. Temple, *Some Lambeth Letters*, p. 178.

Elsewhere he wrote

To fight is, at best, the less of evils.

Ibid, p.102.

It was with this clear moral guidance that my father, Hugh, took up his new post as Vicar of Epsom in December 1938.

His first ambition was to transform the *St Martin's Parish Magazine*, and in January *No 1, vol 1 (new issue)* was published in a fresh format. From January 1939 until October 1950 he wrote a monthly Vicar's Letter to introduce the Magazine, 143 of them, and they chronicle, month by month, what it was like to live through those terrible years. It is an impressive archive, a narrative of moral guidance to his parishioners through the darkness that for nearly six years seemed to have no end in sight. It shows a faith tried in the fires, and unblinking leadership.

The author's father, Rev Hugh Warner, in 1939

Epsom Parish Church Magazine

February 1940
From the Vicar.

My dear Friends,

It is probable that for many of us these coming months will strain our Christian loyalty to the breaking point. Self pity, bitter hatred against fellow Christians, distrust of the love of God, and even doubt as to whether the Christian values of freedom and humanity are worth suffering for, may each in turn corrode our souls . . . God is calling us to years of special heroism. Lent this year must be observed by us all as no Lent has ever been before . . . Here are the questions to which we must try to find the answers this Lent:

a. What power is there in my life which would help me successfully to face the loss of my family?

b. What inner resources have I to offset the hopelessness that comes to some when business crashes?

c. If I feel convinced that it is God's will for me to take a share in the destruction of my fellow men, how can I do this and yet keep hatred and bitterness out of my heart all the time? . . .

June 1940

My dear Friends,

I want to be very practical in my letter this month, as there seems no doubt now that before I write my next letter to you we may have to face air-raids. There are two ways of facing them; – as Christians, and as pagans . . .

1. A Christian is one who believes that the unseen things of the spirit are more important than the material things we see and handle every day.

2. Bombs are only able to destroy these more or less unimportant material things, like buildings, roads and human bodies.

3. I say 'more or less', because in ordinary times material things, just because of their beauty and usefulness, are tremendously worth caring for and valuing. But we are not living in 'ordinary times' when at grips with the spirit of evil on such a vast scale.

4. Bombs *can't* destroy any of the really important things like hope, courage, service of other people worse off than ourselves, faith or the human soul.

5. Our job, therefore, is to go on building up other people's faith, hope, and courage no matter to what extent destruction of material things is going on around us.

6. Three things may happen to us; – we may escape unscathed, in which case we shall throw ourselves into the task of helping others; – or we may suffer physically through being wounded, in which case we will remember that Christ passed the same way before on His way to Victory from the Cross, and we are but sharing His sufferings with the knowledge 'our strength is made perfect in weakness': – or we may be killed, in which case there need be nothing but the uttermost confidence and fearlessness if we have taken the trouble to be prepared by our daily prayers, our weekly Holy Communion and our unselfishness all along the line.

7. There is one other possibility – we may lose one or more of our relations. If this happens, fortify yourself by the conviction that death cannot break the bonds of love if this love has been expressed in some close connection with Christ . . .

8. Don't mix up physical fear with moral fear . . . Physical fear (the sort, for instance, that makes our knees go wobbly and insides go queer) is best dealt with by rationally thinking through what it is that we are frightened of, and realising why we need not be because of what I have said in paragraphs 6 and 7 above.

9. Moral fear *is* something to be ashamed about. It is the sort that stops caring whether the cause of justice is worth suffering for, or

whether the things of the spirit are really more important than the material things which bombs destroy, and which cloaks itself in venomous hatred for our enemies.

10. There need be no alarm if sirens go off when we are in Church, since our plans are made. If it is a Holy Communion service, we shall take no notice but carry on. Obviously there is no better place to be in whether for life or death than the realised presence of Jesus.

11. Those whose emergency duties call them at once, may leave the Church without disturbing others. Sit in the middle of the Church, and the risk of hurt from falling glass will be negligible. After the service wait in the Church until the priest has decided if it is safe to cross over to the crypt in the Church House . . .

12. Every worshipper must bring his or her gas-mask to all Church services. Children will be sent home from Sunday School if they come without their mask. Parents will not be allowed to fetch their children home from day or Sunday School after an air-raid warning has been given. Ample shelter accommodation has been provided for all of them. If you parents come along you will only take up space in the shelter which the children ought to have. The teachers will keep them happy, so don't worry, but stay at home.

13. If you see the Church flag flying, this means the emergency arrangements are in force.

Now think of Peter on the water, and Jesus saying 'Why are ye fearful, O ye of little faith?' and throw yourself again into the business of being a real Christian in every way.

                    Yours sincerely

                              Hugh Warner

Emergency arrangements included the War Office directive that church bells throughout the land should be silent. If they rang, that announced the

German parachutists had landed. Most people took this to mean the invasion would have begun.

Over at West Grinstead, 28 miles away:

> Tom Lock, the only [Home Guard] bell-ringer to live conveniently close to St George's Church . . . was told to ring only after he had received a written order, delivered by dispatch rider . . . It was not a task he relished: the bells at St George's are positioned on the ground floor and a German sniper would easily have been able to pick him off through a window . . . how long should he ring. 'Oh, just give it a good whacking' his superior told him.
> Midge Gillies, *Waiting for Hitler*, London, Hodder and Stoughton, 2006, p.121.

Church bell ringing is not just tugging on a rope. It is a skill. To start, each bell must be 'set', its mouth face upward. This itself can be hard work. My eldest brother, David, had tried – with my father standing by him – pulling a bell-rope. It came down, then slipped through his fingers, and flung him over backwards.

He was not fazed. As my Aunt Robine wrote, in her notebook, about the effect of the night bombing on us children:

> David was too busy to be very frightened. He was always collecting gas masks, shepherding the other boys and generally being useful. But Andrew was the only one who wondered what would happen if we lost the war, so I think he worried quite a bit.
> *Notebook*, pp.20–21.

For Michaelmas Term, 1940, David was to leave us for his first boarding school, the Prep. School at Amberley, near Stroud, Gloucestershire, called St George's. From then until July 1944, except in the holidays, Andrew was senior brother at home.

In that month my father's Vicar's Letter in the Parish Magazine speaks of 'our newly-disturbed nights' as the VI rockets, Hitler's 'secret weapon', the 'doodlebugs' as we called them, hit Epsom. Next month's August 1944 letter opens:

'In the midst of life we are in death . . .' Strange how sentences
like that suddenly come to mean something very true . . . In these
days, right up against it, none of us but has to come to terms with
it in one way or another. They say, to look at a thing you fear
straight in the face is to be no longer afraid of it. Let's try . . .

On June 27 a VI had fallen on the London railway terminus we all used,
Victoria station, killing 14 travellers and maiming others.

One result was that David did not come home in July but spent the
summer holidays in Wales with relatives. Andrew was sent to be with him,
and from there, in September 1944, he joined David at St George's Prep.
School in relative safety, playing Balthasar's attendant while his elder
brother David played Kaspar in the school's nativity play that Christmas.

This meant that from July 1944 until late spring 1945 – a V2 rocket fell
on London's Smithfield market on 8 March killing 110 people eight weeks
before the German war ended on 8 May 1945; during the last year of the war,
throughout that culmination of slaughter, I was the senior boy living at
Epsom Vicarage, with Martin, later to become the academic philosopher,
next, and – to our joy – our first sister, Megan, who had been born on
4 September 1943, the year of the Sandhurst Road School massacre.

This time the new baby did not arrive between the alert and the all clear
of the sirens, but while Andrew and I were sitting in our apple tree.
However, as Megan was coming into the world in the Worple Road Vicarage,
in the garden Andrew fell out of the apple tree and broke his arm. Will
you confirm, Andrew, that I did not push you? The inconvenience of this
timing to my poor parents can best be left to your imaginations.

For the first two years of her life, Megan slept with my mother's sister
in a cupboard under the stairs: as a baby, in a metal cradle shaped like half
a walnut with bullet-proof transparency over the face section. It came
complete with oxygen pump in case of gas attack.

As my mother said ruefully when the flame-tailed roar and rattle of a
doodlebug passing over us began to hum off to destruction while she
and I bathed the baby by candlelight:

Everyone expects one war in a generation, but two is really too much.

But daily life had to go on. In 1944, Robine's notebook tells us:

Epsom now [was a] more dangerous town with V bombs about day and night. Shopping one day I saw one of our pilots gently edge one of these nuisances with his left wing to fall onto an open space and then come back waggling his wings at the shopping queues: and we all waved. *Notebook*, p.25.

During the last year of the V bombs, my sister and the 3 boys (David was away at boarding school) slept in the Morrison shelter in the dining room. It took up the whole room in the smaller house into which we had moved. The new baby, Megan, and I slept under the stairs in the broom cupboard. *Notebook*, p.21.

During June and July 1944, Andrew and Martin slept with their heads at one end while my Mother and I slept at the other. We all had to keep our feet still. From late July, when Andrew was sent to be with David in Wales, my mother had one end to herself, albeit with four feet poking her, in the table-cage in which we spent our nights, and at which we ate during the day.

My father slept at the end of the garden in the 'damaged and unsafe' Anderson shelter. These half-underground, bent-corrugated-iron-roofed huts were surprisingly effective, if damp and cold. They cost £7 each, unless your annual income was under £350, in which case they came free.

Ever ready with fresh ideas, he wrote in his Vicar's letter of October 1940:

In order to allow more room in a small shelter for sleep have you tried a hammock?. . . You can sling it across a normal Anderson shelter by piercing the sides of the shelter for the metal hooks and fixing a small metal plate on the outside before screwing the nut on . . . Has anyone tried . . . heating a shelter with a candle placed in a slightly-raised flower-pot with another flower-pot inverted over the top? . . . the inverted pot soon gets so warm that it generates a flow of hot air round about.

He slept out there so, as his biographer put it, he could:

> dash off to the scene of action . . . even before the sirens had ceased their alarm. He sensed uncannily where a bomb was going to fall, and was usually on the spot before either doctor, air-raid wardens, or rescue-squad . . .
>
> Nancy Le Plastrier Warner, *Hugh Compton Warner: The Story of a Vocation*, London, S.P.C.K, 1958, p.125.

From this tree-shaded Anderson shelter he would visit his parishioners.

> Can't we think of some plan of providing simple refreshments for those who have to sit for six hours or so in the Public Shelters? I have already found how welcome even one biscuit or a packet of potato crisps is to people caught away from home and bed like this . . . Would you like to help me provide something like this – especially for the children and mothers with small babies? As I am patrolling the parish continuously during all the raids, I could take a snack satchel round with me to the Public Shelters.
>
> *Epsom Parish Church Magazine*, Sept., 1940.

His parishioners responded, and their church attendance was impressive. In August, 1940 he writes:

> On every hand I sense a growing feeling of high courage and spiritual renewal. It isn't only that every Sunday our church is packed twice over with about one thousand a time, but every day brings some new evidence of generous kindliness and good humour . . .

In October 1942 he tells us:

> Who would have guessed that the Day of Prayer last month

was to have been such an overpowering experience? A church packed to overflowing twice within two hours, and after that over three hundred communicants, and great services in other churches in the town . . .

There was one group of non-Christians for whom he had a passionate mission. In June 1941 he writes:

> Many Jewish refugees have lately come into our midst, and I am sure we would be eager to do all we can to help them after the persecutions they have been through . . . I was glad, therefore, to be able to offer the use of part of the Church House on Friday evenings and Saturday mornings (the Sabbath) to a delegation of Jews who came to ask me if I could help them find premises for the conduct of their services.

Next year he is holding special services 'For the Jews in Germany and countries occupied by the enemy.' By 1943 he cries out in bold type at the opening of the Parish Magazine:

IS IT NOTHING TO YOU. . .?

An Urgent Appeal to all Christians in Epsom.

Mass shootings, mass poison gassing, mass electrocution, transportation in cattle trucks with lime and chlorine, 150 to a truck . . .

Pregnant mothers; babies, children, the sick and very old . . . there is no discrimination. They are Jews. That's enough.

In Nazi-occupied Europe there were at the beginning of the war six million Jews. Already between one and two million have been murdered deliberately by the Nazis.

This policy is now **BEING SPEEDED UP**. It is reaching its climax. Can nothing be done for those who are left? . . .

Send a post-card to each of the following . . . Sir Archibald Southby, The House of Commons, The Home Secretary, Whitehall SW1, The Foreign Secretary, Whitehall SW1 urging two things, namely:

That our own regulations for the admission of refugees should
be relaxed.
That the boldest possible measures of rescue be adopted . . .
Epsom Parish Church Magazine, March, 1943.

When the evils against which we are fighting rear their very ugly
heads in our own midst, it is the duty of every Christian to 'go for'
them, and kill them . . . Are we in England completely untainted
by the same poison of Anti-Semitism? . . . The latest example I've
come across has been the accusation that the shelter disaster
in London was due to the Jews . . . it is wicked not to get hold of
the real facts . . .'
Epsom Parish Church Magazine, April, 1943.

As a greater awareness of what the Nazis had been doing in the concentration camps grew, incredulity turned to anger, desire for punishment, and
revenge. Did not the German V1 and V2 rockets mean V for Vergeltungswaffe or 'revenge weapon'? As Quentin Reynolds, the American war-
reporter, wrote of the British mood at this time:

They were through taking it. They wanted to give it.
Gavin Mortimer, *The Blitz*, Oxford, Osprey, 2010, p. 144.

In the Magazine as early as October 1941 my father asks:

Are we beginning to do what two years ago we promised
ourselves we would never do? . . . In those days we could hold our
heads high in the midst of bombs and anxiety, because our cause
was untarnished by a blind seeking for revenge . . .

Churchill, having asked to see a film showing the bombing of German
towns, 'suddenly', according to the diary of Australia's representative on
our War Cabinet: Richard Casey,

. . . sat bolt upright and said to me 'Are we beasts? Are we taking
this too far?'
Martin Gilbert, *The Second World War*, London, Phoenix, 2009, pp.440–441.

Though at the request of the Russians Churchill had agreed with the American Chiefs of Staff to deflect some of our bomber force to attack the German lines of communication in the Berlin-Dresden-Leipzig region, and had given Air Marshal Harris a free hand, when he heard of the obliteration of Dresden Churchill did his best to restrict area bombing:

> Minute to Chief of Air Staff Sir Charles Portal and Chiefs of Staff Committee. 28 March 1945.
> It seems to me that the moment has come when the question of the bombing of the German cities simply for the sake of increasing the terror, though under other pretexts, should be reviewed. Otherwise we shall come into control of an utterly ruined land . . . The destruction of Dresden remains a serious query against the conduct of Allied bombing.
> Patrick Bishop, *Bomber Boys*, London, HarperCollins, 2008, p.352.

But the bombing campaign that was finally to escalate into Hiroshima and Nagasaki, bringing the war to an end, had spun beyond the control even of Churchill.

In August 1944 a Vergeltungswaffe rocket nearly destroyed our Worpie Road Vicarage, and once again all our windows were blasted. This was a near miss too close.

My grandmother, living with us, dying of cancer, sent one of us children downstairs with a message to our mother to tell the boys in the street outside to stop revving up their motorcycles. 'It is very inconsiderate of them to make such a noise'. Alas! It was more than motorbikes; though she was right: it was very inconsiderate.

So we decamped to her house in Hove, Sussex, on the South Coast. Even to us children it seemed an odd choice of refuge as it was much nearer to the enemy. When in early November we returned, I had missed twenty-three days of Epsom schooling.

In retrospect I can see my mother wanted to sort out some of her mother's papers and possessions before she died. Grandmother's death

came on 30 September. With that, Aunt Robine who had been nursing her
came to Hove leaving my father on his own in the windy Vicarage carrying
on his desolate tasks; so it was while he was alone that on 26 October the
news came to him of the death of his beloved Archbishop Temple.

My mother later wrote:

> Immediately he took a train to Westgate to be of what help he
> could to Mrs Temple, and to look his last on the serene and ever-
> youthful face of his 'dear Arch'.
> Nancy Warner, *Hugh Warner*, p,130.

In addition to two brothers in the navy, my father had two sisters
who, from a distance, were a support. The elder, my Aunt Rosalie, was a
Lieutenant-Colonel in the Queen Alexandra's Royal Army Nursing Corps.
She was sent to a serious war zone to replace the Matron of Mogadishu
Hospital who had just been murdered. After that posting, Rosalie was Matron
of Malta's Military Hospital – where Gunner Andrew Warner my brother
(now Canon Warner) while on active service visited our aunt on the island,
touching down in a noisy York Troop Carrier on his way to the Suez Canal.
Lieutenant-Colonel Warner and Gunner Warner met on the tarmac. To his
relief he did not have to salute as she was in civilian clothes.

Finally, Rosalie was promoted to be Matron of Q. A. Military Hospital,
Millbank, London. She came through the war unscathed.

His younger sister, our Aunt Maud, nearly did not. As a First Officer she
was, with others, entrusted with censoring letters from our troops prior to
D-Day – 6 June 1944.

It was vital that Hitler should continue to be deceived and expect the
main invasion force of the Allies to land and attack at Pas-de-Calais. It is,
after all, the shortest sea route between England and France.

Censorship and deception succeeded. To the relief of the Allies, Hitler
continued to keep his Fifteenth Army defending Pas-de-Calais in empty
anticipation for twenty days after the Normandy landings had been
established.

Maud sat at Dover in her high-backed chair overlooking the sea making sure soldiers' handwritten letters home contained no indication of troop movements.

One day, after having sat for a long stint, she left the room for a few minutes. During those moments an exploding bomb threw a vicious piece of shrapnel through the window-glass, knocking over her chair. She kept the shard, and gave it to me. Be careful it does not cut your fingers.

So shrapnel from Dover on the eve of D-Day arrives in Cambridge sixty-seven years later.

It is a popular myth that Cambridge did not suffer in the Blitz; but if you visit me in my college rooms at St Catharine's you can still read, painted on the door-frame of my staircase, C Staircase, opposite the list of names, directions to the college's air raid shelter.

According to Jesus College's 41st Annual Report, quoted in the *Cambridge Alumni Magazine*, no. 60 of Easter, 2010:

> There were 424 air raid alerts at Cambridge during the war, during which the enemy dropped 118 high explosive bombs, 3 oil bombs and about 1000 incendiaries, and 29 people were killed. The Round Church, the Union Society and houses in Jesus Lane were hit in July 1942.

We can add many more incidents – that a Dornier 217 bomber was shot down, landing in Warren Road, off Milton Road, though the newspapers were made to say only that it 'came down on some allotments in the country.' You can see photographs of it in the scrap book compiled by Ian and Brian Gerrard (and their father before them) that they have lent for display here today; for which we thank them.

Lady Chadwick kept a meticulous diary which tells of many raids and events that are otherwise unrecorded, or were hushed up. A brief sample:

> 18 June 1940 100 planes came over E. Coast and 7 were shot down. One bomber dropped bomb on [Mill Road] and 7 people killed. It was shot down by a spitfire.
>
> 11 Oct 1940 C.U.M.S. sang Stanford's 'Songs of the Fleet' with

Henry accompanying. Siren in middle but we took no notice.

29 Oct-28 Nov 1940 [She lists all the dates] Sirens, due to planes passing over [Cambridge] to Coventry . . . Sirens, slept in corridor [of her college] all night.

15 Jan 1941 Incendiary bombs dropped on Cambridge Perse Boys School.

7 Mar 1941 Boris [Ord] conducted for last time before going to Air Force.

Boris, who was my musical mentor, had been a pilot in the Royal Flying Corps in the First World War, during which time he had been twice wounded, the second time seriously. He rejoined the R.A.F. as Flight-Lieutenant, 1941–46, and participated in the Normandy Landings and the ensuing campaign.

He is remembered today as the supreme choir trainer of his time. On his demobilization in 1946 he returned to King's, building up and sustaining the choir until his final illness in 1958. I bow to the memory of a patron, and a brave veteran pilot of both World Wars.

I have spoken of my maiden aunts – there was a shortage of potential as well as actual husbands after the First World War – of my mother's sister, Robine, and my father's sisters Rosalie and Maud. These were important role models: but an even more influential example to us was our unflinching, loving mother. She wrote a weekly letter to each of her six children every week of her life until she was approaching 90.

The author's mother, Nancy, with another new son

What strain did the Blitz impose on even a deeply happy marriage? This afternoon you will hear her speak on this for the first time. But before that, an introductory digression.

The first volume of my *Collected Poems* was published by our loyal publisher, sitting here, Colin Smythe, in 1985. My poetry is classical, so I was fortunate in having as my proof-reader A. H. Buck from Catford, 'Buckie', my old classics master from Christ's Hospital (where he had also been as a boy), at this time in retirement a proof-reader for Oxford University Press.

Buckie had been called up at the close of World War One and received a commission. He discovered on demob that he could not take up his classics scholarship to St John's College, Oxford until October 1919, as Oxford was over-full of war-survivors. With a school friend fellow-officer he therefore returned to Christ's Hospital to finish his time as a schoolboy. (We must remember that call-up was on one's eighteenth birthday.) One master asked them whether they would mind sitting at the back during lessons as having veteran commissioned officers from France in his front row as he expounded Caesar's *Gallic War* he found unnerving.

In 1985 Buckie sent my corrected proofs back to me with the note: 'I have done my best with all your poems except the one written in German, a language I detest and refuse to read.'

Against this may I place on record that over the years I have had a number of German doctorate students teaching for me, and I have found them among the finest men you could hope to know. Evil breeds, it is never static, as the war showed. But there is another truth that age brings: it is that over the longer time-period goodness can, too, though only at the cost of cutting out the cancer. These grand-children and great-grandchildren young Germans are to me one of the miracles of history, and proof that, with the birth of new innocence, the innate potential for goodness and compassion in human beings finally triumphs.

To return from this digression. On the publication of *Collected Poems 1960–1984* my mother wrote me a letter enclosing some poems she had written over the years about which we knew nothing. One I shall read you. Her letter introduces it with these words:

> I came across the enclosed 'poem' I wrote years ago – in Epsom –
> when war-time conditions, babies, etc. had got me down . . .

Wife to Husband

I vexed you, dear, I know this morning.
I wept: you could not fathom why.
You felt aggrieved, exasperated:
I don't look pretty when I cry.

'Good Lord!' you thought, 'these tears, these women!'
You didn't *say* so – no, that true.
Control's an admirable virtue:
I wish it were consoling too.

Years past, in Love's strong arms infolded,
I should have sobbed each foolish thing,
And we'd have kissed and laughed together
Till all the pinpricks ceased to sting.

But there's no time these days for courting.
Minds jaded, bodies tired, nerves frayed
Oppress fond hearts, and youth's clear vision
By wedded care is overlaid.

'Deep down', you dear old moralizer,
You say, 'Our love is just as big.'
I know – but oh, how deep it's buried,
And I am far too tired to dig.

It's hid 'neath duties, cares, engagements,
Scant leisure, overburdened time,
Bills, sickness, worries, screaming babies,
 – 'And wives that cry at Breakfast-time'!

*Hugh and Nancy, the author's
father and mother*

O come, dear! Only one wife surely!
Suppose you had a whole harem –
There! Now you're laughing! O, thank Heaven!
I thought that I was going to scream.

Be tired, be cross, but don't be solemn,
A joke dispels so many a fret.
Give me one kiss, warm, gay, forgiving,
And I'll not cry again – just yet.

Daddy was much touched by it, and gave me a good hug!

They were to give us yet another baby when hostilities finally ceased: Alison, our peace-baby, here today with her husband. My late parents now have many grandchildren, and three of their great-grandchildren are present: Mariam, Lina, and – with my daughter her mother, and her father – Alice: all of them children of the peace announced by Churchill in:

A World Broadcast, 8 May 1945: Unconditional Surrender

Yesterday morning at 2.41 am at Headquarters, General Jodl, the representative of the German High Command, and Grand Admiral Doenitz, the designated head of the German State, signed the act of unconditional surrender of all German land, sea, and air forces in Europe . . .

The German war is therefore at an end . . .

Finally almost the whole world was combined against the evil-doers, who are now prostrate before us. Our gratitude to our splendid allies goes forth from all our hearts . . .

Then to Parliament:

I recollect well at the end of the last war, more than a quarter of a century ago, that the House, when it heard the long list of surrender terms . . . did not feel inclined for debate or business, but desired to offer thanks to Almighty God, to the Great Power which seems to shape and design the fortunes of nations and the destiny of man; and I therefore beg, Sir, with your permission to move . . . the identical motion which was moved in former times:

'That this House do now attend at the Church of St Margaret, Westminster, to give humble and reverent thanks to Almighty God for our deliverance . . .'

Churchill, *The War Speeches*, Vol. III, pp.435–7.

At that moment it seemed the overwhelming mechanisms of war, with all their horrors, had been defeated by three strengths – all, indeed, we could offer and which *were* offered throughout those six years of what we under-statedly called 'the duration' – offered with humour, with endurance and, through grief, in that supreme quality in combatant and civilian alike, personal courage.

The three weapons which had proved unbreakable were: the sustaining love generated within family life, and through widespread outgoing and unselfish good-neighbourliness; the idealistic faith embodied by our univer-sally loved spiritual leader William Temple (and, in our own case, by his young and devoted chaplain); and the hope, in our darkest agony, massacres, and defeat, against all reason, ignited, cherished, and finally triumphant, breathed through the wireless on us by Winston Churchill.

I shall close with words delivered by a university lecturer over two thousand three hundred years ago, also spoken some seventy years after a major war – by Aristotle, whose tutor, Plato, had as a child lived through the closing years of the Peloponnesian War, that struggle between the oligarchs of Sparta and the birthplace of democracy, and had known the fall of his city, Athens:

And we ought not to listen to those who counsel us 'O man, think as man should', and 'O mortal, remember your mortality'. Rather ought we, so far as in us lies, to put on immortality and to leave nothing unattempted in the effort to live in conformity with the highest thing within us. Small in bulk it may be, yet in power and preciousness it transcends all the rest.

Aristotle, *Nichomachean Ethics*, trans. J. A. K. Thomson, London, Penguin, 1953, p.305.

On a Ferry Boat, Summer 1944

I did not see the bombs fall on the Thames,
But I did feel next morning's cranes of fire
Each side our boat. My bones seemed to perspire
As buildings yelled skeletal requiems,
Roared, cracked, exploded through the wind's whiplash,
And leaping flames, black smoke, framed Tower Bridge.
My father hoped our Lambeth ferriage
For Temple to St Paul's was not too rash . . .
Day rockets! We turned back. Nazis return
Again each night. Godmother will feed me.
Mother near home with baby on her knee,
Bombed out, is no more safe than us. All burn.
      I slipped. He lifted me. Down my lip curled.
      This surely is the ending of the world.

Sonnet, line 8: Archbishop William Temple. See Notes.

Epsom, Ewell, and the edge of Cheam as seen in German aerial photographs captured at the end of the war. Trenches dug on the Downs to stop the landing of aircraft in an invasion can be seen bottom right   *© Bourne Hall Museum, Ewell*

The following photographs were taken during the Blitz by William Vandivert, an American photographer then working for *Life* magazine. While in London, he met and married Rita André, a cousin of my father. In 1947, William and Rita Vandivert, along with Henri Cartier-Bresson, Robert Capa and others, founded the cooperative photographic agency Magnum. After William Vandivert's death, his daughter and sole heir, Susan Vandivert-Olin, gave me copies of these photographs (some of which have not been previously published), and she has kindly given permission for them to be reproduced here.

John Thompson

Blitz Requiem

REQUIEM AETERNAM

May souls in peace rest beyond reach of time,
Healed from the horror of their parting hence.
On these may light perpetual, sublime,
Shine and deliver from all past offence.

ABSOLVE AND KYRIE

Deliver us from menace in the dust,
Long hours in the cold waters of the sea,
The failing parachute, the bayonet thrust –
May we know our sin nailed you to the tree.

Lord have pity on us
Lord have pity on us
Lord have pity on us

For malice in revenge and cruel laugh
Teach us our own responsibility,
For those who now take life on our behalf,
Those who are dying so we may be free.

Christ have pity on us
Christ have pity on us
Christ have pity on us

From our indifference to consequence
Of our retaliation, make us pause.
Forgive us glorifying Judas' pence.
Christ, make ourselves more fit to serve your cause.

Lord have pity on us
Lord have pity on us
Lord have pity on us

DIES IRAE

What fresh terror sirens' moaning
Heralds? Earth and heaven groaning
At near raiders' engines' droning,

Night sky lit with flames ascending,
Wrath and fear in ashes blending
With each dive-bomber's descending.

Underneath a dining table
On a mattress, while the babel
Of a thousand aircraft able

To destroy a sleeping city
Streams above, a mother's pity
Rolls her in birth-agony.

From the dog-fight high in summer
Blue, where milk streaks spread in slumber,
And small boys look up in wonder

As one youth explodes in fire,
And another flying higher
Mushrooms down from funeral pyre;

From the flame-tailed rocket's rattle,
And the whine of bombs in battle
On civilians' lunch time prattle;

Packed between pews sleeping, church nights,
From the dark sky probed by searchlights,
Spare us further blinding eye sights.

Flying low with high explosive
Clearly aimed by creed corrosive,
Two eyes blast dawn's peaceful olive

On the playground; pencils scattered,
Homework, little things that mattered
Like these bodies, shrapnel–shattered

In school uniforms of cotton.
Trust in mass graves dead and rotten.
Shall these children be forgotten?

Lest our true compassion deaden
Let not hate make mercy leaden.
Spare us, Lord, in Armageddon.

SANCTUS

Almighty God whose goodness fills the height,
Creator of the world shielding our sight,
We bend our eyes down in your mercy's light.

AGNUS DEI

Good shepherd's dearest, dead in agony,
Our evil cleansed in perpetuity
May we arise with you in ecstasy.

RESPONSORIUM *Bass solo*

In this red curse of combat, Lord, forgive
Each one of us who kill in hope to live –
Blind with tears. Your coming wrath must shake me
For what I do in fear. O Jesus, make me
Compassionate to captives in our power
In soul-scarred sins I choose this violent hour –
My shattering explosives leaping higher
Trembling me as you judge the world by fire.

REQUIEM AETERNAM

May souls in peace rest beyond reach of time,
Healed from the horror of their parting hence.
On these may light perpetual, sublime,
Shine and deliver from all past offence.

IN PARADISUM

May saints and martyrs in this extreme time
Cry out in anguished prayer for us above
As earth's foundations shake in shame and crime.
Crucified Jesus, pity in your love
The fireman struggling as forlorn hope dims,
Doctor and priest each doing all he could,
Nurses and teachers sorting out torn limbs,
Mothers and children digging to grow food
On their allotments with potatoes, hens;
Old journalists stumbling to find the facts –
The ordinary, decent citizens,
All of them blasted in unselfish acts:
Good people who have paid the highest price.
May angels lead them into Paradise.

REQUIEM AETERNAM

May souls in peace rest, beyond reach of time,
Healed from the horror of their parting hence.
On these may light perpetual, sublime,
Shine and deliver from all past offence.

March 2011

Remembrance Sunday Sermon

King's College Chapel, Cambridge, 13 November 2011

On 6 February 1945, Winston Churchill, aged 70, went to his desk and wrote:

> 'Tonight the sun goes down on more
> suffering than ever before in the world.'

For over five years he had guided us through the Second World War, and sustained our morale. This simple sentence of his realization carries unimaginable grief.

By 1945 this country had given its all. We had his courage to sustain us, but little else. Ingenuity was our chief weapon, stoicism our way of life.

David Isitt, undergraduate, Kingsman, and also Chaplain here after the war, tells us that:

> 'Coal was rationed, so was bread and butter and jam and meat and clothes and milk and eggs and cheese and tea, so there wasn't very much to eat. Your coal ration might heat your room for two evenings a week. For the rest, we crowded into the Ronald Balfour Reading Room where there was a gas fire, and we read for the Tripos, smoked our pipes, and smelled rather bad in our unwashed clothes. It was wonderful, and I loved it.'

On 11 October 1940 Boris Ord, the choirmaster here, and later my mentor, conducted Stanford's 'Songs of the Fleet', with Henry Chadwick accompanying at the piano. Sirens went off during the performance warning of enemy aircraft overhead. The sirens were ignored.

Boris had been a pilot in the Royal Flying Corps in the First World War, and was twice wounded, the second time seriously. After this concert he left

King's to join the R.A.F. as a Flight Lieutenant, and was to fight from 1941–5, not least through the Normandy landings and ensuing campaign.

He was not going to have this concert spoilt.

On Cambridge 118 high explosive bombs, 3 oil bombs, and over 1,000 incendiary bombs were dropped. In July 1942 alone, the Round Church, the Union Society buildings, and houses in Jesus Lane were bombed.

A German Dornier 217 bomber was shot down, landing in Warren Road.

But before the serious air-raids began, these magnificent stained glass windows had been taken down and dismantled, to be hidden from reach of explosives; which is how we still have them today.

In their place were huge black canvas screens which flapped loudly in the wind. Wooden panelling continued round right up to the altar, behind which stood three desolate empty wooden niches, before completing the circuit back to these stalls on the other side.

However, you could not always see this because the winter fog was so thick – this was before the Clean Air Act – so thick that you couldn't see from one side of the chapel to the other.

Fingers were numb. The Chapel was dark, and dirty with grime and old smoke. There was no heating, no electric light – the only electricity was saved for blowing the organ – and the cold fog seeped in everywhere, circling the choir's spluttering candles.

The Battle of Britain lasted from early July to the end of October, 1940. Throughout that astonishingly beautiful summer and autumn the Royal Air Force and the Nazi Luftwaffe could be seen by everyone, spiralling above us killing each other.

Overlapping these dates, from 7 September began the night Blitz, concentrated on London for fifty-seven consecutive sunsets until the all clear sounded at four or five in the morning. Thereafter frequent heavy bombing continued until May 1941, and intermittently until around 8 May 1945 when a V.2. rocket hit London's Smithfield Market, killing 110 people. During these five years Britain was at bay, fighting all-out war for survival.

Epsom, where my father was the Vicar, was the first and last target of the enemy raiders coming across the Channel for London. As a result I and my brothers and sister experienced the Blitz at first hand. It shaped our childhood: indeed my younger brother was born under the dining room table while we sheltered below in the cellar during one of the heaviest raids of the war – 27 September 1940.

The main target was Epsom's railway junction, which fed Clapham, Victoria and Waterloo stations. In our four square miles over twelve thousand homes, including our first and second Vicarages, suffered. When we were bombed out we slept in the Parish Church.

Schools were a particular target. During my first term at school, Petworth Boys' School to the south-west on the flight path over us was destroyed in a daylight raid, killing the Headmaster and 31 others, boys and staff. A stick of eight bombs causing devastation just missed Epsom Convent School, but in my second term, on 20 January 1943, Sandhurst Road School, Catford, twelve miles north-east on this same enemy flight path, was machine-gunned and bombed leaving 31 children and 6 members of staff dead on the playground. Seven children died later in hospital.

Cambridge was more fortunate. On 15 January 1941 several incendiary bombs were dropped on the Perse Boys' School, but to the best of my knowledge no one was killed.

Why am I sharing this with you? Because I am of the final generation that 70 years ago survived the Nazi bombardment of Britain, one of the lucky children who – in the middle of it – survived the Blitz, the rockets, being bombed out twice; who had to duck machine-gunning on our way to morning school – the Nazi's favourite time to attack. 'It will break their morale' they said.

Those memories are as immediate and clear today as the first glass splinter of bomb blast that cut my shielding hand. But memory is not enough. It is what you do with your memories that matters.

Last week I was talking to Mrs Molly Linn[1], who was at Sandhurst Road School, Catford on 20 January 1943. We were reminiscing, and I asked her if she had any thoughts I could pass on to you today. This is what she said.

'We'd made a shepherd's pie in cookery class that morning, but

1 Mrs Marie-Louise (Molly) Linn, née Kinnuman, b. 9 January 1931, youngest of eight children, married Andrew Derek Linn, 27 August 1958, widowed 14 August 1986. Her father was a Finnish

I was too excited to eat because we were going to the theatre to see *A Midsummer Night's Dream*. It had been my birthday 11 days earlier, and I had a new coat in royal blue, which made me feel so grown up.

The siren went. I thought "I'd better get my purse and gloves from my desk to take to the shelter", and walked as far as the classroom door.

I saw children hanging out of the window, as Betty, the head girl, was telling us to get to the shelter. As she spoke, I looked out of the window and saw a plane. A girl, a seven-year-old, in the playground waved assuming the swooping plane was an R.A.F. bomber.

The pilot was wearing a leather helmet and goggles, but it didn't occur to me that he was German. His mouth was drawn back and for a few seconds I thought he was grinning . . . I saw him reach forward and do something to the controls . . .

The next thing I knew, I was buried. Betty, who had been standing by me, was killed.

I was eventually rescued and taken to Lewisham Hospital. I remember my clothes being cut away, which upset me. I thought, "It's a new coat. What are my parents going to say?"'

Molly had two crushed and broken arms, and two legs so mangled that they had to be amputated.

'The Queen came to visit. She brought bananas, and said someone had brought them from Casablanca for the Princesses, but they wanted us to have them instead. The younger ones thought you ate them with their skins on, but she showed us you didn't.

The Head Mistress came to see me and said "That was a nasty day, wasn't it."'

Merchant Seaman. Her 21-year-old brother was Able Seaman Kenneth Kinnuman. His ship, the SS Rio Azul (London), was torpedoed off the Azores, and Kenneth was one of those who boarded a raft. He survived for two weeks on the open sea, dying on 14 July 1941, a day before those still alive were rescued. By the end they had been surviving on a teaspoonful of water a day.

Astonishingly Molly still lives in Catford. Her memories reveal no hatred. She has used them to be the source of energy to build a life without legs, to marry, have a job, retire, become a widow, and then to work in a hospice – and, as she says, 'not make a fuss'.

The Psalmist sings of those 'who going through the vale of misery use it for a well: and [find] the pools are filled with water. They will go from strength to strength.' (Psalm 84 *vv* 6 & 7) Molly Linn is one of them.

As Aeschylus put it 2,500 years ago:

> Man must suffer to be wise.
>
> . . . when time has waited long
> There grows from the root of wrong
> The flower of suffering.

Choephori

There are people in this congregation, perhaps many here this morning, who have lost loved ones; some of them in war: who have known suffering. To you I speak.

Memory, however sacred, is not enough. Christian remembrance is about the transformation of suffering. It is not static, but dynamic. In the heart of despair, indeed from the very depth of the sorrow, we can find the strength to turn the emotion round, to recreate life.

War dismembers, as it dismembered Molly's twelve-year-old limbs. This day in Chapel we re-member, we put together from memories, realize in our own personalities the fact that we are still alive, to bear witness, celebrate the good in those lost but loved lives, to tell their story and in so doing pass on the hope, the Christian hope, that all can, by grace and a supreme effort of will, be re-deemed, re-thought, by those disfigured limbs crucified on Calvary, the remembrance of which has given us the faith that built, and sustains, this glorious chapel, its music, its art, its windows bringing in this cascade of light, the light of hope, now in the present, and for the future; and of our love for those gone, for our children, and friends, even, finally, our enemies, being the life-force of God that will, if we let it, create a better world.

For Molly Linn, née Kinnuman

Twenty-eight fighter bombers overhead
Swooped up our flight path, low, seeking our schools.
Where were the sirens, anti-aircraft tools –
Radar – when we were queuing to be fed?
Minutes south of us, Petworth School last term
Was blasted. Boys and teachers in mass graves
Frost the raw grief. Outside a Junior waves
And is machine-gunned. You, in rubble, squirm
And lose both of your legs. Your playground fills
With sad tarpaulins. Far in the Azores
Your brother Ken's torpedoed. Without oars
They last on their raft two weeks, till thirst kills.
    Quiet, we know – our deaths not far away –
    Love is life's only pulse from dark to day.

28.2.2012

Epsom

In war civilians will be killed, we know;
But if you find your home is the front line,
As we did, London's last defence design –
Known to enemy, bombing us below –
Runs through our church, each breeze of life's intense;
And infinitely precious simple things,
Also our friends, are fresh under dark wings.
Small, daily chores take on a heightened sense.
The Manor Park's concrete tank barricade
Still stands. On open ground trenches criss-crossed
To de-wheel planes invading. 'All's not lost
If each takes one down with us as we fade.
    Children, if caught, throw sand into his eyes
    Then snatch his gun – and make sure that he dies.'

8.3.2012

For Miles Hursthouse

Your doctor cousin from Invercargill
Who ran the hospital in Singapore
When he surrendered, offering his skill,
Was idly bayoneted to the floor.
Next, all his patients; and your friends were caught –
Observers, like you, on far islets. Stopped,
Their hands up, were beheaded for good sport.
No wonder you were glad the bomb was dropped.
Yes, I know heart's tight thud on losing friends
To war-games bland, malicious violence,
And understand 'forgive, forget' offends
Their memory, seems fatuous pretence.
    Now in the winter of my years, I weep
    We find forgiveness hard through tears so deep.

                                        20.1.2012

For Francis Bacon

'A dog born in a stable's not a horse.
No, I've no Irish blood, though Dublin born.
The stable-boys who horsewhipped me were coarse
Doing my father's bidding in his scorn.
I came to London aged five, and sweat fear
At stealthy shade of Zepplins overhead,
Floating. Worse, through high searchlights I would hear
The whine of coming bombs in my young bed.'
I too was flogged, with twisted belt by boys,
Woken from school sleep – Monitors' vigil;
And, twice bombed out, know well how blitz destroys –
But blessed my shielding parents; miss them still.
    Our stems were not unlike. Our difference
    Shines in the blooms that grew from violence.

Charles Lamb, Essayist, Poet and Dramatist, 1775–1834, by Charles Hazlitt (detail)
Courtesy of the National Portrait Gallery

Christ's Hospital Three-and-Sixty Years Ago

A lecture given to the Charles Lamb Society
for the birthday celebration of Charles Lamb
at 14 Prince's Gate, Kensington, London, 13 February 2010

I had a guinea-pig of whom I was fond. I was eight years old. I also had two parents (my father was Vicar of Epsom), two elder brothers, one younger brother, and one even younger baby sister. Of these, all except one I saw only in the holidays, as my slightly older brother and I were boarders at a Prep School in Amberley, Gloucestershire.

I first travelled there on my own, by train, in freezing fog – it was March, 1946 – locked in the guard's van with a caged Alsatian dog and an addressed label tied by my mother with furry brown string firmly round my wrist. On arrival I could scarcely see anything through the dark, save the steam from the engine swirling across the thin, mist-heavy lights over the station platform.

Though there were fewer than sixty boys in the school, I seldom saw my brother; save when a letter came from home, jointly for us both, sometimes containing stamps. Then he and I would be allowed to meet, and he would select two stamps at a time, always allowing me first choice. This generosity astonished me, though I never told him.

At the end of one Latin class the teacher asked me to remain behind. He told me I had to travel to London to take an exam. 'You'll never pass', he added.

My mother met me, and we walked up from Victoria Station, leaving behind its great iron roof-girders wrecked and twisted by bombing, all the way along Victoria Street with its mountains of rubble on either side until we reached Westminster Abbey.

Tired as I was, this undamaged church mightily impressed me, an experience somewhat dappled by the stern lecture my mother was giving me about being on my best behaviour when we met Mrs Willis, Mrs Gladys Willis, who was a Presentation Governor of Christ's Hospital, which meant she could chose a needy boy from a list of three for a place at this school, all fees paid. If I were the one she liked, I should still have to pass the exam.

What with the long journey, the joy of seeing my mother again tempered by her strange severity about my possible behaviour with this stranger, and the stark reminder all around me of our five years under bombardment by the Nazis which I had recently been trying to forget, I fell silent, scarcely speaking when I was introduced. My mother spoke charmingly but uncharacteristically fast to Mrs Willis, and she was courteous to my nervous mother. Mindful that it seemed to matter to her that I made no mistakes, I stayed dumb; toyed with my slab of cake.

Finally, Mrs Willis addressed me directly. It was I, after all, she had come to see. 'How is your guinea-pig?' she asked, not too grandly. On the long walk through the rubble I had asked my mother the same question, and she'd told me it had died. My reply to this sudden change of conversation was to burst into tears. And so I came to Christ's Hospital.

Charles Lamb's Governor–patron was Samuel Salt, who had two sets of chambers in London in the Temple, and lived directly above the Lamb family in Crown Office Row. He had a large and fine book collection to which the Lambs had access, as Charles's father, John Lamb, was for fifty-five years Samuel Salt's manservant. As Charles (or Elia) tells us in his essay 'The Old Benchers of the Inner Temple':

> When a case of difficult disposition of money, testamentary or otherwise, came before him, he ordinarily handed it over with a few instructions to his man Lovel, who was a quick little fellow, and would despatch it out of hand by the light of natural understanding, of which he had an uncommon share. It was incredible what repute for talents S[alt] enjoyed by the mere trick of gravity . . .[1]

1 *The Works of Charles Lamb* (one volume) London (George Newes) and New York (Scribner's), no date. p.122.

Lovel is, of course, Elia's name for Charles's father. Samuel Salt, now a widower, took a friendly interest in 'Lovel's', or rather John Lamb's family. In fact it was not Salt himself but his friend, Timothy Yeats, who was also a Presentation Governor of Christ's Hospital, who sponsored Charles, as Salt had already used up his current quota of presentations. It is never easy to secure one, and Charles Lamb had to wait for a vacancy. His much older brother had entered the school at the age of five. Charles put on our long blue coat and yellow stockings to become a Bluecoat Boy on 9 October 1782, aged seven years and eight months.

Both Lamb and I were boys at Christ's Hospital for around eight years, he until nearly fifteen, I from just nine until I was sixteen. With one major exception, the school I attended sixty-three years ago was far closer to the milieu that Lamb experienced than to life at the school today.

The exception is, of course, that Lamb's Christ's Hospital was in the City of London, in Newgate Street, housed in the old buildings that had been the Greyfriars' before Henry VIII dissolved the monasteries. Henry's son, the boy King Edward VI, whose face looks out from every one of our school buttons, founded the school for 'the fatherless and other poor men's children' in the City, to be taken in and given meat, drink, clothes and lodging, 'learning and officers to attend on them.' This was in response to a powerful sermon preached before him at Westminster by the Bishop of London, Nicholas Ridley, in 1552, on 'Charity'. The intelligent young teenage King 'suddenly and of himself' said: 'You have had some conference with others what ways are best to be taken therein, the which I am desirous to understand, and therefore I pray you say your mind'. When told, Edward at once wrote the necessary letter, which the elated Ridley took to his friend the Lord Mayor of London Sir Richard Dobbs. The school was given its Royal Charter on 26 June 1553 by the fifteen-year-old King, eleven days before he died. To this day the school only accepts those whose parents' income is beneath a limit laid down by the Council of Almoners. It has kept faith with its compassionate boy-founder.

This London school, child of the City of London and housed in old Greyfriars, the mediaeval Franciscan monastery, was Lamb's. It originally

The Choral Scholar. Francis Warner aged sixteen, about to leave school for music college, before taking up his Cambridge choral scholarship at eighteen

included both boys and girls, but that co-education had ended just four years before Lamb's arrival in 1782. By that time all the girls had been moved out of London to Hertford.

In 1902 the boys also were moved out of London, to a magnificent estate of new red brick buildings, created with all the confidence and grandeur of a Britain at the height of Empire, on a vast open site near Horsham in the Sussex countryside. This forms an entirely self-contained community, self-sufficient, with its own farm, electricity generator, water tower central point high above the great dining hall, railway station, infirmary, armoury, technical school, playing fields, lake, fields, woods, and finally ring-fence, our outer boundary.

At and across the centre of this runs an avenue, flanked by lime trees, of sixteen lofty boys' houses, each containing two dormitories (a junior and a senior one) of thirty beds each, a senior and a junior Housemaster, the dayroom, and ancillaries. These, each paired A & B in an H-shaped forma-tion, are on the Avenue's north side. On the south are the homes of the Senior Masters including, next to the huge chapel, the Headmaster's.

At the centre of this, the chapel and dining hall forming two sides of it, is the largest academic quadrangle in England, save only for that of Trinity College, Cambridge. And here, for the next eighty-three years, until 1985 when the girls' Christ's Hospital at Hertford closed and they joined the boys on the Horsham site, making the school once more co-educational, as it had been in origin; here during my time 840 boys lived for nine months of each year under strict military discipline, as rigorous as that of any public school in Britain. In our white neck-bands and long blue coats, our silver buttons, knee breeches and yellow stockings, we had daily drill, marched to all meals, marched to daily morning chapel, and lived a Spartan and severely controlled life, without exeats, half-term, or female company, for twelve, thirteen and fourteen week terms for eight years.

Into this new, country setting, in 1902 Lamb's school was moved. He has written of his schooldays in two essays, the first, 'Recollections of Christ's Hospital', composed in 1813; the second 'Christ's Hospital Five-and-Thirty Years Ago', under his pseudonym 'Elia', in 1820. This second is written obliquely, as though Coleridge, his friend at school and after, were casting wry shadows across that grave and eulogistic first essay. Together these two writings form a vivid, sometimes terrifying, evocation of school life.

This aspect I shall approach now, but keep short. The life of a military-disciplined, female-less boarding school was harsh; by today's standards almost unappreciable. If you do want full details of our systematic beatings by the masters and senior boys, the punishment drills, and all the other negative features of our rigorous, closed male environment, then a large book by Norman Longmate called *The Shaping Season* will give you all you could care to know. I threw my copy away, not because it was untrue – it is accurate – but because there was more to Christ's Hospital than that; and that more is what I loved.

However, for a few moments I shall compare memories with Lamb. In the earlier essay Lamb writes:

> . . . at a school like this, where a boy is neither entirely sepa-rated from home, nor yet exclusively under its influence, the best feelings, the filial for instance, are brought to a maturity which could not have been attained under a completely domestic education . . . absence, not drawn out by too great extension into alienation or forgetfulness, puts an edge upon the relish of occasional intercourse . . .[2]

Lamb was exceptional in having close links with his home even while he was at school. As his later essay points out:

> He had his tea and hot rolls in a morning, while we were battening upon our quarter of a penny loaf – our *crug*, mois-tened with attenuated small beer . . . smacking of the leather jack it was poured from.[3]

and

> In lieu of our . . . *quite fresh* boiled beef on Thursdays (strong as *caro equina*), with detestable marigolds floating in the pail to poison the broth . . . he had his hot plate of roast veal . . . cooked in the paternal kitchen . . . and brought him daily by his maid or aunt.[4]

This special treatment was not only because of the proximity of his home,

2 *Works*, p.428. 3 Ibid., p.18. 4 Ibid., pp.18–19.

but also of the influential school governor, Samuel Salt's, interest in his manservant's children's welfare.

As a result Lamb did not suffer the two key experiences that most of us had, of homesickness, and hunger.

Set beside this the words of a boy who was at school with me, Bryan Magee, taken from his recent book *Growing Up in a War*:

> You visited your family three times a year; and the total amount of time you spent with them added up to about a quarter. For three-quarters of the year, in uninterruptedly long stretches of time, you were at school, and not allowed out of bounds. So it became your world. This made it a conditioning experience . . . And at Christ's Hospital that conditioning went deeper than at other public schools, because it started younger and went on for longer.[5]

> In various ways all the separate little aspects of our lives seemed to be governed by rules. We had to clean our shoes at a certain time each day, and when we had cleaned them they were inspected by a monitor . . .[6]

As for our food, he writes:

> The food . . . language quails. Words cannot describe it. The fish pie stank. The stew consisted of lumps of grey gristle floating in a fatty brown grease with skin on top. The spaghetti we called 'worms in carbolic'. Whatever leftovers there were from these nightmare dishes were recycled into an all-purpose pie. It defies serious understanding . . . But we ate it . . . we were hungry children and there was nothing else; and in any case we were not allowed to leave food on our plates.[7]

Bryan Magee writes at greater length, and evokes it all too clearly.

---

5 Bryan Magee, *Growing Up in a War*, London (Random House), 2008. p.174.
6 Ibid., p.159.   7 Ibid., p.185.

As for homesickness, we were allowed to bring from home one blanket. When I was in the Prep, before I had reached the mature age of double figures, I laid across the bottom of my bed each morning a blanket that my mother had folded, before she sent me off to school with it. During my entire time in the Prep I never unfolded it, even during those savage winters, because I knew that the last person to have folded it was my mother.

These dormitories, huge corridor rooms with fifteen iron beds down either side, each with a horsehair mattress on wooden slats in place of springs, and what we called lav-ends at either end; these dormitories were ruled by boy monitors – what in other public schools are called prefects. Here is Charles Lamb, or rather his fictional persona, Elia, on them:

> Lamb's governor . . . lived in a manner under his parental roof. Any complaint which he had to make was sure of being attended to. This was understood at Christ's, and was an effectual screen to him against the severity of masters, or worse tyranny of the monitors. The oppressions of the young brutes are heart-sickening to call to recollection. I have been called out of my bed, and *waked for the purpose*, in the coldest winter nights – and this not once, but night after night – in my shirt to receive the discipline of a leathern thong, with eleven other sufferers, because it pleased my callow overseer, when there had been any talking heard after we were gone to bed, to make the six last beds in the dormitory, where the youngest children of us slept, answerable for an offence they neither dared to commit nor had the power to hinder.[8]

Edmund Blunden, another Old Blue, who addressed you at this birthday feast in 1966, was at that time sharing my Oxford college rooms with me while he was Professor of Poetry. I remember packing him off to you for this event, not dreaming that forty-four years later I should be making the same journey. Edmund wrote a history of Christ's Hospital, published in 1923, in which he writes of 'a tradition of savagery on the part of the monitors.'[9]

8 *Works*, pp.20-21.   9 Blunden, Edmund, *Christ's Hospital*, London (Christophers), 1923, p.162.

Bryan Magee writes of my time:

> In those days the monitorial system was exceedingly powerful.
> Almost every aspect of life in the school outside the classroom
> was organised by the older boys. They had what felt like total
> power over us, including the power of punishment. We saw it
> as them, not the masters, who ran our everyday lives. When
> they left the school they went straight into the army, where
> they arrived ready-trained in exercising authority over their
> fellows . . . [and] sprinted up the ladder of promotion.[10]

Masters, of course, beat us regularly, but not so often. This form of
punishment we seldom resented. It paid a debt, cleared the air, and was
forgotten. Only on one occasion did I feel resentment. My nearest brother,
of whom I have already spoken, Andrew, was at school at St John's,
Leatherhead, with my other brothers. In term we never saw each other; so,
on one occasion only, he and I arranged that if he were to make the long
cycle ride over to Christ's Hospital on a Sunday, I should meet him in the
Avenue, outside my house, Middleton B, at 3.00 pm. With typical generosity
he made the journey. We met for perhaps five minutes. Then he cycled back.

Unfortunately, the Junior Housemaster of Middleton B, a keen rugger
man who had played with the Harlequins, was watching out of his window.
As I came in he seized me, took me into his study, and made me turn out my
pockets. 'Where are the cigarettes?' he demanded. 'I don't have any', I
replied. 'Yes, you have. I've just seen you take some from an intruder on a
bicycle. Give them to me!' 'Search me; I don't have any.' 'Don't you be
cheeky to me, boy. I'm going to beat you anyway.' He did.

This calls to mind Lamb's description of the Upper Grammar–master of
his time, the Rev'd James Boyer:

> Nothing was more common than to see him make a headlong
> entry into the school-room from his inner recess, or library,
> and, with a turbulent eye, singling out a lad, roar out. 'Od's my
> life, sirrah' (his favourite adjuration), 'I have a great mind to

10 Bryan Magee, *Growing Up in a War*, p.152.

whip you,' – then, with as sudden a retracting impulse, fling back into his lair – and, after a cooling lapse of some minutes, (during which all but the culprit had totally forgotten the context) drive headlong out again . . . with the expletory yell – '*and I* WILL, *too*.'[11]

As you can see, not much had changed.

It is not that on other occasions I didn't deserve it. Later, on Saturday nights, I would stuff my blue coat down my bed, go to the lav-end, climb down the iron drainpipe to the ground lavatories where I had hidden my civilian clothes and bicycle, balance my trumpet on the handle-bars, and cycle into Horsham to play for the second half of their evening in a dance band at the Drill Hall. For this I was paid seven shillings and sixpence. But I was never caught.

Once last punishment I shall mention. It was collective, and called a Gloom. If no boy owned up to some misdemeanour, the whole house had to sit at the dayroom tables for a length of time in total silence, hands clasped, with nothing to do, until the guilty boy cracked, or the allotted time was up. After a few of these glooms I realised that I could use this time profitably. It seemed highly likely that, when I left, I should be in a war. I had known noth-ing else; and all the masters had at some time fought. If I were dropped behind enemy lines with a friend, it might turn out to be important to know exactly what five minutes was. By hard concentration I found out that it was singing silently to myself 'Ten Green Bottles' as fast as I could five times. Some boys were puzzled why my mouth was moving.

On 24 January 1948 a telegram came to Prep B (something unheard of) for me. It read 'YOU HAVE A NEW BABY SISTER STOP MOTHER AND BABY WELL LOVE DADDY.' I still have the tiny diary in which I wrote down this event.

The telegram was given to me by the Junior Housemaster of Prep B, Mr Eagle, a handsome, slim, ex-RAF officer who himself had a new-born baby called Johnny. Mr Eagle was a perceptive man, younger than most masters,

11 *Works*, pp.28–29.

and he spoke to me on our own for a few moments. He must have observed how homesick I was, though I thought I had concealed it. In a sudden moment of trust I told him that having new babies had been our way of answering Hitler's bombs. We were a close, happy vicarage family, and from earliest days I had been fully aware, through five years of bombardment just south of London, that adults from another country were trying to kill us.

Invasion had been threatened from France, just as Lamb's own generation had been. He was a Deputy Grecian when the Bastille fell. Napoleon waited at Boulogne for a whole year with his flat-bottomed boats and Grand Army to invade and conquer Britain. Charles Lamb knew what this waiting felt like. On 14 July 1940 we had gathered round the wireless at home to hear Churchill tell us of 'the impending assault':

> Perhaps it will come tonight. Perhaps it will come next week.
> Perhaps it will never come.

In every kitchen in the land was pinned up, by order, that sheet of instructions from the Ministry of Home Security: IF THE INVADER COMES – WHAT TO DO AND HOW TO DO IT. We young children were also being prepared by such means as Alison Uttley's 'Little Grey Rabbit' book *Hare Joins the Home Guard*:

> An army of weasels was marching along the old grass-covered
> Roman road. Their teeth shone white, their noses were raised,
> their little fierce eyes looked here and there, as their long thin
> bodies moved swiftly over the ground . . .

> Mouldy Warp was working furiously at a trench which cut the
> old road. Deeper and deeper he went, and a band of rabbits
> with wheelbarrows were piling the soil high. Old Hedgehog
> stood with his prickles like a gorse bush. He rolled himself into
> a ball and hid in the shadows. Overhead flew Wise Owl, with
> never a sound of his soft wings.[12]

12 Alison Uttley, *Hare Joins the Home Guard*, London, 1941, pp.60–63.

The regular arrival of new baby brothers and sisters was our joy in the blackout, the family's affirmation of hearth-fire hope through Armageddon. This was home, even when we were bombed out of it. I still love babies.

Mr Eagle understood. 'You can baby-sit for my Johnny if you like' he said. So I did from time to time, when not tearing at high speed with John Ind on my roller-skates across the asphalt during breaks, jamming my heels together while splaying my toes out to make a sudden turn at the last minute, 'making a corner' as we used to call it.

These times alone by Johnny's cot were my private link with home. A few years later Johnny was riding his bicycle across this same Prep asphalt at high speed, but failed to turn in time. He hit the wall and was killed outright.

Lamb tells of 'the doleful tune of the burial anthem chaunted in the solemn cloisters, upon the seldom-occurring funeral of some schoolfellow'.[13] Johnny's was the only one I knew.

Lamb writes well of school friendships, and observes:

> The Christ's Hospital boy's friends at school are commonly his
> intimates through life.[14]

This has certainly been true of me. My House Captain in Middleton B was Brian Trowell, now retired from being Oxford's Heather Professor of Music. He lives near me. I was his 'swab' – what other schools call a 'fag', cleaned his shoes, lit his study fire, washed up, and so on. Owing to rheumatic fever Brian Trowell lost a year's education, and was 19 years 5 months old when he left the school for Cambridge.

Sophisticated John Ind, present here this afternoon, and with me in the Prep, invited me on arrival (I was three weeks late owing to illness – measles) to share a cigarette with him in the underground tunnel that links all the avenue houses called The Tube. 'Might we be expelled?' I asked. 'I have three brothers in this school, and they tell me they never expel anyone under ten' was the answer.

Roger Martin (who was also at Cambridge with me, as was Trowell) who acted in productions of mine in the post-war years, went back to Christ's

13 *Works*, p.435.   14 Ibid., p.432.

Hospital (bar four years teaching in Africa) for the rest of his working life as a master. These, and some twenty more, are still my close friends. Why? Lamb suggests an answer.

> In affectionate recollections of the place where he was bred up, in hearty recognitions of old school-fellows met with again after the lapse of years, or in foreign countries, the Christ's Hospital boy yields to none; I might almost say, he goes beyond most other boys. The very compass and magnitude of the school, its thousand bearings, the space it takes up in the imagination beyond the ordinary schools, impresses a remembrance, accompanied with an elevation of mind, that attends him through life. It is too big, too affecting an object, to pass away quickly from his mind.[15]

There is often a pressure of thought behind the words Lamb uses, which find their outlet in subtle perceptions that go beyond the obvious. A good example is Elia's meditation on Garrick's statue. Lamb's two essays on Christ's Hospital well exemplify this, not least in his understanding of friendships. I would add that the quotation I have just read does not only apply to the boys.

When I first moved up from Prep B to Middleton B in the senior school, my Senior Housemaster was a gentle ineffectual man who left all discipline to the monitors, and played the 'cello. As I had played the 'cello since before coming to the school, I felt we had something in common. He was replaced by Edward Malins soon after, an elegant teacher of English and the director of school Shakespeare plays, in which I acted. (Boys also played the female parts, as in Shakespeare's day.)

Malins had been to Worcester College, Oxford, and later served with the Royal Scots Greys during the Second World War as a Lieutenant in the Indian Army – in his free time playing polo at Poona. He would arrive at school corps parade, replete in shining leather belts, riding a stallion.

As Senior Housemaster he took over much of the beating, often following

15 Ibid., p.432.

Edward Malins

it with a glass of sherry, if he was not too annoyed. On leaving Christ's Hospital a few years after I did, he became my research student at Cambridge; then, when I moved over to Oxford, followed to become my research student there, publishing his thesis on *English Landscaping and Literature* with Oxford University Press in 1966. He owned a fine antique harpsichord and played it sparklingly. At school I sang or played in several concerts in which Malins accompanied the soloists, choir and orchestra with panache, and particularly one that all of us still remember with joy, Purcell's *King Arthur*.

This was conducted by a master who had, perhaps absent-mindedly, a considerable influence over my life and over the lives of many of my friends; an influence that was wholly good, indeed inspirational. His name was Cecil Cochrane, a handsome, blonde clergyman who had been a chorister, then later a Choral Scholar, in the choir of King's College, Cambridge. He had a fine, rich, bass-baritone voice.

Lamb says of 'our good and old steward' Mr Perry, of whom he was clearly fond:

> five hundred boys [would] feel towards him each as to their individual father. He had faults, with which we had nothing to do; but, with all his faults, indeed, Mr Perry was a most extraordinary creature.[16]

He might have said the same of Cecil Cochrane, whose universal nickname reveals his weakness (though none of us ever saw him actually drunk): Corks.

It was not what he said but what he was that made him so charismatic; what he stood for, the music he loved – Vaughan Williams, who used to visit

16 *Works*, p.430.

Cecil Cochrane

us, Constant Lambert, an Old Blue; Brahms, Bach, Handel – above all, Elgar; and Corks's magnificent organ playing, and solo singing. He was always, without fail, on the side of the boy in trouble, and ridiculously kind. Though a Junior Housemaster, he flatly refused to beat. Catching me smoking behind the Music School he said nothing, but later called me to his study to share with him at the piano some of his favourite arias. It was a delightful, long session in which I was introduced to much music I did not know. Throughout he smoked, as usual, but this time giving me cigarette after cigarette as our music unrolled. I went back to my house and was violently sick. Never since that day have I smoked a cigarette.

On one choir outing we ended the day by visiting his mother on her birthday. He had bought a birthday cake to give her with a large, edible rose on top. On the train he was, of course, tempted, dividing it between us all, and at the station presented her with the rose. She was most touched.

His flaws were so obvious that we loved him. A new Headmaster got rid of him, and he went as a Minor Canon to St Paul's Cathedral, where he found no outlet at first for his musical gifts. When I heard of his unhappiness I invited him to conduct my Cambridge orchestra and choir in Elgar's *Dream of Gerontius* in Ely Cathedral. I stepped down to conduct the Semi-Chorus; and a large number of his former pupils sang and played. Lamb's claim that 'The Christ's Hospital boy's friends at school are commonly his intimates through life' once again crossed the master/pupil divide.

At Corks's memorial service Edward Malins said:

> During this golden decade [he was] at the height of his powers,
> the finest choral trainer of any school in England.

This was true. Our chapel choir, in which I sang under Cochrane for five years, and from which I won the Choral Exhibition which gave me a Cambridge education, broadcast on the BBC at Christmas, and was the first school choir to issue gramophone records.

No fewer than thirteen of us won Choral Scholarships to Cambridge and Oxford, at least seven of them to sing under Boris Ord in King's: and there was a succession of organ scholars.

Lamb asks the reader's 'leave to remember our hymns and anthems, and

well-toned organ'. That same organ came to our new site at Horsham, and presides over the vast hall, the meeting-place, we call Big School. An even finer, five manual organ accompanies services in the chapel. I used to rise early and practice quietly on it, then stay for optional Holy Communion which either Corks or the chaplain would take, before walking over to the dining hall, thus skipping breakfast parade.

Lunch parade was to the music of the full military band, in which, from 1949-54, I played the trumpet, with John Ind as my co-trumpeter. For tea parade only three of us played, each blowing one of the school's 'silver bugles' while standing on the steps of the central fountain. Bryan Magee writes:

> Christ's Hospital was at that time barred from entering the annual public schools' band competition because it had invariably won when it did.[17]

This is because we practised and played together every day, week in week out, for the lunchtime march-past into dining hall.

The chapel played a large part in our lives, not only for those of us in the chapel choir, and organists. Charles Lamb in his 'Recollections' writes:

> The Christ's Hospital boy is a religious character. His school is eminently a religious foundation; it has its peculiar prayers, its services at set times, its graces, hymns and anthems, following each other in almost monastic closeness of succession.[18]

A childhood regulated thus leaves its permanent mark. At my previous Prep school at Amberley, the beautiful short evening service of Compline had, at that very early and impressionable age, been hard-wired into us:

> Visit, we beseech thee, O Lord, this dwelling, and drive from it all the snares of the enemy: let Thy holy angels dwell herein to preserve us in peace . . .

These 'snares of the enemy' we knew only too well, and were merely bemused why a ground-based metaphor should be used of aerial bombard-

17 Bryan Magee, *Growing Up in a War*, p.169.   18 *Works*, p.426.

ment. Those ringing phrases still sing in the blood: 'Lighten our darkness, we beseech thee, O Lord' (Compline was always by candlelight), 'and by thy great mercy defend us from all perils and dangers of this night; for the love of thy only Son, our Saviour, Jesus Christ'. 'Perils and dangers of this night', and those 'deeds of darkness', when I hear them still evoke the noise, and smell, and flashes of the blitz and the V 2s, our childhood anxiety in the darkness gently offset by love; and the dramatic visual evocations of Compline warmed our small hearts.

> Look down, O Lord, from thy heavenly throne, illuminate the
> darkness of this night with thy celestial brightness, and from
> the sons of light banish the deeds of darkness . . .

At Christ's Hospital this was magnified a thousandfold. Were not some of the hymns we sang written by Old Blues who had sung in this chapel? Sydney Carter's 'Lord of the Dance' for instance? Did not Vaughan Williams compose for us?[19] Admittedly, the Christianity was often unorthodox. Handel's duet for two basses sung by Corks and future King's choral scholar John Walker, 'The Lord is a man of war', or Charles Woods' anthem 'O Thou, the Central Orb', or Addison's hymn 'The spacious firmament on high', are scarcely in nodding distance of the sermon on the mount. This was a much more practical, muscular Christianity. In the classroom, for Divinity, we spent a great deal of time on St Paul's missionary journeys. He had, after all, visited a swathe of the British Dominions, even though on a Roman, rather than a British, passport.

> Now the Rome of slaves hath perish'd,
>   and the Rome of freemen[20] holds her place.

Yes, we learned Tennyson's praise of Virgil by heart. We, who were being groomed to be the new Proconsuls, needed to know such things. To the disgust of several masters, I won my year's Divinity Prize the year I left, as I had delighted in and mastered these coloured maps. The books I ordered for prize-giving were *Bach's 48 Preludes and Fugues* in two volumes, which I set

19 See Notes.   20 Imperial London.

out to learn by heart. Typically, I never mastered them all. Was this hubris? I also set out to learn every instrument in the orchestra. I only mastered two, trumpet and 'cello, and played in a very amateur way some of the related families of instruments. Yes, it was ridiculously over-ambitious; but at that age we felt, if we applied our minds to it, we could do anything.

Prayer clearly worked, especially if you were Church of England. Hadn't we stood alone, like Horatius in the face of impossible odds, against the whole might of conquered Europe from the North Cape to the Spanish frontier with only a few Spitfires, and won? 'Every prayer is answered (even if not always in the way we want); every curse returns' we were taught in our Shakespeare class.

The sermons on occasion were so impressive that we remember them today. We were inspected on parade by Field Marshal Montgomery, Chairman of the Governors of the school my three brothers were at, St John's School, Leatherhead – his one comment to an occasional victim as he walked the ranks was 'Get your hair cut!'; and later an American Colonel preached to us in Chapel. We remember his sermon sixty years or so later partly because of the preacher's name: Colonel O. Heck. He began in his slow, southern drawl:

> If I were a millionaire, I would build a monument, one mile long, one mile broad, and one mile high; and on it I would write in letters of gold: 'Samson the Mighty: Samson the Failure'.

We were stunned. Who could forget that?

The Headmaster's sermons, washed – indeed sometimes overwhelmed – through a sea of metaphor, were unique. Roger Martin mischievously tape-recorded one on his Grundig, a recording I still have. Flecker is preaching on Elisha.

> Even the very youngest [of you] are not far from the river of life, and the older are on its very brink. Life rolls before us cold, turbid, unfriendly. There, at our feet, lies the mantle. Are we

great enough to grasp it, and smite the waters? This mantle is an allegory, the mantle of tradition. If you want to be a man, you must do as that young prophet did. You must take up the mantle, and use it. You must *smite* the waters of life with all the best that you have learned.

There are ships enough that ply upon the river: luxurious launches of materialism, trim packet-boats of respectability, skiffs for the athletic to scull, punts for the idler, and, for the clever people, graceful yachts that tack to and fro, catching each veering breeze of fancy or false doctrine. At the worst, there is the raft of indecision which will drift us somewhere, and *may* keep our feet *fairly* dry . . .

No great men ever sail the river. They *smite* the waters and go through a-foot.

It is not an easy path across the river. On this side and on that rise walls of seething water, shot with the mud of social strife, livid with hate and mortal anger, frothing with lies. The storms rage, the lightnings flash, the waves threaten to engulf the hardy traveller, but he who in lonely faith has grasped the mantle and smitten the waters finds he is no longer alone. At his side is one that he seems to know . . . Here is the joy of perfect manhood.

Our headmaster was a tall, pipe-smoking classicist called H. L. O. Flecker. He spoke to you, the Charles Lamb Society, for these birthday celebrations when I was a boy under him at the school in 1950. To be fair to him, he saw the school successfully through the war, in the full knowledge that, being not too far from the south coast, and a wholly self-sustaining and self-contained estate, it would be Hitler's barracks in the first wave of his invasion. The concrete shed in the Headmaster's garden by the Chapel still has on its walls, if you move the logs over, the dates, inscribed by Flecker at the time, recording each of the many nights he slept there during air-raids, planning the battle.

The weary and disorientated Nazis would have encountered nearly one hundred First World War veterans only too keen to have another crack at the Boche, this time on home ground; and eight hundred and forty tough, young, highly disciplined, trained, fit, and motivated boys – for many were at the school because they had lost their fathers.

We had our own well-equipped armoury run by a real Sergeant-Major, and we knew the terrain; every underground passage and back stairs. We all spoke German, for German, not French was the school's second language taught and learned for just such an eventuality. Like the ancient Greeks, this is what, on sports field and parade ground, in classroom and chapel, we had been steeled for. Boys and masters were ready, and could have pinned down a battalion of the Wehrmacht.

> And how can man die better
> Than facing fearful odds
> For the ashes of his fathers,
> And the temples of his gods?

Flecker also translated St John's Gospel from the Greek, and taught the Grecians Divinity from his translation. He was the brother of the poet James Elroy Flecker, who was homosexual. Flecker could not bear to hear his brother mentioned.

What, you may ask, of the Chaplain? In my long time at the school we had more than one, and I can remember little, save one excellent piece of wholly unorthodox advice on what was the only time I asked for spiritual guidance. 'Should I come to Holy Communion if I was not in a state of grace?' I knew the terrifying edict of St Paul in *I Corinthians* 29 promising damnation.

> Good heavens, boy, none of us are. Of course. Keep coming.

So I did not give up, after all.

We had our own language, the same for Lamb as for myself, and, I dare say, it may still be in use in the school, though I know it is no longer a sealed community such as nourishes a private language. Edmund Blunden drew up a list of words, and it is a long one. Here are some:

Crug	–	bread
Bodge	–	paper, both writing and lavatory
Flab	–	butter
Kiff	–	tea or coffee
Housey	–	(adj. or noun) Christ's Hospital
Skiff	–	to scrape leavings off your plate
Sicker	–	the infirmary
Spadge	–	to walk
Taffs	–	potatoes
Fotch	–	a blow across the head with the flat of the hand: the usual minor punishment by masters and boys alike.
Gag	–	meat, especially fat.

Eight years is a long time, whether Lamb's or my own, to compress into a lecture; but three-and-sixty years ago Lamb's school's way of life was in most respects still ours. It shaped him, and Coleridge, as it shaped us, giving us a remarkable education, and start in life, for nearly all of us a lifetime of good health; a value-system, self-discipline, expertise, and lasting friends. Who could not be grateful – as I am to Chutney, my guinea-pig, whose far-reaching death happened while I was struggling with my text-books by B H Kennedy, and Hillard and Botting, far from home at my first Prep School. Doesn't Hamlet remind us that

There is a special providence in the fall of a sparrow?

So I thank, in Charles Lamb's words:

> Our Founder, that godly and royal child, King Edward the Sixth, the flower of the Tudor name – the young flower that was untimely cropt, as it began to fill our land with its early odours – the boy-patron of boys – the serious and holy child who walked with Cranmer and Ridley – fit associate, in those tender years, for the bishops, and future martyrs of our Church, to receive,

or (as occasion sometimes proved), to give instruction.[21]

And I close by thanking you for inviting me; thanking Samuel Salt – Lamb's mentor–Governor and Timothy Yeats Lamb's Presentation Governor to Christ's Hospital; and thanking my own, Mrs Gladys Willis, whose generosity, and whose compassionate understanding on that fateful day with my mother, opened to me the hospitality of Christ.

The beauty of shared music never lies but transcends time balms grief and makes amends

Two lines from a poem by Francis Warner carved in stone on the entrance to the Music School at Christ's Hospital.[22]

21 *Works*, p.436.   22 See Notes.

Memorial Service Address for
The Very Revd Professor Henry Chadwick
K.B.E., D.D., Mus.B., etc.,
23 June 1920 – 17 June 2008

Great St Mary's, Cambridge, 22 November 2008

HENRY THE MUSICIAN

HENRY CHADWICK was prepared for ordination, and made Deacon on 19 September 1943, by a man he admired and honoured for the rest of his life: William Temple, Archbishop of Canterbury. My father was Temple's personal chaplain – and so Henry and I first met.

Temple died on Thursday, 26 October, 1944. Shortly before, on September 23, Temple gathered his candidates round his sick bed on the eve of their ordination to remind them of the responsibility they were taking on with their vows. Henry says he was filled with panic. In his words:

> William Temple described his father's sermons as 'granite on fire'. The phrase would equally describe William's charge to his ordinands.

(*All unattributed quotations are from Henry's letters to me over the years.*)

Henry then became curate of Emmanuel Church, South Croydon. My father was Vicar of nearby Epsom, and was again mentor to Henry, charged with giving pastoral care to some of the young curates in the vicinity. They needed it. Between that September and the following March, 2,855 people were killed, being within range of the German flying bombs, the V1 and V2 rockets, whose flight path, directly over Epsom and Croydon, followed the railway lines into London. Our area was known as 'bomb alley'.

It is against this background of cacophony, falling houses, chaos, sirens and fear that Henry's love of music should be seen. It was refuge in an

alternative world of pure form and its delight, expressing intense emotions
with graciousness and truth. Or to use not my words now but Henry's:

> . . . among the arts music possesses this extraordinary power, a
> power utterly to absorb, for the very good reason that it cannot
> be performed well unless it does utterly absorb the performers
> and will not be understood by the listeners unless they allow it
> to become a controlling medium through which their souls
> aspire to the divine beauty.[1]

To this background of fear, and savagery from the air, in Henry's case we
must go back and add a more personal well-spring.

Henry had arrived at Eton as a King's Scholar in 1933. The following year
his housemaster summoned him to his study to tell the boy that his father
had died. Henry's mother, a gifted pianist, had filled their bustling family
life – there were four brothers and two sisters – with music-making. Grief,
and the natural home-sickness of a boarding-school boy at such a time,
drove him deeper into music for consolation.

He took up the bassoon, and quickly became good enough to play in the
school orchestra; indeed, this tall boy with his long instrument would have
gone on playing the bassoon after leaving school had he not had to give it up
because he could not afford to buy so expensive a woodwind.

But his future was to lie with the organ. He was named 'Keeper of the
College Organ', and had four years in Eton's fifteenth-century chapel learning on that magnificent William Hill instrument under the guidance of
Henry Ley. He would travel with him when Ley went to give recitals at various cathedrals. More than sixty-five years later, in 2001 when reminiscing in
a Senior Common Room talk about the royal invitation to him to assume the
Deanship of Christ Church, Henry told his listeners:

> I had of course been in Tom Quad, first taken there in 1935 by
> that great musician Henry Ley to visit Thomas Armstrong in
> the Cathedral organ loft.

1 Henry Chadwick, *Tradition and Exploration: Collected Papers on Theology and the Church*,
Norwich, Canterbury Press, 1994, p.207.

While at Eton Henry would often walk over to St George's Chapel, Windsor, to turn the pages for that organist, William Harris. Harris composed anthems such as the double choir motet, 'Faire is the Heaven', and music for two coronations, those of 1937 and 1953. Both Henry Ley and William Harris became important father figures to Henry during these adolescent years. He could not have had better mentors.

In 1937 Henry won a Music Scholarship to Magdalene College, Cambridge. In all but name it was the Organ Scholarship, carrying with it the customary duties of running the chapel choir, which he did for three years.

The practical examination for the scholarship took place in Trinity College chapel, on the Harrison organ:

> a competition in which I competed with the later head of BBC music who had the bad luck to hit a fortissimo B flat at the final entry of the St Anne fugue.

Henry, who himself was about to offer Bach's St Anne fugue, heard this mistake while waiting his turn, and so made very sure that

> my left foot found the fortissimo A flat thereby gaining me a scholarship that secured me a university education.

You will have the opportunity to listen for that moment played by David Goode at the end of this service.

He went up to Magdalene in October 1938 and came under two key influences. One was Francis Turner, M.C., D.F.C., a veteran of the Royal Flying Corps in the First World War, and severely injured. He ran the Music Scholarship at Magdalene, and became the college father figure to Henry.

The other was Boris Ord, who conducted the King's choir, and was also the University Organist. He, too, had been in the Royal Flying Corps, returning to the R.A.F. as a Flight Lieutenant in the Second World War, and he was seriously injured. Neither Boris nor Francis allowed that to interfere with their University musical careers.

Of Dr Ord Henry wrote in another letter:

Boris Ord with his two senior choristers from King's College choir, Cambridge[2]

> Boris was the greatest influence on me . . . In my time reading music as an undergraduate no one had a more magical effect as a teacher than Boris . . . [He] was simply one of the greatest practical musicians in our lifetime. His choir was unsparing in quest of perfection.

Through Boris Henry met London musicians such as Constant Lambert, before whom he played one night in Boris's rooms, F.6., over jumbo arch:

> It was in my first term as a young Music Scholar at Magdalene. I got back to the College about 9.00 pm and the porter told me to 'telephone Mr Ord at King's' whose lectures on Score reading I was attending. I walked round to the Gibbs building and there found Boris and a group of dinner party friends. B[oris] explained they wanted to hear on his 2 pianos Chabrier's arrangement of his *España*. Being one of the green things on the earth, as in the Benedicite, I had never seen it and had to sight read, despite some technical difficulties. Paddy Hadley had dined well. He turned over my pages – very necessary as the music is fast. He shouted 'Bravo' as he turned each page, simultaneously smiting me in the back every time. It was all an education to a boy of 18½.

2 Boris Ord, 9 July 1897 – 30 December 1961, with his two senior choristers from King's College choir, Cambridge, at the Three Choirs Festival at Worcester in 1957. On his right is Christopher Cornwell and on his left Richard White 'probably the finest King's treble voice in the twentieth century' (see Notes). They are listening to Walton's *Belshazzar's Feast* while following in the score.

Sacheverell Sitwell was one of the party. I had read his book on Domenico Scarlatti. He was very kind. I got back to Magdalene, where my rooms were under the Pepys Library, on the last stroke of midnight – at that date (1938) the prescribed limit.

Many years later, when he was Dean of Christ Church, Oxford, he 'teamed up with Sidney Watson to give a memorable concert in the Upper Library.'[3] They played the second Rachmaninov suite for two pianos, and then Chabrier's arrangement of his own *España*: indeed, they played it with such vigour (Henry's head doubtless full of memories of that undergraduate evening in King's) that a retired Colonel announced at the end that the effect was comparable to drinking a full bottle of Scotch.

In 1939, having been up at Cambridge only a year, he won the John Stewart of Rannoch Prize for his knowledge of Elgar's and Newman's *Dream of Gerontius*. Boris Ord and Edward Dent were his examiners. During Henry's first two years, Edward Dent was his supervisor for Composition, and for History of Music: Edward Dent, tall, thin, bespectacled, delighting in startling remarks; governor of the Sadler's Wells Opera, and a director of the Covent Garden Opera Trust; this Etonian Fellow of King's enlarged Henry's musical techniques and widened those horizons.

Henry also attended an Ear Test class with Paddy Hadley, Fellow of Gonville and Caius, who would from time to time, to keep up his sock, disconcertingly push drawing pins through it into his war-time wooden leg. In one such class Paddy Hadley asked them to name the keys of the last three chords of Debussy's *L'Après-midi d'un faune*. No one knew them – except Henry.

> For a whole year (Henry writes) I had the luck to be the piano-accompanist for C.U.M.S., and I learnt rapidly that I must know the music by heart, for the reason that one's eye could be nowhere but on Boris's beat. He was doing Beethoven's *Missa Solemnis*. The 'Dona nobis' was terrifying . . . quite taxing – especially the 'Et vitam venturi.'

3 Mark Rowlinson, *Christ Church Magazine*, 2002.

Just as Henry was starting to write his examination fugue for the Mus.B. in the Old Music School in Downing Place, the cinema organist next door in St Andrew's Street began practising, shattering his peace. With typically impressive concentration he composed the fugue to completion and handed it in. As we know, he passed. Even as a boy, as evidenced by his King's Scholarship to Eton, he had this gift of intense concentration. It was the key to his extraordinary achievements.

Henry could not be named in the Class List for the Theological Tripos, which he read for and sat. In his words:

> I was not allowed to be a candidate for Honours in Theology, having spend my first 2 years getting a Mus.B.. Charles Raven told me that I had a First in Theology but it couldn't be official or published.

Bedford College, London, had been evacuated to Newnham College, Cambridge, just as the evacuation from Dunkirk had begun, and Henry met a multi-talented musician from Bedford College at a Sunday tea party at St Paul's Vicarage. She was singing in C.U.M.S. when Boris was conducting Handel's *Israel in Egypt*, just as the war was making it topical. Boris's C.U.M.S. accompanist proceeded to court Peggy on two pianos in Magdalene. Margaret Brownrigg, as Peggy was then, had herself studied at the Tobias Matthay Piano School in Wimpole Street, London, and twice performed in pupil concerts at the Wigmore Hall. Afterwards Peggy took her L.R.A.M. as a soprano, and amused their theological friends in later life by saying that she had married her accompanist.

When Henry returned to Cambridge in 1946, as a Fellow of Queens' College, he often performed at the Music Club concerts. John Dykes Bower came from St Paul's Cathedral in London to play the Bach 3 piano concerto with Boris Ord and Henry. They also played Bach's A minor 4 piano concerto.

He loved to play the Brahms Horn Trio with a good violinist. At Oxford in the 1950s he met the composer Zoltán Kodály, then at the height of his fame with many English Public Schools performing his *Missa Brevis*, its music dappled with the understated anguish of our recent war. Kodály turned the pages for Henry in a performance of Schubert's E Flat Trio at one of the soirées Margaret Deneke held in her North Oxford house on Sunday afternoons.

> 'On one occasion at Christ Church', Mark Rowlinson writes, 'I brought some songs along after dinner by Schumann, including one or two that Henry had not previously encountered. "I don't know this one. What key would you like it in?" Schumann is notoriously difficult to transpose, especially at sight, because of its harmonic twists and turns – this was accompanying at the level of Geoffrey Parsons or Roger Vignoles.'

At Christ Church, and at Peterhouse, after a Governing Body meeting, he would go straight to his Steinway Grand and play a difficult piece of music with fortissimo bass chords; and prior to performing at a college concert at Peterhouse, Peggy remembers, Henry put in some very serious practice to play Beethoven's Kreutzer sonata with a highly gifted undergraduate violinist. At the Peterhouse May Week concert in June 1993, when, aged 73, he was retiring from the Mastership, he played Mozart's Sonata for 2 pianos in D major with Marie Noelle Kendall, a professional pianist, and the wife of one of the Fellows. It was his last public appearance as a pianist.

Writing of St Augustine Henry wrote:

> It is probably of himself that he writes when he says (*de Libero arbitrio*, ii, 13, 35) that there are 'many for whom happiness consists in the music of voices and strings, and who count themselves miserable when music is lacking in their lives.'[4]

Surely it is not only Augustine but Henry who is speaking of himself.

For many years Henry and I have lived opposite each other in St John Street, Oxford, and in our retirements he has frequently come over the road for a mid-morning musical break.

What did we talk about? One thought he shared turned up soon after in

4 *Tradition and Exploration*, p.207.

a lecture he gave, in 1981, and was then published, so I can share it with you. It shows Henry's intellectual clarity when being self-aware of his own emotional response: not an easy thing. He uses the old title of what you and I know as Mozart's wind serenade in B flat major, the "Gran Partita", K.361; Mozart's wedding gift to Constanze, his bride:

> The slow movement of Mozart's Divertimento for thirteen
> wind instruments makes a moving anthem for Trinity Sunday,
> *Quis te comprehendat?* I confess I find the music even more
> moving for wind instruments than when sung by a choir with
> organ accompaniment . . . [It has parts for *two* bassoons.] . . .
> But no one could plausibly urge that its employment as an
> anthem is inherently unsuitable, for the opposite is clearly the
> case. The music expresses a sense of awe and quietness with
> exquisite adoration.[5]

The very last time, Lady Chadwick, Peggy, brought Henry across to sit with Penelope my wife as I put on a recording – as we could no longer make music together as we did – of the King's choir conducted first by Boris, and then an anthem conducted by one of the greatest of Cambridge musicians – a brave man, who won the Military Cross in battle – Sir David Willcocks. We listened to the motet 'Faire is the heaven, where happie soules have place' – words from Pembroke College's perfect poet, Edmund Spenser's *Hymne of Heavenly Beautie*, set by Henry's old father figure from St George's Chapel, Windsor: William Harris.

Faire indeed now is Henry Chadwick's heaven, where his happie soule has place; probably already in the sub-stalls as a probationer for the angelic choir. I'll end with words from a sermon he gave in King's Chapel, May 1991.

> Of all the arts, music is the one to which order and regularity
> matter most deeply. But it is also the art with the greatest
> detachment from objects which we can touch and see. It there-
> fore has a power to take us into a world beyond matter. At least

---

5 *Tradition and Exploration*, p.207.

for a few fleeting moments it can deliver us from the chance
and chaos of our lives, and by its very transitoriness point us
towards that which abides.

St Cecilia's Day, 2008

Henry Chadwick at Albert Schweitzer's piano playing Bach's Prelude and Fugue in
C minor *at Schweitzer's house at Günsbach, near Freiburg. September 1999*

The Song that is Christmas

When a poet thinks of Christmas, he very often thinks of the carol. Indeed, the very term 'carol' today means little more than a Christmas song.

So a carol service may include lyrics as different in tone as 'In the bleak midwinter, Frosty wind made moan' and 'God rest you merry, Gentlemen, Let nothing you dismay;' and as diverse in technical form as 'While shepherds watched their flocks by night' and 'O little town of Bethlehem' (both hymns); 'I saw three ships come sailing in', a street ballad: and traditional lullaby, such as *Rocking:* 'Little Jesus, sweetly sleep, do not stir.'

Many have been handed down from the Middle Ages. But the word then had a different meaning. Far from being a term exclusive to Christmas and alluding to subject matter, it was simply the name for any lyric which had a chorus or *burden* which could be sung by dancers as they held hands in a ring.

So a 'true' carol would be distinguished by its form. It would have a burden sung at the beginning calling, perhaps, the partakers in the coming dance to join hands: then as the first verse was sung the singers would dance a complete circle; pausing at this stage to repeat the burden while they gained breath before dancing in the opposite direction for the second verse.

When this is remembered, and the derivation of the word from the old French *carole*, meaning a ring-dance, is borne in mind, then one's attitude to some of the more apparently unusual carols alters.

Poems such as 'Lord Jesus hath a garden full of flowers gay,' 'Tomorrow shall be my dancing day', and 'Willie, take up your little drum,' far from being oddities included in modern carol books by a quirk of the editors are rather the original types of what has now become a somewhat misleading term.

For in the mediaeval world it was the carol that sang of summer, of dancing and the open air; and in direct contrast to it was the ballad. Whereas the form of the carol depended on a burden which was external to the narrative

stanzas (and its definition depended on this burden), the ballad either had
no chorus at all, or, if it had one, it was a part of the stanzas themselves, often
the second and fourth lines:

> 'What will you leave to your brother John?'
>   With a hey ho and a lillie gay.
> 'The gallows-tree to hang him on.'
>   As the primrose spreads so sweetly.

The atmosphere conjured up by the ballad was one of darkness and unease,
of a single singer on a winter night standing by the fire after a communal
feast, relating tales of sudden violence and unquiet graves to a silent
company, while outside

> 'The wind doth blow today, my love.
>   And a few small drops of rain . . .'

But in place of one man singing to the listening darkness, the carol
presupposed open-air and gaiety, young folk holding hands and singing
their own music for the dance. Fear of death and world beyond is replaced
by joy in life, and a celebration of

> The rising of the sun
> And the running of the deer . . .

Where the ballad is impartial and doom-laden, the carols sing of more intimate and lyrical subjects — of lovers, of mothers suckling children, and
hence, on occasion, of the Virgin Mary and her Child.

But carols were not limited to religious subjects. We still have one in the
manuscript of Henry VIII which has a burden opening:

> 'Blow thi horne, hunter, and blow thi horne on hye!
> Ther ys a do in yonder wode . . .'

Another burden seems to have come into rather indecorous being
because choirboys were asked to sing too many plainsong notes to too few
syllables.

Then, as now, if boys are asked to sing wordless *melisma*, or too decorative a tune to no words, they make up mnemonics. So from an over-decorated setting of Kyrie Eleison came the burden (and with it a whole carol):

> Kyrie, so kyrie.
> Jankyn synget merie
> With Aleyson.

Secular May-day dance has found its way into the Penitent's cry for mercy.

On the other hand, a great many carols were not popular in origin, such perhaps as this one and many if not most of the early ballads, but rather popular by destination.

So a secular ring-dance with a well-known tune might be 'converted' to religious ends by the alteration of certain key words. Many a Christmas lullaby began life as a lover's *aubade*, the traditional tender song of daybreak-parting and safe-keeping:

> This endris night
> I saw a sight
> A star as bright as day;
> And ever among
> A maiden sung
> 'Lullay, by, by, lullay.'

Indeed, many of our finest and most poignant carols depend for their purity of tone on the blend of romantic with mother-love.

> I saw a fair maiden
> Sitten and sing:
> She lulled a little child,
> A sweete lording:
> Lullay my liking, my dear son, my sweeting:
> Lullay my dear hert, mine own dear darling.

And perhaps the most fragile, the most uncannily beautiful of all, is that

15th century distillation of this blend, that carol which draws on the atmosphere of dawn, on May-song, lover's compliment and mother's lullaby.

> I sing of a maiden
>   That is makèless;
> King of all kings
>   To her son she ches.
> He came all so stillè
>   Where his mother was
> As dew in Aprilè
>   That falleth on grass.

Such poems are not all the result of Christian re-writing of secular song.
Rather, the re-casting of such songs created the climate in which such a
distillation might occur.

But quite other forms could result, not the least common being the
macaronic, or poem written in more than one language, often Latin and the
vernacular.

Sometimes a tag from the liturgy (until the time of Henry VIII, of course,
sung and said always in Latin) would fill up an offending line, at others
the juxtapositioning of sonorous Latin with homely everyday English
would bring out the divinity of the Christ-child, together with his ordinary
humanity:

> *O lux beata Trinitas*
> He lay between an ox and ass.

and in the famous German-Latin carol (or hymn)

> *In dulci jubilo*
> Now sing with hearts aglow!
> Our delight and pleasure
> Lies *in praesepio* . . .

where the roles of the two languages are reversed, the homely stable manger
being honoured, on account of its great guest, with its resonant Latin name.

Some of the most popular of the carols, too, are those that were originally pagan, but have been drawn into the service of Church's Year, such as that haunting and strange blend of the pagan ballad world and the Christian carol, a pagan dance of male and female tree-worship, 'The Holly and the Ivy':

> The holly bears a berry
> As red as any blood,
> And Mary bore sweet Jesus Christ
> To do poor sinners good.

In this poem the two traditions, clerical and pagan, are for once not blended at all, but simply set side by side. The first half of each verse is utterly different in diction, meaning and style from the third and fourth lines even in the burden; and the first and last verses have remained unaltered.

> The holly and the ivy
> When they are both full grown
> Of all the trees that are in the wood
> The holly bears the crown.

Into this world of superstition and fear, fertility and tree-worship, the 'merry organ' and 'sweet singing in the choir' enter with charming incongruity.

So the carol began as a May dance in the open air, and was brought indoors into the church to lend its joy to the mid-winter festival. Yet it never wholly lost its origins. Whenever one sings a carol burden, the dancing ghosts take hands, and as the Latin phrases are taken up, memories of some choir-boy's whipping may return.

The lover and the Wise Men, the mistress and the Virgin, the Mother with her young baby and the old father, the pagan desperation and Christmas joy all lend their strength to body forth the central paradox of the life-force crucified, of the infant and new-born God; not only in solemnity, but also with delight:

Green groweth the holly,
So doth the ivy;
The God of life can never die,
Hope! Saith the holly.

Francis Warner on tour in America, as guest at the organ of St Mary the Virgin, Aldermanbury: the Wren church (1677) bombed in the London blitz, then transported to Westminster College, Fulton, Missouri, USA as a memorial to Winston Churchill. The mother and child in the mirror are the organist's wife Penelope and their daughter Miranda; April 1987

A Cambridge Friendship:
Kathleen Raine and Francis Warner

'Well do I remember sitting in the garden of Clare with you when you were Peter Pan.'[1] It was 20 July 1961, and we were sharing a garden seat on the grass beside the formal pool, planted as it still is with irises, reeds and water-lilies, and protected from sounds of punts on the nearby river by an enclosing yew hedge, in the Fellows' Garden of Clare College, Cambridge.

I had just heard I was to be proposed for a University teaching post, although I was only twenty-three and had been (on account of my College teaching position) for the last two years by far the youngest member of what was then a very elderly English Faculty. Kathleen Raine handed me a beautifully printed book, the Nonesuch Press edition of Geoffrey Keynes's *The Complete Writings of William Blake* (1957), inscribed for me by her with the place — Clare Garden — and the date. It was an older poet's blessing on a younger, thoughtfully prepared and staged by her.

Five years ago (after I had remained nearly a decade at Cambridge, and lectured at Oxford for a further thirty-four years until retirement back to my old Cambridge College) she began a letter to me with the words: 'What a pleasure to be writing to you once more at St Catharine's College! I hope they have given you a lovely set of rooms. So long ago since Tom Henn presided, and it was through him we met!'[2]

The rooms St Catharine's has generously given me for my retirement years are in fact the same rooms on C staircase, overlooking Main Court, that had for many years belonged to Tom Henn; rooms in which he had supervised me, and had introduced me to Kathleen.

She at that time had been working on what was to become the massive two-volume publication by Princeton University Press, in the Bollingen Series,

1 Kathleen Raine to Francis Warner, 9 October 1998   2 K.R. to F.W., 9 September 1999.

Tom Henn

of her A. W. Mellon Lectures in 1962, *Blake and Tradition.* Her working habit was to write down the quotations from memory. As a result, someone was needed to check them. 'If you were serious in your kind offer to help with my bibliography, etc. I would be more than grateful. Could you telephone me about this? I am starting work on it now, and the checking seems likely to be formidable.'[3]

Towards the end of the project she sent another note from Girton, where from 1954 to 1961 she had been a Research Fellow: 'I told the Bollingen people yesterday that you might be willing to help again, but that if they called on you they must pay you — but this probably won't arise — but I wanted to feel that Peter Pan might return if more magic were needed . . .'[4]

Blake and Tradition, the work of which C. S. Lewis, my research supervisor, had said, 'When the Big Book finally appears I think all the pre-Raine views of Blake will be obsolete for ever',[5] was finally published in 1968.

Kathleen's letter recalling that 'laying on of hands' in Clare Garden continues:

> The other occasion I remember so clearly is one evening in Oxford when you took me home and showed me Benedict in his cradle adorned as for a holy child, as he was, and the special glow of that room [my study] with your sleeping child. Memories never die, and all lie there awaiting resurrection. Some are terrible and shameful, are the awaiting hell, but others are fresh and lovely, and knowing you, Francis, is one of the precious strands woven into my life.[6]

3 K. R. to F.W., undated.   4 K.R. to F.W., undated.   5 C. S. Lewis to K.R., 5 December 1958.
6 K.R. to F.W., 9 October 1998.

In Cambridge the friendship was that of a beginner poet with an older, established one. Not only did she make sure my poems were published, she also offered to write a paragraph for the dust jacket of the American edition to promote them in the USA.

In Oxford, the relationship was between two close colleagues. I invited Kathleen to lecture for me on David Gascoyne, and published her lecture in *Studies in the Arts* (1968), a volume made up of lectures by my old Cambridge colleagues whom I had invited over to speak in Oxford, to try to put pressure on the English Faculty to update its syllabus beyond the year 1900.

Suheil Bushrui

Over the years we often travelled together on poetry-reading tours to Beirut, the USA, Switzerland and elsewhere. Often our host was Professor Suheil Bushrui, whom we had met at the Yeats International Summer School at Sligo, in Ireland, in the early 1960s; he became one of our closest friends: 'His unique gift is the ardour of spiritual fire. He has a way of appearing from time to time, like a Djinn from the desert, at significant moments — or perhaps the moments become significant only with his arrival . . . Like Gibran, Suheil himself is a bringer of wisdom, healing and harmony into our world of ignorance, conflict and fear.'[7]

When Suheil was Professor of English Literature at the American University of Beirut, we visited him several times. The last time, as my wife Penelope and I were leaving the house for Heathrow, the telephone rang. It was Suheil, to say that the fighting in Lebanon had engulfed Beirut airport so we should not come. Kathleen, however, had already left her home and landed in the heart of the conflict: 'I am so glad in retrospect that I did go to Beirut for the cancelled conference, and that I was given a glimpse of civil war and hatred, the living reality of what Suheil stands for. I don't remember

7 Kathleen Raine, *Poetry and Peace* (typescript).

the details of how many times his house was bombed, or of the year he left for America — I should have consulted you . . '[8]

There were peaceful days, too. Kathleen took my small daughter Georgina for a walk beside the Cherwell river at Old Marston one sunny winter's day and taught her a lesson she has never forgotten — which nettles sting. Next day Kathleen wrote: '*Pink-flowered* dead-nettles don't sting, either! Only nettles without flowers sting! Think of it — it ought always to be so![9]

She could appreciate me teaching a class with W. H. Auden, but not his poetry: 'I detest Auden's work, incidentally; it's all I believe poetry should not be.'[10]

Oxford itself, though, meant much to her:

> I have enjoyed your *Oxford* [poem] immensely . . . I have felt
> that Oxford is a part of what I am, and must be for all of us who
> were at Cambridge. It is a part of what used to be the life-blood
> of England and being English. Much as I have rebelled, I recog-
> nize it as being there. Rebel though I have been, and imperfect
> as my 'belonging' is. It is in spite of myself that I feel I do
> 'belong' in a way that pulls at my heart more than I would
> have expected. In a way it completes your plays about our
> civilization and its key moments.
>
> I hope your picture of Oxford remains true . . . the continu-
> ity of values, concern for the young, not the star performers,
> but the small things like reading a colleague's piece of writ-
> ing to check the notes, and whatever is the opposite of name-
> dropping: Bowra appearing because he was kind to his mother,
> Edmund Blunden because of his courage in suffering his trau-
> matic memories of the First World War, Lewis very much
> present in the background, Auden roused from a fit of gloom
> by a Martini to give a glowing teaching session to students
> sitting on your floor . . .

8 K.R. to F.W., 2 July 1997. 9 K.R. to F.W., 28 December 1966. 10 K.R. to F.W., 18 May (no year).

I have in a sense rejected and dropped out of that civilized continuity, and your poem stirs a sad nostalgia in me for something I might have been a part of had I been more generous and loving and humble. There will always be people like me who cannot or refuse to be a part of that texture, but please God there will always be people like you, Francis, who delight in the weaving of it, from friend to friend, from generation to generation . . .[11]

Even so, it was my return to Cambridge – 'it's where you belong' – that brought out her most passionate memories:

I found your birthday present when I got home and could not wait to read your poem on Cambridge. Although you were a generation (at least) younger than I, it amazed me how our lives flowed into and through one another, which is indeed what a University essentially is. For example, Boris Ord plays a great part in your life, and he did in mine — I joined his Madrigal Society in my first year (or conceivably my second) and that was one of the wonderful experiences of Cambridge for me. I had never heard of, much less heard, madrigals before, and the beauty of both English, but more especially Italian, madrigals remains with me to this day . . . I was also a modest second soprano in C.U.M.S. under Dr Rootham, and I remember doing Vaughan Williams's *Sea Symphony*, and the composer coming to conduct us . . .

I think that, besides the beauty of the colleges and Cambridge itself as a place, it is music which meant the most to me of what I learned there. Bach's *B minor Mass*, Purcell's *Dido and Aeneas*, and simpler carols at Girton which we sang.

Tom [Henn] was indeed a part of that life, but for me that was later, when I had come back to Girton as a Research

11 K.R. to F.W., 19 August 2002.

Two guest poets recover after their poetry-reading double act. Switzerland, September 1990

Fellow. That was when we knew one another, and of course
Sligo . . . Happy days . . .

I also encountered another Cambridge, the cerebral liberal
and Marxist Cambridge of Empson and Bronowski and the
'Heretics', but the marvel of my first two years was the newly
founded Festival Theatre, which was I now realize a child of
the Irish renaissance . . . I think that was all over by the time
you arrived. C. S. Lewis was there by then — another marvellous moment . . .

With all my love; that poem is truly matter from the heart,
and the true heart of Cambridge.[12]

Her clarity of mind and perception remained sharp:

I can see now how all your work has built up into a unity.
It is about civilization — or perhaps *a* civilization, the one

12 K.R. to F.W., 24 June 2001.

we inherit — and selects certain moments, certain people, who represent and have carried that civilization right from its beginnings. It is quite something to have done, Francis, and I am grateful, even though I prefer Vermeer to Rembrandt myself, while realizing I am probably wrong in doing so; but the 'warts and all' aspect of our heritage is not congenial to me. Just as I prefer Shelley to all the other poets of his century, and don't like Dickens.[13]

Her gift of friendship never failed:

You, as I realised only very recently, are now I think my oldest friend. And a long and close link it is, deeply fraternal in shared memories and much in common after all in our shared culture and shared values. Shared values we didn't even know we held. The invisible ones are the most real, and what brings them to light is a total change in that background . . . the class structure represented by Oxford and Cambridge served England very well and that is where we both belong, although you more than me, because I was a late comer. My Mother was Scotch, my Father was a son of the working class, and that is where his sympathies lay. The culture of the Methodist (Wesleyan) Church. But he rose by way of education, which meant English Literature, Shakespeare and Wordsworth in his case, and Latin and Anglo-Saxon . . .[14]

Her compassion was there to the last:

Little did I think when I suggested that Brian [Keeble] and Stephen Overy should invite you to speak at the launch of my *Collected Poems* that Stephen would bring news of your illness — cancer is a dread word, but truly our life in this world, however long, is only a moment and we must look beyond, not in longer continuity but into another dimension, in which of

13 K.R. to F.W., 5 September 2002. 14 K.R. to F.W., 19 August 2002.

Colin Smythe

course we already are. But what a precious moment it is, and
we are here to perform a task, to make our souls, finally to do
the will of God. Long may you be here in this world, Francis,
where your gifts and your wisdom are much needed, and may
a cure be found; but we know that there is no cure for what we
are. We pass through, as the sparrow through the hall of the
Northumbrian King. Where do we come from and where do
we go and who are we? But it is here we meet and love one
another, and what a miraculous world this one is . . . Like
Blake's Angels all I can say is 'Holy, Holy, Holy is the Lord God
Almighty!' As I know you also do, dear friend.[15]

Kathleen died on 6 July 2003. Her last letter, of 9 May 2003, confirming our
lunch together eleven days later, was filled with her vibrant, forward-look-
ing personality:

What a joy it will be to see you after so long . . . It must have
been a delightful visit from Colin [Smythe], in those much

15 K.R. to F.W., 7 September 2000.

loved rooms, in this golden spring talking of past, present and future things. And let us do the same for a while.

Would you consider giving Temenos a series of Yeats lectures next year? or even one? I am nominally retired but Grevel Lindop consults and listens to me.

I will be ninety-five next month, and begin to feel my excessive years a burden, but still find this world miraculous and beautiful. I can still promise with some likelihood that I will still be here on May 20th!

With my love and blessing,

Kathleen

C. S. Lewis and the Revision of the Psalter

Commemoration Lecture for the centenary of the birth of C. S. Lewis,
Great St Mary's, Cambridge, 22 July 1998

It was in September 1958, nearly four years after he had, on his fifty-sixth birthday, given his Inaugural Lecture in Cambridge '*De Descriptione Temporum*' that C. S. Lewis published his *Reflections on the Psalms*, a work he had been writing during the previous autumn. The following month, Lewis was invited by Geoffrey Fisher, the Archbishop of Canterbury, to become a member of the 'Commission to Revise the Psalter'.

I became Professor Lewis's research student a year later, and saw him regularly almost until December 1961, when he wrote to me:

> The position is that they can't operate on my prostate till they've got my heart and kidneys right, and it begins to look as if they can't get my heart and kidneys right till they operate on my prostate. So we're in what an examinee, by a happy slip of the pen, called 'a viscous circle'. Still, it's not quite closed. Meanwhile, I have no pain and am neither depressed nor bored.[1]

The First Report of the Commission to Revise the Psalter, containing their revision of the text of Psalms 1–41, was presented to the Convocations of York and Canterbury in May 1961, and the committee was encouraged to continue along the same lines. With further revisions of the first forty-one psalms, the entire Psalter of 150 psalms was presented before Convocations in May 1963. On 22 November that year, just six months later, C. S. Lewis died.

As the Psalms have always been my delight, I was particularly fasci-

1 See Notes. Warner has written of his tutorials with him in Walter Hooper's *C. S. Lewis: A Companion and Guide*, London, HarperCollins, 1996, pp.92–94.

nated by the events taking shape around me, not least by the Archbishops'
order:

> To produce for the consideration of the Convocations a revi-
> sion of the text of the Psalter designed to remove obscurities
> and serious errors of translation, yet such as to retain, as far
> as possible, the general character in style and rhythm of
> Coverdale's version and its suitability for congregational use.

So may I begin by trying to bring to life a little of what was happening
at this time?

First, as in all good drama, one should know the *dramatis personae*.

The Archbishop of Canterbury, Geoffrey Fisher, bespectacled, gaitered,
and frock-coated, was a man who gave orders that were obeyed. The seven
members of the Commission invariably called him 'the Headmaster'. To
him their reports on the Psalms, and if necessary on the Psalmist, were to be
sent: and on time, please. Those invited to undertake the revision were:

The Right Reverend F. D. Coggan, Bishop of Bradford, Chairman. (In
1961 Coggan became Archbishop of York, and — after our period — in 1974
Archbishop of Canterbury.) A tall man with a deep, musical voice even
today as he approaches ninety, he had, from St John's College here in
Cambridge won a first-class degree in the Oriental Languages Tripos in
1931, and gone on to be Assistant Lecturer in Semitic Languages and
Literature at the University of Manchester for three years. He thus had
a firm grounding in Hebrew.

Next was Bishop G. A. Chase, Master of Selwyn College, then Bishop
of Ripon until 1959 — a charming, courteous, eirenic, clear-prosed man,
wholly good and reliable: 'a safe pair of hands'. He wrote a *Companion to the
Revised Psalter* (1963), with a little introduction to each of the 150 Psalms.

C. S. Lewis was there on the committee under two hats. One was as a
scholar, who had, for instance, written amusingly about Coverdale. The
other was as a creative 'literary man'. The two Bishops, Coggan and Chase,
then, were to be offset by two 'literary men', and two scholars, Lewis in fact
doubling.

The other 'literary man' was T. S. Eliot, the American who had long taken on British nationality, leader of the Modernist Movement in literature with his *The Waste Land*, and, even today in 1998, in the openly displayed Nobel Prize Winners' Book at the top of the great staircase at London's Athenaeum Club, seen as an iconoclast and perhaps a dangerous maverick.

T. S. Eliot, Anglo-Catholic, royalist, meticulous scholar, fastidious literary critic, poetic genius, anything but a maverick, was expected by Lewis to be one who would throw out the old and loved. When I asked Lewis what Eliot was like on the Commission, he said that whenever he, Lewis, suggested a change, Mr Eliot always wanted the Prayer Book version retained. This was the reverse of all that the committee had expected. When I told this anecdote to Mrs Eliot she laughed and said: 'True, too true! I remember him coming in late one night from a meeting of the Commission, and when I asked him how it had gone he said with a tired grin: "Well, I think I've saved the twenty-third psalm." '

Archbishop Coggan tells me the contrast between the two 'literary men' was startling. C. S. Lewis would come in dressed in tweeds and looking like a tubby, red-faced countryman, with his bag of books slung over his shoulder. T. S. Eliot, supposedly the avant-garde poet, would arrive from a very different world, a slim, dark-suited, select gentleman from the City of London, with rolled umbrella.

The other hat that C. S. Lewis wore was square: the mortar-board of the Cambridge Professor of Mediaeval and Renaissance Literature. He was one of the two scholars on the committee, the other being Cambridge's Regius Professor of Hebrew, Professor D. Winton Thomas, of St Catharine's College.

Professor Winton Thomas was a fierce Welsh Nationalist, a rugby player with the build of a second-row forward. To him I was going, at this same time, for instruction in Hebrew. Winton Thomas was not by nature an historian, certainly not a poet. His strength was Semitic languages and philology. When he gave a lecture in Cambridge on the Dead Sea Scrolls, it was — to the sadness of his audience — not the parallels with the New

Testament period that interested him, but only the language and philology. 'It cannot be emphasized too strongly, or too often, that very few archaeological discoveries bear directly upon the Old Testament narrative,' he would say – and indeed write, in his introduction to *Archaeology and Old Testament Study*, Oxford, 1967.

This strong, heavy, forceful character was not always wholly loved by his colleagues. At one meeting of the Faculty Board of Divinity, presided over by Michael Ramsay (later to become Archbishop of Canterbury) the question was raised whether there might be created another post in Hebrew and Old Testament Studies. (There was ample money for new posts in those days.) 'Would we like one?' asked Ramsay. Quick as a flash Professor Winton Thomas spoke out: 'No!' he said. 'We have already scraped the barrel with the last appointment.' The blushing scrapings of the barrel was sitting between him and the Chairman. 'Yes, yes, yes, yes,' said Michael Ramsay, and moved on to the next item on the agenda. Even so was that extra lectureship lost.

There were the bishops, then: Coggan (the Chairman) and Chase. There were the two 'literary men' T. S. Eliot and C. S. Lewis. Professor Lewis (same man) and Professor Winton Thomas, the second Hebraist and by far the most powerful (only Lewis could stand up to him) were the scholars. And then there were the 'music men'. Originally there had been just one: Gerald H. Knight, Director of the Royal School of Church Music; but 'headmaster' Fisher had noted his absences, and in 1960 J. Dykes Bower, Organist of St Paul's Cathedral, was appointed as an additional member of the Commission, since Gerald Knight's duties required a fairly long absence from England.

There is your cast. Imagine them seated round the table in Selwyn College, or at Lambeth Palace where the Lambeth Conference is now taking place. The parallel that comes to mind is that seventeenth-century room in which the blind John Milton, his secretary the exquisite poet Andrew Marvell, and John Dryden all met and worked in the office of the Latin Secretary, where diplomatic correspondence was prepared. All three were Cambridge men.

And how did our cast proceed? The Chairman tells me the literary men would make suggestions in opposite directions, Tom Eliot, Prayer Book very firmly in hand; Lewis, like Coverdale, willing to try his hand at a new phrase. Then Winton Thomas would come in to say when they were being inaccurate. When all that was finally settled and agreed, the music man would pipe up: 'But that can't be sung!'

The archbishops had asked for a text suitable for congregational use. Gerald Knight would always ask: 'Does the stress fall on the right word' (here C.S. Lewis was in his element), or avoid 'an unnatural prolongation of a syllable to fit the chant?' (Here Lewis was not so at home.) Let me give you an example:

The last verse of Psalm 15 is unsatisfactory for choirs. The full verse reads: 'Whoso doeth these things: shall never fall.' The second half of the verse is too brief for Anglican chant. Lewis suggested, in place of 'shall never fall', the words 'shall never be cast down'. Tom Eliot fully approved, and Winton Thomas did not object. Even the music man concurred. So it was submitted in that First Report of Psalms 1–41 in May, 1961; only to be sent back by 'the headmaster' with the comment that it suggested 'mental depression'. So they tried again, and what we have now in the final published Revised Psalter is 'shall never be overthrown'. Here I detect the Welsh rugby-playing Professor. Anyway, it is much easier to sing.

'They were very lively occasions,' says the Chairman, Lord Coggan; and Bishop Chase wrote that the Commission was 'a work which we ourselves found both refreshing and rewarding. The bond of friendship and happiness established between ourselves was never broken or even strained.'

The preface to the report says:

> It has not been our duty to make a new translation, but to mend an old one. This distinguishes our task from that of those engaged on the translation of the Psalms for the New English Bible. Their work has been generously placed at our

disposal and, as we were instructed, we have given it full consideration so far as questions of linguistics, and textual scholarship and interpretation are concerned.

In fact it is recorded that they had in front of them the OT AV, the Revised Version of the Bible, the Revised Standard Version, the Septuagint (Greek third century BC), and the Vulgate Latin translation made by Jerome c. 392 AD but based upon earlier Latin versions. Walter Hooper lent me Lewis's Prayer Book, and there, printed at the back of that copy of the Book of Common Prayer, is also printed in full, in addition to the prayer book psalms,

A New Version of the Psalms of David – N. Tate & N. Brady, Oxon MDCCCL (1850)

This volume is introduced as the 'Book of Common Prayer, according to the use of the United Church of England and Ireland. Oxford MDCCCXLIX' (1849). The Tate and Brady version, then, was the very latest revision of the time – and in between these pages were still some carbon copies, corrected, of the typescripts used by Lewis on this committee.

We must remember that they were advised not only by scholars. In their First Report they had left the Prayer Book's word 'fowl' in verse 8 of Psalm 8. 'The fowls of the air, and the fishes of the sea'. 'But', says Bishop Chase, 'we received a letter from the Antipodes protesting that the word meant – "dead chicken"! So we have changed it to "birds" here and throughout the psalter.' I note they did not change 'fishes' to the more modern 'fish': Eliot, perhaps, fighting a rearguard action.

In the first introductory words of the book which brought Lewis on to the Commission, *Reflections on the Psalms*, he writes:

> This is not a work of scholarship. I am no Hebraist, no higher critic, no ancient historian, no archaeologist. I write for the unlearned about things in which I am unlearned myself . . . I am 'comparing notes'; not presuming to instruct.

It would be a fascinating exercise to compare what this 'one amateur to another' (as he calls himself in 1958) discovered through the experience of revising with the professionals. The subject is huge – worth a doctorate. What would be intellectually dangerous would be to use the book he wrote earlier to draw deductions on his later thinking, under technical guidance, as he combed and revised the Psalter. Of Miles Coverdale he had written, long before,

> He had not learning enough to have solid grounds of his own for choosing between the various interpreters who all lay together on his desk: ignorance, in a sense, left him free to be accommodating.
>
> It may also be suspected that ignorance left him free to indulge aesthetic preferences, to follow this or that interpretation according as it agreed with his own, often exquisitely melodious, English style . . .[2]

Behind the opening apologia of *Reflections on the Psalms*, then, lies an echo of his view of Coverdale's freedom.

What Lewis soon learned, under the guidance of Winton Thomas – if he hadn't before – is that in the old Hebrew scrolls, to save space, Hebrew letters were written without spaces between words. What is more, in Hebrew until the seventh century AD there were no written vowels. The Psalms have come down to us from scrolls made up of an unbroken sequence of consonants.

Around the seventh century AD vowel points – that is, strokes or dots inserted above, below, or inside consonants – were added, but these could easily be mistaken. A squashed ant could change a meaning.

So, depending on where you make a break in the consonants to form words, you can derive different meanings. An example the Commission worried over was Psalm 55, verses 19b and 20.

The *Prayer Book* reads:

> 19   It is he that hath delivered my soul in peace from the battle that was against me: for there were many with me.

2 C. S. Lewis, *Oxford History of English Literature*, Vol III, 1954, p.208.

> 20 Yea, even God that endureth for ever, shall hear me, and bring
> them down: for they will not turn, nor fear God.

The *Revised Psalter* now reads:

> 19 He shall redeem my life in peace: for many archers are come
> about me.

not 'for there were many *with* me'

> 20 Even Ishmael, and the tribes of the desert, and they that dwell
> in the East: who do evil continually and fear not God.

It seems incredible that we are reading the same Hebrew text: but I assure
you it is. A slight change in vowel points, a different division among
the unending line of consonants, and you can do it. 'What's this about
Ishmael?' you may ask. Ishmael comes from combining into one word the
two Hebrew words 'God' and 'will hear'. Ishmael is interpreted as 'God
hears' in Gen. 16.11:

> And the angel of the Lord said unto her [Hagar] 'Behold,
> thou art with child, and shalt bear a son, and shalt call his
> name Ishmael: because the Lord hath heard thy affliction.
> And he will be a wild man: his hand will be against every
> man . . .

Now we see the point.

Fascinating to Lewis were the animals. One of his finest poems is about
the unicorn. Unfortunately the unicorn was not known to the ancient
Hebrews, so it becomes wild oxen. The metaphor of the horn comes from
the image of powerful oxen, wild and dangerous, whose strength and
ferocity came, they thought, from power hidden within their horns. The
Prayer Book gives in Psalm 22:

> 21 Save me from the lion's mouth: thou hast heard me also from
> among the horns of the unicorns.

This becomes in the the *Revised Psalter:*

> 21 Save me from the lion's mouth: and my soul in misery from the
> horns of the wild oxen.

Notice also that the 'God who is the horn of my salvation', who is 'strong to save', and as a result of his help exalts 'the horn of his People' — that is, making them strong and victorious — is not waving a unicorn's horn.

Notice also that 'salvation' has not the religious meaning we associate with it, bred as we are on the New Testament. Its primary meaning, in the words of Bishop Chase, 'is victory or deliverance. Sometimes this is pictured as accompanied by spiritual blessings, but it is the thought of material deliverance that is uppermost.' The word salvation is replaced by such words as victory.

> *Prayer Book:* Salvation belongeth unto the Lord (Ps. 3.8)
> *Revised Psalter:* Victory belongeth unto the Lord (Ps. 3.8)

Out goes 'salvation' along with 'unicorns'. What, Lewis wondered, would happen to the 'dragons'? He was fond of dragons, too.

> *Prayer Book:* No, not when thou hast smitten us into the place
> of dragons: and covered us with the shadow of death. (Ps. 44.20)
> *Revised Psalter:* No, not when thou hast smitten us into a place
> of jackals: and covered us with deep darkness. (Ps. 44.20)

So jackals drive out much-loved dragons.

You will also notice that 'the shadow of death' has been rejected, and replaced by 'deep darkness'. We recall of course, 'Yea, though I walk through the valley of the shadow of death, I will fear no evil' of the twenty-third Psalm. But Winton Thomas pointed out that the Hebrew phrase is primarily 'darkness', 'the darkness of the Judean ravines where night after night the shepherd kept watch over his flock'. So, in spite of Tom Eliot, verse 4 becomes: 'Yea, though I walk through the darkest valley, I will fear no evil.'

Let us think a little about the language in which the Psalms are written. Arabic has twenty-eight consonants, Hebrew only twenty-two. Hebrew has a limited vocabulary — perhaps some five thousand words. The syntax-structure is not at all complex. There are few connecting particles.

One must repeat, balance, contrast, work in short movements. The Hebrew images are predominantly vivid, noun-related, sense-objects based on the everyday life of the community and the individual. As Tom Henn, a friend of C.S. Lewis, has written in *The Bible as Literature:*

> For a people at first nomadic and then agricultural, cave, desert, river, well and fountain, storm and rain and drought, tower and wall have a special immediacy . . . Fire, gold, honey, birds . . . we are in a primary world of quick apprehensions, deception and immediate reaction.[3]

May I remind you, too, that classical Hebrew has no tenses or moods. Past, present, future are not clear-cut, nor is the difference between a statement and a wish.

> *Prayer Book:* He shall send down from on high to fetch me: and shall take me out of many waters. (Ps. 18.16)

becomes

> *Revised Psalter:* He sent down from on high to rescue me: he took me out of the great waters. (Ps. 18.17)

The Commission settled on past tense throughout this psalm, whereas the Prayer Book version hops between past and future.

> *Prayer Book:* The Lord shall reward me after my righteous dealing. (Ps.18.20)
> *Revised Psalter:* The Lord rewarded me after my righteous dealing. (Ps.18.21)

The Psalmist moves easily from direct statement about God in the third person to address in the second person, and vice versa:

> *Prayer Book:* For thou hast maintained my right and my cause (Ps. 9.4)
> But the Lord shall endure forever. (Ps. 9.7. 'sitteth enthroned', *Revised Psalter*)

3 T.R. Henn, *The Bible as Literature* London: Lutterworth Press, 1970, pp.63–64.

The commission threw out the Prayer Book's 'Tush'. The Prayer Book has: 'For he hath said in his heart, Tush, I shall never be cast down' (Ps. 10.6). This becomes: 'He hath said in his heart "I shall never be shaken".' 'We have consistently omitted the word, since nowadays it is regarded as slightly comic'. (Chase)

Psalm 7, verse 10, 'For the righteous God: trieth the very hearts and reins' is altered. 'Reins' is the old word for kidneys, which in Hebrew thought were the organ of feelings, as the heart was of the intellect. This becomes: 'For the righteous God: trieth the very secrets of the heart.' Which do you prefer? 'Lust', which in Coverdale's day meant any strong desire, is replaced by such words as 'arrogance' or 'pride': Ps. 10.2:

> *Prayer Book:* The ungodly for his own lust doth persecute the poor.
> *Revised Psalter:* The ungodly in his pride doth persecute the poor.

Lewis was quick to point out that our word 'its' was not current or really available to Coverdale. Almost throughout the Revised Psalter 'his' has been changed to 'its' where modern idiom would anticipate it.

Hebrew thinking did not distinguish soul from body as we do.

> *Prayer Book,* Psalm 6:
> 2b O Lord heal me for my bones are vexed
> 3a My soul also is sore troubled . . .

It looks like a contrast.

> *Revised Psalter:*
> 2 O Lord heal me, for my bones are shaken with terror
>   (surely T. S. Eliot)
> 3 Yea my soul is sore troubled.

And Lewis had written perceptively in *Reflections on the Psalms* on the Hebrew attitude to the afterlife. Now he could put his thinking into practice. Sheol, more like the Greek Hades, is no longer the Prayer Book's Hell, but becomes 'grave', 'pit', or 'death'.

On one occasion at least they defied 'the headmaster'. Fisher had sent back the word 'buckler', said it was 'obsolete', and asked for a more understandable translation. They debated, and then – with great temerity – wrote back to the Archbishop of Canterbury to say that there was no modern equivalent to buckler meaning 'a small, round shield used to ward off blows', and so it remained.

Let us step back for a moment and see Lewis away from his committee at this time. Henry Chadwick and his family were living in Cambridge, and his daughters were going to school in Cambridge, when he was appointed Regius Professor of Divinity in Oxford. He travelled to and from Oxford in Hilary Term 1959 by means of the train (two hours via Bletchley on the line abolished by Dr Beeching) known as the 'Cantab Crawler'.

Lewis was doing the same in the opposite direction, and had written to Edward Allen in December 1955:

> I find myself perfectly content in a slow train that crawls through green fields stopping at every station. Just because the service is so slow and therefore in most people's eyes *bad*, these trains are almost always empty and I have the compartment (you know the funny little boxes into which an English train is divided?) to myself where I get through a lot of reading and sometimes say my prayers. A solitary railway journey I find quite excellent for this purpose.

Henry Chadwick and C. S. Lewis would often coincide on the same platform. The ritual was always the same. They would nod, get in the same compartment; Henry being the younger and junior would not, of course, speak first: always the same carriage. Silence. Then, as the train at last came into Blunham, Lewis would close his work, look up, and say to Henry 'Lovely village, Blunham', and they would then talk for the last twenty minutes of the journey. What Lewis had been reading, though, on some of these train journeys, was the draft of the Revised Psalter.

I will end with a letter C.S. Lewis wrote at this time to the distraught and bereft Sir Henry Willink, the Master of Magdalene College, Cambridge

(Lewis's college and also Henry Chadwick's); consolation written when Lewis heard the Master had lost his wife. Henry had gone to preach at Magdalene, and they had stayed the night with the desperately lonely widower. The text fell out of the Visitor's Book when Lady Chadwick went to sign it; and – very wisely – while the men were talking she copied it down; and later gave me a transcript. I will read it, as it shows Professor Lewis's state of mind at this time, and so much wisdom; and then I will cease.

C. S. Lewis to Henry Willink on the death of his wife, 3 December 1959:

> I have learned now that while those who speak about one's miseries usually hurt one, those who keep silence hurt more. They help to increase the sense of general isolation which makes a sort of fringe to the sorrow itself.
>
> I know that what you are facing must be worse than what I must shortly face myself, because your happiness has lasted so much longer and is therefore so much more intertwined with your whole life. As Scott said in like case "What am I to do with that daily portion of my thoughts which has for so many years been hers?"
>
> People talk as if grief were just a feeling – as if it weren't the continually renewed shock of setting out again and again on familiar roads and being brought up short by the grim frontier post that now blocks them.
>
> I, to be sure, believe there is something beyond it; but the moment one tries to use that as a consolation (that is not its function) the belief crumbles. It is quite useless knocking at the door of Heaven for earthly comfort; it is not the sort of comfort they supply there . . .
>
> I think it is tiny little things which (next to the very greatest things) help most at such a time.

A Blessing on C. S. Lewis's home in Oxford, The Kilns

Sheldonian Theatre, Oxford, 17 June 2002

It is a great honour to be asked today to say a few words as we share this service of thanksgiving and dedication of The Kilns, the home from 1930 to 1963 of my supervisor and friend C. S. Lewis, when and where on Friday, November 22, he died a week before his sixty-fifth birthday. Apart from a week or two, my age today.

This service, then, is also my own personal thanksgiving for all he taught me and shared with me as we met regularly, for over two hours, every Wednesday morning in term in his college rooms in Cambridge. But I was only one, very young and very minor, friend. During that time I did not know The Kilns. Older and far longer friendships were enjoyed there: with Hugo Dyson, Charles Williams, Tolkien, all those unfolded so succinctly and evocatively in Walter Hooper's revised edition, recently published, of Roger Lancelyn Green and Walter Hooper's *C. S. Lewis: A Biography* (Harper-Collins, 2002) and also in the three volumes of Lewis's letters now published.

C. S. Lewis

He had a gift for friendship, perhaps an unusual one. The emotional side, in my case, was reserved entirely for letters. Face-to-face, he was not emotional at all. People reading the letters that he wrote to me, with their lengthy and meticulous annotations of my poems, or telling me of his illness, say, "What a close relationship." But it was only so on paper; personal contact was for debate – the trying out of ideas: the exploration of joint enthusiasms, even, though largely in a factual way. He was not cold; he was disciplined; courteous; well mannered; eager for debate – debate in which the egos were not involved, and all energy was intent on what he called 'pursuit of the fox, truth – that elusive quarry'.

From him I learned every time we met. As the relationship was one between teacher and pupil, this was a gift more precious than gold. It was not quite the same among colleagues in the Oxford Magdalen Senior Common Room, who may not always have wanted debate over lunch and logic based on facts. Not that Lewis forced himself on people at all, but he did not like cant or sloppy emotion. One must not exaggerate this – he had a long and warm and happy experience of Magdalen, Oxford, and we must not forget that. He also had that at Cambridge. In the Senior Combination Room of Magdalene College, Cambridge, he found congeniality, even if the same, I'm afraid, could not be said of the Cambridge English Faculty, riven as it was, as I well remember, by faction. But in his two Magdalens he could find that collegiality that he so loved. In college, at Cambridge and Oxford, and at The Kilns, he found true collegiality, places where each person respects, helps, shares, and delights in the work of each, and problems are shared. This is what The Kilns can be, now that the C. S. Lewis Foundation under, if I may say so, the inspired direction of its president, Stan Mattson, has been restored. Not a museum, but a living *locus amoenus*, a delightful place of hospitality where likeminded scholars can appreciate what it meant to Lewis and, in turn, like Castiglione and his Urbino, bring out the best in us.

For thirty-four years in my college rooms here in Oxford I have looked out on Erasmus's Arch, in New Inn Hall Street, which used to be called "Seven Deadly Sins Lane." Teaching in my rooms, walking up and down and glancing out of the window, my eye would fall not only on Erasmus's Arch but on the buildings beyond, now called Frewin Hall, but in Erasmus's time, St Mary's College. In October 1499, Erasmus arrived in Oxford with a letter of introduction to a lecturer two years his senior, John Colet, who was addressing large audiences here on the epistles of St Paul. Erasmus stayed at St Mary's College, the timber roof of which is now the roof of Brasenose College Chapel with a superb added plasterwork of the 1650s by John Jackson.

The Kilns

St Mary's was founded by Thomas Holden and Elizabeth, his wife, primarily for canons of the Augustinian Order. Erasmus wrote a letter to John Sixtin about a dinner party which, though Sixtin was invited, he was unable to attend. Colet, later dean of St Paul's, the affectionately respected leader of the Oxford circle, presided. On his right sat William Charnock, who was the prior of St Mary's. On his left was an unnamed divine, who was an advocate of the old scholasticism. Next to him sat Erasmus; as Erasmus said in the letter, 'so that a poet should not be wanting at the banquet.' Erasmus, at this stage, still saw himself primarily as a poet.

We all know what grew out of these debates over the dinner table in this small community and others like it: the English Reformation, with all its political complexities, English humanism, and the bringing in, by such men as Colet, of the Florentine Platonism that in my own subject was to flower in the poetry of Sir Philip Sidney, Edmund Spenser, and so many more. From such meetings of minds scholasticism, humanism, Platonism, overlapped and reshaped our outlook.[1]

1 For an example of Warner's contribution to Renaissance Latin studies in the early sixteenth century see Francis R Le P Warner, 'Das Gedankengebäude des Agrippa von Nettesheim,' ANTAIOS, Band v, no 2, Juli 1963, Stuttgart, Ernst Klett Verlag, pp 122–142.

The Kilns has just such a future. It is ideal. Its inspiration is a single man – a great Christian who was, and is, an inspiration to millions. Its location is Oxford – still today the centre of the intellectual world, a position which it shares with its younger sister, Cambridge. Its attraction to like-minded inquirers has started in such modest beginnings as began many of the colleges around us now: like-minded scholars seeking after truth, sharing an environment, and becoming friends; collegiality, books, gardens, leisure, shared meals, above all, conversation; but more. Let me give you two anecdotes about C. S. Lewis that demonstrate his ideals; ideals that can guide the future of The Kilns. One is academic, and the other is personal.

We have all here heard and read about the Inklings, but today I want to remind you of another group: and anyone seeking a topic for research might like to explore this further. This other group was simply called The Society. It met once a term with a different host in a different college each time, and the host had to read a paper which started the discussion of the evening. The minute book of the Society is right behind me in the Bodleian Library. It contains a feast of material. John Bayley gave a talk on Shakespeare's puns on the word 'will'. Sir Thomas Armstrong bent the rules and entertained everybody to a visit to Covent Garden to watch Margot Fonteyn and Nureyev dance. John Sparrow, Tolkien, many of the familiar names were members.

I had tea a few days ago with Jonathan Wordsworth, my colleague. For a while he was the secretary of this Society. When his turn came to entertain the group, in Exeter College, he chose as his topic one that Lewis rather liked, called 'quaintness'. Lewis was a regular and sometimes a rather brooding presence. Nevill Coghill was the ideal host: facilitator, master of ceremonies, meeting all with his boundless goodwill and Irish charm.

And the second anecdote is this: Last week I also saw my old colleague, Douglas Gray, and he told me that Frank Quinn (Is Frank Quinn present, by any chance, before I tell this anecdote? You never know in Oxford.) had been a postgraduate research student at Magdalen in the 1940s. He was one of the very first. The don assigned to him, responsible for his well-being, was C. S. Lewis, of whom he was terrified. At the end of term, Lewis summoned him to Staircase Three of Magdalen's New Buildings, outside which, as Lewis described in a letter to his own father, he could see "one little stag (not much bigger than a calf and looking too slender for the weight of its own antlers) standing still and sending through the fog that queer little bark or hoot which is these beasts' 'moo.' It is a sound. . . as familiar to me as the cough of cows in the field at home."

When Frank Quinn had knocked, wearing of course his gown, and entered, Lewis asked how he was getting on.

> 'It's quite difficult, really, but I'm working hard,' said Quinn, 'and the work's progressing.'
>
> 'I mean socially. Have you made any friends?'
>
> 'Not really. What with a wife and small child, and coming to Oxford from outside and being stretched over money, because of that I don't socialize much.'
>
> 'Oh, don't worry about that. I have a fund set aside from royalties. You can borrow as much as you like to help you through, and there's no need to pay me back until you can afford to.'

Two anecdotes – so typical of Lewis. We remember Wordsworth's comment in 'Tintern Abbey':

> . . . that best portion of a good man's life,
> His little nameless, unremembered acts
> Of kindness and of love . . .

though they are remembered by his pupils and the recipients. Two anecdotes to show the outside and the inside of collegiality; and all is based on reciprocal relationships.

To end, I will quote Lewis's favourite sentences from Cicero's *De Amicitia:*

> Those people are worthy of friendship who have within their own souls the reason for their being loved . . . It is characteristic of true friendship both to give and to receive advice, and on the

one hand to give it with all freedom of speech but without
harshness, and on the other hand to receive it patiently and
without resentment.

And lastly –

> Friendship was given by nature as the handmaid of virtue, not
> as the comrade of vice, because virtue cannot attain her high-
> est aims unattended, but only in unity and fellowship.

So, may the warm hospitality and environment of The Kilns bring the
blessing of such union and fellowship. In one hundred years' time there will
perhaps be another such service of thanksgiving for the dedication that
brought this Christian community into being. Small in size it may be, but in
power and preciousness it will transcend all man-made memorials to Lewis.
It is a living inspiration, and the remembrance of a great soul.

Hugh Wybrew:
Liturgical Texts of the Orthodox Church:
3 vols. Foreword

Three Greek words, each of three syllables, mark the climax of Eastern Christendom's year. In candlelit darkness the Easter troparion begins, to be repeated over and over, building to a heart-pounding wave of sound that bridges mortal and eternal, annihilating the universal fear in every human. Echoing the racing drumbeat of the pulse, whether in a tiny church on an island in the Cyclades or, with Justinian, under Hagia Sophia's dome itself, the cry breaks the night:

θανάτῳ θάνατον πατήσας

'By His death He has trodden death under His feet.' Here is the sublime centre from which all liturgy derives, which all rites reflect and celebrate.

If one compares this with the central truth proclaimed in Western, English liturgy, different facets are emphasized. Equally ringing and sublime is the claim, 'I am the resurrection and the life', but the words and viewpoint are Christ's, not man's. Listeners can accept or reject it. Orthodox liturgy assumes the group is sharing the good news and passing it on.

The two languages, too, differ in their strengths. Every translator knows the fluid music of Greek. This derives from the proportion of its vowels to consonants, which in Latin and English is smaller. The majority of Greek words end with a vowel; 'n' and 's' (with its compounds) are almost

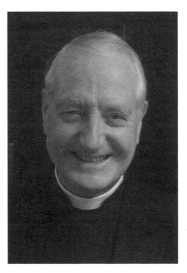

Hugh Wybrew

the only consonants that end words. These final syllables trip the rhythm along in a way utterly different from the marmoreal quality of Rome's Tridentine Mass, or our own *Book of Common Prayer* with its stress on the open vowel (a technique learned from Virgil). All three liturgies have virtues, but they are different.

This book of Orthodox liturgical texts, together with the earlier two in the series, *Orthodox Lent, Holy Week and Easter* and *Orthodox Feasts of Christ and Mary*, all prepared by Hugh Wybrew with commentary, bring the spiritual cast of mind of Orthodox Christianity within reach of Western readers, and provide pasturage for hungry and enquiring souls who are open to fresh enrichment of their deepest beliefs and meditations.

The Byzantine poets, those self-effacing monks dedicated to adorning and enriching the liturgy, simply called themselves 'melodes'. As Greek evolved from a quantitative to an accented language, so the greatest of these hymn-writers, the prolific Romanus, *poeta vere Christianus* of sixth-century Byzantium, slimmed down (though still discursive and metrically elaborate himself) the over-decoration of such predecessors as Ephraem the Syrian, and showed how fewer words led to greater effect. His hymns are 'sermons in poetic form'. So, too, are Hugh Wybrew's lucid, uncluttered translations from the wealth of Orthodox texts. These are arranged so that the whole celebration of Christ's visit to earth and our response to it can be seen through three cycles – Easter, Christmas, and the festivals of the Blessed Virgin Mary – to their culmination in Pentecost and All Saints' Day. To go through this experience with Hugh Wybrew as our guide is to emerge grateful, wiser and humbler as we realize once again that in our Father's house are many rooms, and, if we open this door, the world of Eastern spirituality can lend us its unfading golden light to bring us joy.

The Bones and the Flesh:
Henry Moore and Francis Bacon

It seems straightforward.

Henry Moore was born a Victorian, the son of a coalminer, in Castleford, Yorkshire, 30 July 1898: Francis Bacon an Edwardian, in Dublin, 28 October 1909, of wealthy, country house stock. Moore was loved, and to the end of his life talked tenderly of rubbing his mother's back to ease her rheumatism. Bacon claimed he was many times horsewhipped on his father's orders by young, unmarried grooms in the stables, and was neglected by his mother.

Moore went to the local state schools; Bacon from 1924–26 to the Public School Dean Close, at Cheltenham. Moore went on to Leeds School of Art, and the Royal College of Art where he later taught. Bacon claimed he had no art training.

Moore was a strong and healthy man, happily married all his adult life, living at Perry Green in the country with Irina and their beautiful daughter, Henry fascinated by and later famously drawing the sheep.

Bacon, unhealthy, asthmatic, loathed animals, and lived a homosexual urban bachelor, mainly in London. Moore, conscientious and socially responsible, was on the Board of many Foundations. Bacon, a solitary, living in a mews near Harrods, moved in the shadows, Soho his recreation, the underworld providing him friends.

Bacon's art depends on the ephemerality of the flesh, on sudden movement, the fleeting moment and its consequences. Moore disliked movement in sculpture: 'frisking, dancing figures and so on'.[1] 'A sculpture jumping off its pedestal is something I greatly dislike'.[2] He sought the timeless, the

---

1 Alan Wilkinson (ed.) *Henry Moore: Writings and Conversations*, University of California Press, 2002, p.182.
2 Ibid., p.305.

landscape, rocks, pebbles, bones, the structure of humans, the sleepers in the Underground.

Both artists repeated and honed their views and anecdotes for public consumption, Moore through years of teaching and press interviews, Bacon at the dinner tables and bars of London, and the baths and brothels of Tangier.

The nation's tribute to the sculptor was 'a service of thanksgiving for the Life and Work of Henry Moore O.M., C.H., 1898–1986' in Westminster Abbey. The painter died suddenly, on a trip to attempt to rekindle a relationship with a young man, in Madrid, 28 April 1992. As he requested, there was no ceremony, and no one was invited to the cremation.

But it is not straightforward. Indeed, the easy reduction of art to biography needs here to yield to a different orientation of thought; and context beyond the personal may provide a starting point.

From our present (and passing) perspective, Moore and Bacon seem the last proponents of the Renaissance tradition: narrowing the timespan, the opposite end of the Pre-Raphaelite experiment – the completion of the spectrum-shift which in part was precipitated by the discovery of photography.

In the later Victorian era focus was still on the supremacy of the human figure as of prime interest. Photography's tonal light and shade was driving artists to an emphasis on outline. This endorsed the contemporary need for clear demarcation, not least throughout the Empire: the cornice dividing – not uniting – wall and ceiling, end-stopped rhymes in stanzaic verse, 'The rich man in his castle, The poor man at his gate', First and Third Class railway carriages (there was no Second Class). Photography was often shadowy, fuzzy, 'unwholesome' like any deviation from gender.

Charles Collins's 'Convent Thoughts' (1851) in the Ashmolean Museum details the outline of every leaf and blade of grass, which is then filled in with colour. William Powell Frith's painting of the racecourse at Epsom, 'Derby Day' (1856) in the Tate Gallery, renders a clearly recognisable portrait of every member of the vast crowd, each hat, shoe, fold and eyebrow. There is nothing impressionistic here. Everybody is doing something definite. He was the virtuoso of teeming life exactly detailed; Dickensian. To us the

Pre-Raphaelite outline seems a last, sharp-edged rejoinder to photography's shadows, before representational art ceded that territory of visual record to emulsion on rolled strip.

Bacon and Moore are the mirror image at the opposite end of the same spectrum. The unquestioned assumption that 'The proper study of mankind is man' is the same, but his or her outline is not. Whereas for Collins one worked inwards from outline to enhance external recognition, the 'realism' of Moore and Bacon derives from the opposite perception.

Bacon loved poetry and plays, and Moore plays and poetry. Moore wrote and acted the lead in a play called *Narayana and Bhataryan* at Castleford Grammar School in 1920, dedicated to the memory of the poet Rupert Brooke. The play was heavily influenced by James Elroy Flecker, son of the founder Headmaster of Dean Close School who retired as Bacon arrived.

Bacon knew the poetry of W. B. Yeats well, and would joust quotations with me. Moore designed the poster for the play I dedicated to him, *Meeting Ends*, and also generously designed the cover for an undergraduate magazine of *Oxford Poetry* for which I, as 'Senior Member', was finally answerable.

Bacon would often quote W. B. Yeats's poem 'The Second Coming', written January 1919:

Francis Bacon, 1952.
Henri Cartier-Bresson

> Things fall apart; the centre cannot hold;
> Mere anarchy is loosed upon the world.

Kathleen Raine introduced us to each other, and when he died she sent me her poem 'Remembering Francis Bacon', which includes the lines:

> At some party years ago you spoke to me
> Of Yeats, and of your sole desire

Once, if only once, to touch the real.
You were speaking from the heart.[3]

For Bacon the 'real' was not the outline, but the centre, the inner heart of energy.

Here the brush-stroke creates the form and does not merely
fill it in. Consequently, every movement of the brush on the
canvas alters the shape and implications of the image.[4]

Moore used to say 'The sculptor identifies himself with the object's centre of gravity, its mass, its weight; he realises its volume, as the space that shape displaces in the air.'[5]

One of the things I would like to think my sculpture has is a
force, is a strength, is a life, a vitality from inside it, so that you
have a sense that the form is pressing from inside trying to
burst or trying to give off the strength from inside itself, rather
than having something which is just shaped from outside.[6]

Talking of Giovanni Pisano he said:

Many early sculptors approached form from the outside. . . but
Giovanni was one of the first Italians to feel the bone inside
the sculpture. . . we could see how the elbow joints pushed out,
that there was an inside structure.[7]

Let us take two ways of looking at a tree. One is the army way, outline.

There are three kinds of tree, three only, the fir and the poplar,
And those that have bushy tops to.
                                        Henry Reed, 'Judging Distances'

The other is to understand the outline simply as the point at which the energy growing up from the roots through the trunk peters out eventually in

3 *Temenos 13*, London, 1992, p.175, ISSN 0262–4524.   4 Peppiatt, *Francis Bacon: Anatomy of an Engima*, London, Weidenfeld and Nicolson, 2008, p.182.   5 Wilkinson (ed.) *Henry Moore*, p.184. 6 Ibid., p.198.   7 Ibid., p.173.

twigs. Yes, one can indeed join the tips of the twigs and notice that they make a beautiful arc, but the outline is not the explanation. One is a static way of thinking, the other dynamic. This is the trajectory travelled from the Pre-Raphaelite ideal to Moore and Bacon, before the concept and assumptions of art in our own time changed completely.

Both drama and poetry grow from the inside, as the young dramatist, later – from 1982 – member of the National Theatre Board, Moore, and Yeats-loving Bacon knew.

Art, like religion, or music, cannot satisfyingly be explained mechanically. They depend on movements of a nexus of mind, emotion, physical perception and intuitive insight. Focus on outline is inadequate. This motion is perhaps the essence of what it means to be alive. It is the inner life of things, rather than the beauty of colour or form or even of significance or morality, that compels our complete attention: what Aristotle called 'giving life to lifeless things'. Our sense of wonder at a fine example is in part that we know such art can outlive the artist, and others unborn may respond the same way: with wonder.

If, in Victorian fashion, we begin from the outside, we note that as Bacon began to secure his reputation he insisted on presenting his pictures in the heavily gilded ogee frames made by Alfred Hecht of the King's Road, Chelsea. Their dimensions, weight of tradition, and resonances were important. They placed his work alongside the old masters.

Both Bacon and Moore were preoccupied with the impact of size, in a way that the present computer-accustomed age may not immediately understand.

To those born before computers became ubiquitous, size had a more immediate impact on the nervous system. Television presents us with a small, child-sized prattler, intruding into the well-lit private living space of a giant watcher who is in total control of extinguishing it; who can only be cajoled into allowing continued existence by, like Scheherazade on her wedding night, keeping the tyrant amused.

Television by its very size invites the laughter of Lemuel Gulliver in Lilliput, where he found the inhabitants were six inches high. The Cheshire

Cat grinned at Alice. The collapse of deference to politicians is in part due to their appearing on television – ingratiating, small, comic and expendable. We swat them with the remote control.

Film stars, by contrast, are larger than life. Our roles are reversed. In order to watch them in a cinema we must, like school-children, leave home at a specified time to be checked, told where to sit, silenced and put in the dark: after a wait, remain for our allotted time gazing up at the gigantic figures who – unlike the attention-seeking child-puppets in our living rooms – take not the slightest notice of us. In war-time, picture palaces showed us Churchill, in the Pathé News reels, only on heroic scale.

This Moore and Bacon well knew. They each tended to reject both television and film in favour of theatre, for two reasons. Theatre is a living, not recorded art, unique, unrepeatable, like human life. No two performances are the same; and attempts to film stage shows fail. What is also true is that the actors are not only unpredictably living, but are our own size. As a result, as in normal daily life, if they speak to us they draw us in. If we applaud they smile; boo, they react. They are us.

So the painter and the sculptor – one in a static and the other in a dynamic way – always bore in mind the relationship of their potential work of art to the size of the spectator.

Bacon's heavy and protecting frames deliberately contrast with the world of his depicted figures who are stark – anything but protected, imprisoned in their cubes and solitary rooms. Bacon, as a homosexual rejected and criminalized by contemporary society, views society from the outside: from what he called his 'gilded squalor'. He knew our community to be for him non-communicating, excluding, violent.

So he makes his viewers stand beside him, join him, drawn to the reassuring traditional and hierarchical frames to peer into a view of our civilization that is anything but civil. As a result he is subversive. We, too, become outsiders, alienated from the world as he paints it. For his figures even pity seems inappropriate.

Henry Moore does not confine his sculptures. His ideal setting is the natural countryside with its ever-changing sky as backcloth. Though he shares with Bacon the view that the art object must be seen, and conceived, in relation to the size of the standing viewer, his in two ways is a dynamic approach. The advantage for the sculptor is that by walking round the object a viewer can see it from innumerable angles. Full appreciation is peripatetic.

Jealousy of this advantage of sculpture over painting drove Picasso and Braque in 1911 to steal Mercator's technique and, by wrapping a grid round the object to bring all sides to the front as the paper was flattened out, gave us the creative distortions of cubism.

Each large sculptural piece by Moore has its origin, its 'genesis', grows from an embryonic form of a small, hand-held plaster maquette, usually based on natural forms, 'found objects' randomly encountered.

These grow. I asked him if he hoped the final, full-sized sculpture would be the same as his maquette. He replied, 'One must always allow room for chance'.

> I did several little plaster maquettes, and eventually one nearest to what the shape of this big one is now pleased the most. . . But in making the big one, the smaller one changes, because you have to alter forms when they are bigger from what they are when they're small, because your relationship to them is a different one.[8]

> It's as though you have something trying to make itself come to a shape from inside itself. This is, perhaps, what makes me interested in bones as much as in flesh because the bone is the inner structure of all living form. It's the bone that pushes out from inside.[9]

Both consciously and instinctively we recognise this, and the result is frequently to elicit from the person viewing, walking round a creation by Moore in its landscape setting – whether the object is a large abstracted Upright Internal/External Form, or a mother and child, a fallen warrior, or even a King and Queen – an undeniable flow of compassion.

8 Wilkinson (ed.) *Henry Moore*, p.215.   9 *Henry Moore at the Serpentine*. Arts Council 8oth birthday exhibition catalogue, London, 1978. Introduction by David Sylvester, p.1.

Lucy and Georgina, Warner's elder daughters, with Moore in his maquettes studio

But once this has been said, the finished work of Moore is intentionally static, unbounded. '[It is] my belief that sculpture should be permanent, should last for eternity.'[10] Bacon's, within its frame, is often in violent movement; lacerated, pulverized, ephemeral, inflicting and suffering pain, even in one case apparently pointing a machine-gun at the viewer.[11] Bacon's extreme personal masochism and sadism are thrown onto the canvas. When he paused, if impressed by what he had just done, he would endow it with his life-giving seed, then cover the spread drops in white paint 'with a gesture like a throw of dice' as he put it, if he felt the gamble had come off.[12]

In the mid-1950s David Herbert tells us:

> Francis was frequently found by the police beaten up in some
> street in Tangier in the early hours of the morning. Bryce
> [British Consul-General in Tangier Bryce Nairn] complained
> to the Chief of Police and asked him to have more police on

10 Ed: C. Allemand-Cosneau, M. Fath, D. Mitchinson, *Henry Moore From the Inside Out*, London, Prestel, 1996, p.71.   11 See p.162.   12 E.g. Bacon's triptych *Two Figures Lying on a Bed with Attendants*, 1968.

duty in the darker alleys of the town. A few weeks passed; the beatings continued. Then the Chief called on Bryce and said, 'Pardon, Monsieur le Consul-Général, mais il n'y rien à faire. Monsieur Bacon aime ça.'[13]

Moore's approach to the life force was at the opposite emotional and creative extreme. He was Lord of the Archetypes, those 'primordial mental images inherited by all'. In the integrity of his mastery of these lies the heart of his greatness.

We may take as an example that large bronze of 1968 wryly called 'Large Totem Head', which it is not, as the objections to its sexual suggestiveness when it was given by a German department store to the city of Nuremburg amply demonstrated.[14] Yet the objections, understandable had they been about Bacon, were misplaced. There is nothing defiant, nor prurient, about it. Moore's work cannot be taken in at a glance. It needs time to encourage thought.

Every person on earth comes into the world the same way, and so carries subliminally, buried within his or her subconscious, a memory of that brutally painful and horrifying journey to the light. The reason for the size of this sculpture is that the spectator must be able to identify with coming out of it.

The oval opening is protected by a vertical bar; but later, when the time becomes appropriate, the thoughtful spectator sees this no longer as an excluding, or imprisoning, virginity, but the honeyed string of a musical instrument, touched giving universal pleasure. As the mind moves from one perception to the other, so the onlooker in walking round finds not what we expected but the back which recalls a sliced avocado pear which, we remember, contains protected within its soft walls a single, hard, tough source of life.

It is tactfully, tenderly, created before us without lewdness or shock. It is

13 David Herbert, *Engaging Eccentrics*, London, Peter Owen, 1990, p.83.
14 As the Greeks called the Furies 'the kindly ones' (Eumenides) lest by naming they be invoked, so Moore on occasion was happy to replace a strongly emotive word with its opposite, usually with a little grin.

Large Totem Head 1968,
bronze, height 244 cm,
Hatfield House, 2011
Photo: Emily Peters

what we leave in terror, and later re-enter in joy. It just is; a basic fact, inviting no more than an aware acceptance. And, with the Psalmist, we marvel.

> Thou has fashioned me behind and before: and laid
>   thine hand upon me.
> Such knowledge is too wonderful and excellent for me: I
>   cannot attain unto it.[15]

This is not a sculpture for a city. On the contrary, of all his works this most needs – as it had in the perfect setting of the garden of Hatfield House in the exhibition of 2011 – a surround of bushes. Calmly standing for what it is, in this secret arbour, on a well-trimmed lawn while above it waved the

15 Psalm 139, vv.4,5.

branches and body of a high tree, it made the profoundest experiences of human living, the arrival and creation of life, one with all nature.

When we think of what Gustave Courbet or Picasso would have done, we are grateful for Moore's deftness of metaphor and sure judgement of tone. For Bacon this subject, let alone the sophistication of approach, would have been impossible. The subject did not interest him. There was an occasion on which he commissioned John Deakin to photograph Henrietta Moraes unclothed.

> He was a horrible little man. He came round and told me to lie on the bed with my legs open. . . I said "Deakin, I don't think that is what Francis wants. I don't think that would interest him. . ." Of course he didn't, so we had to start all over again. Later on I found Deakin selling copies of the first lot of photos to some sailors in Soho for ten shillings a time. I was furious. . .[16]

To see how Bacon approached such fundamental facts one has only to look at his *Diptych* 1982–4. Here the solitary man who has no head, no body above the chest, crouches as a wicket keeper, knees apart, wearing nothing but cricket pads on which he rests his hands open in a gesture ready to catch. With its full frontal pose and stark orange background, few paintings are more flamboyantly, uncompromisingly aggressive. Curiously though, it could not be called salacious. Bacon's figures walk a tightrope between these two provocations.

The lord of the archetypes did not receive them from the Platonic world of Forms as a gift from heaven; though, as Aristotle said, the gift of seeing one thing in terms of another – metaphor – is an ability (like melody) that cannot be taught. Moore had to quarry his subconscious, and on occasions he leaves us with an insight into that process.

One of the most revealing of these is his lithograph 'Pandora and the Imprisoned Statues' of 1950, for the translation by André Gide of Goethe's *Prométhée*. It is a book illustrated by Moore and published in Paris by Henri Jonquières in 1951. This lithograph – coloured in light and dark beige,

16 Peppiatt, *Francis Bacon*, p.258.

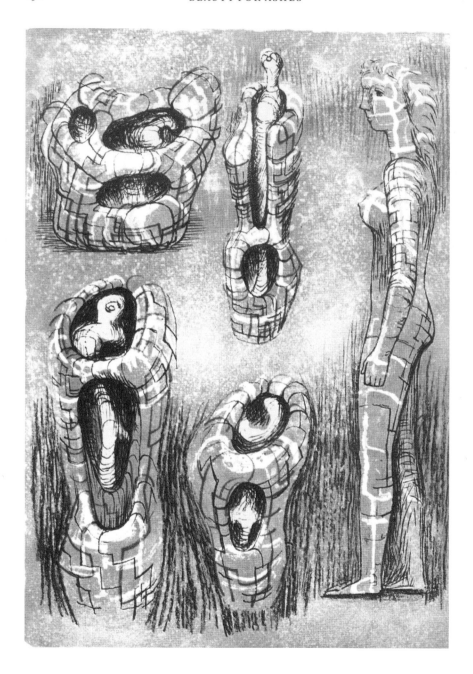

Pandora and the Imprisoned Statues 1950, 31.4 x 22.2 cm. For an understanding of the growth of his art, Moore's most interesting lithograph: his 'Eureka!' moment. Photo: Menor

green, light blue, light yellow, orange and black – one 'reads' from right to left.

His starting point is a standing nude woman who faces in to the page and is seen in profile filling the side of the page from top to bottom. Her head is set against a background of green lines that suggest the natural world. Her left foot, just in front of her right, makes, with the delicacy of a ballet dancer, a slight step towards the four other objects, two above and two below, that fill the rest of the sheet.

In front of her face is an upright external form enclosing a contrasting internal, yellow one that protrudes its neck and head out of the top as from a partly opened overcoat.

Beneath this is a fatter, more rounded shape with a view through two holes into cavities that contain a yellow object in each; the upper suggesting a curled embryo. (His daughter Mary had been born in 1946.)

Raising our eyes to the left hand side of the lithograph we find a further treatment of the theme, fatter, more squat, with three apertures, like a head with eyes of very different sizes. In the larger is the curled embryo in a different position.

Beneath this we have the imaginative leap that was to give him an archetype he was to refine for the next thirty years until, four years before his death, when he was in his eighties he gave us that masterpiece drawn from this, the bronze *Large Upright Internal/External Form*, 1981–82.

Its internal form was cast first as a sculpture in its own right in 1981, and called Large Interior Form; but as the name shows it was conceived to be enclosed. Its vulnerability, as of a stamen enfolded by petals, or an embracing parent, protecting, yet allowing the head to peer through, crosses the categories of nature's species to present an eternal truth: innate care for the future of an organism. In the hauntingly beautiful setting of the exhibition in Kew Gardens, September 2007–March 2008, it was the most admired of the 28 large scale Henry Moores on show, matched in popularity in that exhibition only by his *Reclining Figure*, completed when he was 85, in 1983, which combined the artist's three most recurring themes: mother and child, reclining figure and internal/external forms.

Large Upright Internal/External
Form, height 673 cm, 1981–82
Photo: Jonty Wilde

A sketchbook of 1935 shows us Moore's earliest exploration of this theme. In an eve-of-war sketchbook of 1938–39 (275 mm high) we see a page in pencil and crayon of six attempts: but the head still sticks out. In his post-war 'Studies for Sculpture: Ideas for Internal/External Forms' 1949, a sheet in pencil, wax crayon, chalk, watercolour, gouache, and ink (HMF 254a), we observe a now bold confidence that he is nearly there in a magnificent page 584 x 398 mm of nine studies, two of which enclose what might be a head. One takes up his theme of the helmet.

But it was to be another few months before he realized that a synthesis that was more than the sum of its parts could be achieved, in whatever size he may cast it, *by rethinking the relationship of its parts to the whole as he enclosed the head*, and so made his breakthrough.

Moore's art evokes tenderness. We respond at once to that late masterpiece *Mother and Child: Block Seat*, 1983–84, 244 cm high, where the stylized mother inclines her body forward just enough to offer the protection of her right shoulder around the abstract child, as her very realistic left arm and hand show coming support, if needed, underneath the baby.[17]

We remember the tenderness of the Rocking Chair sculptures made for his daughter Mary; and also of the exquisite terracotta models for family groups of 1945: even of the *Suckling Child*, 1927, at one disembodied breast.

But in his hands this theme could also be anything but tender, while still instinct with compassion. The memory of broken nights gave us his bronze *Mother and Child* of 1953, 50.8 cm high, where a greedy baby reaches for, and is held back from, the breast by a mother so sore and tired that her head is simply represented by the top of a toothbrush whose bristles are fangs – Moore's shorthand for what she is thinking.

Bacon's mother and child, a painting titled (not necessarily by him) '*After Muybridge – The Human Figure in Motion: Woman Emptying Bowl of Water, and Paralytic Child Walking on all Fours 1965*' arises from a very different emotional climate; detached, ironic. Here is no sympathy, and only the strangest kind of empathy.

The naked child crawls on all fours as gingerly as a cat on a ridge round the circular metal rim of a table that has lost its glass top, or a trampoline stripped of all save its hooped frame, while the woman – balancing on the same metal circle on the opposite side, her dress blown up to reveal her buttock – leans perilously over to empty a bowl. Her face, which we can just recognize, is distorted as she is in the process of turning as the water tipped out begins to flow down, then as though caught by the gust of wind rises up the canvas against a stark orange background.

In their precarious balancing the viewer sees both woman and child inhabiting a hostile world in which, from birth, everything goes wrong, is insecure, while both are locked in to the contrasting implacable truths of mathematics in Bacon's lordly geometric design.

The picture is Bacon's ironic reversal of Botticelli's wind through cloth-

17 See p. 184.

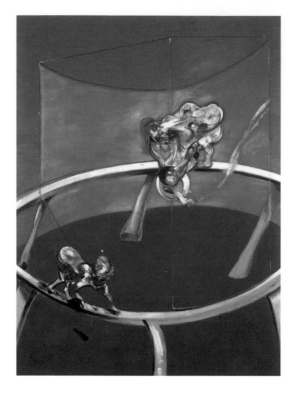

After Muybridge –
The Human Figure in Motion:
Woman Emptying Bowl of
Water, and Paralytic Child
Walking on all Fours 1965. Oil
on canvas 198 x 147.5 cm

ing which, for Neo-Platonic reasons, is always beneficent.[18] It also takes the tradition of Giorgione's and Titian's *Concert champêtre*, 1510, in the Louvre, and Ingres' *La Source*, 1856, in the Musee d'Orsay, where a serene nude woman pours water out and down from a container; and both in direction and mood Bacon violently reverses it. The implied result of such a symbol of human fecundity is a neglected, 'paralytic' child.

Moore carved his first *Reclining Figure* in 1926–27. It was in Mansfield stone, twelve inches long, and male; it has not survived. Soon afterwards in the autumn of 1928 he met Irina Radetsky who was studying painting at the Royal College of Art, where he was teaching sculpture. When they married in July 1929 Irina was twenty-two, Henry about to be thirty-one. Her effect on his art was dramatic and permanent.

It was not that Moore had only concentrated on the male form. His

18 See Warner's play on Botticelli, Ficino, and the Medici, *Living Creation*, Colin Smythe, 1985.

Reclining Woman of 1927, 25 inches long in cast concrete, was certainly sensual:

> Leaning on her right elbow and side, breasts squeezed upwards,
> left thigh tipped voluptuously over right, she looks sultrily
> alluring.[19]

Now something more fundamental took place. He saw in a photograph the Toltec-Mayan statue of Chacmool, the Rain Spirit (11th or 12th century), and in 1929 the deep impression this statue made on him, with his square-blocked ears and flat head turned to the right of his half-raised body as he reclines, with his feet flat, his raised knees together, and his hands on his lap; this fascination combined with the even deeper impression Irina created.

Moore's version of Chacmool's posture, though obviously derived, is startlingly different. With *Reclining Figure* 1929, in brown Horton stone, 83.8 cm long, Leeds City Art Gallery, he makes the figure undeniably feminine, with one hand behind her head, rising breasts, large knees parted with the upper, left one, bent and raised, and the entire body conceived in rounded curves.

It is one of his finest stone carvings, and in its fresh and loving sensuality Moore's transmuting reaction prefigures Picasso's, three years later, to his new young mistress Marie-Thérèse Walter in 1932, in his painting *Nude Woman in Red Armchair*, Tate Gallery, with its uninhibited caressing curves that even subsume the chair.

The parallel in Bacon's oeuvre is his painting '*Two Studies of George Dyer with Dog 1968*'. In Bacon's case the erotic passion was not new, but here it is at its height, and revealed in its emphatic use of curved outline.

It is not just the Victorian use of outline to demarcate. The seat of the hard wooden chair on which Dyer sits, nude, is so carefully rounded, both as a circle and in the depth of its rim, that it draws the eye to see it as criterion for and key to the rest of the painting, beginning with Dyer's right buttock.

Firmly stroking the brush line up round his model's upper thigh, Bacon without stopping caresses it over the knee crossed over Dyer's left thigh and

19 R Berthoud, *Henry Moore*, London, Faber and Faber, 1987, p.103.

Two Studies of George
Dyer with Dog 1968.
Oil on canvas
198 x 147.5 cm

on round his right ankle, foot, and up the other side till he breaks the flow to raise the brush and paint the letter Y with short stem: the shorthand hetero-sexual painters use for a woman's vulva;[20] but Bacon's Y is upside down.

Here, punningly, both the imagined continuation of the right leg (which in reality one could not possibly see) – the upper part of the inverted Y — and the lower also leading to something this position prevents us from seeing, between his thighs, to tease the imagination; both lines invert gender, and tradition, in a bravura assertion of his homosexual physical infatuation.

A fresh firm brushstroke outlines the lower right thigh back to our start-ing point. Now looking at the completed thigh we see he has filled in its outline with an enormous oval bruise.

20 A good example is in Picasso's *Nude Woman in Red Armchair* (see p.157); taken in context, the three most tender lines in all Picasso.

The same can be seen with Dyer's left leg (unbruised), back, shoulder and – tellingly – around the top of his head, his stroked but slightly ruffled hair, beneath which is a grotesque black eye, and bloody nose, mouth and neck.

The line leaves Dyer's arm to become the strong brown ellipse of his floor, his arena, prefiguring the bull-fight arena paintings of the coming year.

In this arena, on the opposite side to the rounded shadow cast by the chair, a shape on the edge of disintegration, a non-outlined, spectral dog, with curved back, and slightly ruffled hair to match Dyer's, looks up – as if it were at Fragonard's swing – between his master's legs, its pink tongue lolling.

Even the quarter-dropped roller-blind, leaving the nude man open to view through the window, makes the same point as Moore's and Picasso's displaying curves; and Bacon's framing cube in which all this takes place bends with the weight of passion to form the outline of an eye looking down, a half-rhyme to the floor's ellipse.

As we stand back from so intimate a celebration and showcase of the artist's sado-masochistic physical attraction to his model, we become aware that outside this arena of passionate imagination is something else. Its ironic otherness is indicated by the rectangular table on which it stands – a vase in which is stuck not a bunch of flowers but Dyer's severed head, a second much more recognizable portrait of Bacon's lover; hence the painting's title.

In typically punning style, Bacon suggests the vase and stump head can in some glances be read as one, as the displaced black liquid that runs down the side of the vase nearest to us splits the base to create the fleeting illusion of two homuncular feet.

This vase with head is, of course, an allusion to Bacon's favourite lines from Keats, about the severed head of Lorenzo, Isabella's lover, in a pot of basil:

> The thing was vile with green and livid spot,
> And yet they knew it was Lorenzo's head.

Dyer's head is indeed 'green' with 'livid spot', but presented to us not as 'vile' but as a bloom for our delectation. Bacon's biographer tells us:

> Of the many and varied influences that had left their mark, this

Warner, Melinda Camber,[21] *Georgina and Moore on holiday, Forte dei Marmi, 1972.*

    self-schooled artist maintained poetry had had the greatest
effect on his imagination.[22]

It was poetry that brought me the friendship of these two artists, and
made me Moore's guest, with my small daughter Georgina, at his exhibition
in the Forte di Belvedere above Florence in August 1972.

We were standing by exhibit 98, *Falling Warrior* 1956–57, when he turned
to ask us what it led us to think about as we walked round it. I forget what
my nine-year-old said, though she made Henry laugh. I replied to his raised
eyebrows: 'Homer'. 'Why?' he asked. 'Because of the many fallen heroes in
the *Iliad* – such as Aretos in Book 17:

    So Aretos reared, heaving up, then toppled down on his back.

'Will you read me some?'

No copy of Homer was available, but someone later found a copy of

Virgil and gave it to Henry. 'All they can find is Virgil', he said. 'That will do' I replied, and translated the final lines for him:

> With rage grief-heated Aeneas plunged his sword full into
> Turnus' breast. His limbs melted to cold. His life
> Fled with a groan of anger to the shades.

'People tell me my warriors are not heroes, not built like Hercules, but somewhat skinny; but in the trenches we were skinny!' he replied.

When he spoke of the trenches of the First World War, I remembered a letter he had written from the Front to Miss Gostick, art teacher at his old grammar school. Not wanting to describe the eye-gouging reality around him of hand-to-hand bayonet fighting in a wet trench after only two hours' sleep, he had told her he was 'more comfy out here than I thought I should be'. Much later he recalled that when the battle of Bourlon

Warrior with Shield, 1953–54
Photo: John Hedgecoe

Wood was over 'only 52 of the 400 men of my regiment were able to muster.' Moore had also been gassed. He was the opposite of 'comfy'.

I told him of a machine-gun and bombing raid in 1943, targeting schools, that flew over mine while I was in it but destroyed another not far away at Catford, killing thirty-eight children, six staff, and maiming many. 'It is your *Warrior with Shield* 1953–4, no. 83 here, that makes me think of all of us who suffered under Hitler's onslaught on our homes. To me this really does speak of that endurance, that dogged spirit with which England endured the Blitz with only the smallest of shields – the R.A.F – determined to hope to the last.'

In the Second World War Bacon volunteered for Civil Defence, and worked in the Kensington area of London with the A.R.P. (Air Raid Precautions), fire-fighting the blazing buildings, and rescuing after air-raids. But he had also experienced the bombing of London in the First World War. His biographer tells us:

> What struck Francis vividly were the blackouts, when the streets and houses stood in gloom and searchlights raked the night sky for Zepplins' stealthy approach. The sight of their monstrous bulk, floating high and silent above the city, terrified Londoners as much as the whine of their falling bombs. For a withdrawn child with a morbid imagination lying in the dark, the suspended threat of death and destruction was to become a lasting reality.[23]

Sam Hunter's photograph of news clippings in Bacon's studio in 1950 includes a page torn from *Picture Post* showing the Nazi Gestapo chief Joseph Goebbels haranguing a crowd. In 1945, before the Second World War ended, Bacon caught, unforgettably, the atmosphere of this time in *Figure in a Landscape* 1945, Tate Gallery.

A suit without a body sits on a reversed iron chair, only his hands painted, as two microphones catch his empty words. In a different treatment of this theme, *Study for Man with Microphones* 1946, (first state), there are four microphones, but in the Tate Gallery painting, seeking ambiguity as so often, he has only two, so they could also give the impression of a characterless pair of hands in white cuffs and suit machine-gunning the art-gallery's spectators.

In this disturbing image of anonymous, sudden violence, Bacon speaks from first-hand experience for the many of us who lived for five years in streets intermittently strafed by machine-gun fire from above, and know that a dictator's amplified words soon become bullets.

Moore's art recording this experience is different. In October 1940 he was bombed out of his Hampstead studio. He responded to this by drawing

23 Peppiatt, *Francis Bacon*, p. 15.

in a series of sketch-books sleepers, women and children, sheltering from the nightly air-raids in the London Underground.

Kenneth Clark saw some of these private sketches; and at Clark's invitation Moore continued them as an official war-artist from 1940–42. The finished drawings worked up from his sketch-books quickly won international attention. They do not record violence: rather, the quiet determination, stoicism, adaptability and common decency of ordinary Londoners facing extreme conditions.

As war-artist he also sketched men, working in extreme conditions underground, Yorkshire coal-miners at Wheldale Colliery where his father had been a miner. His first day down the mine is vividly recalled:

> . . . all this in the stifling heat. I have never had a tougher day in
> my life, of physical effort and exertion – but I wanted to show
> the Deputy that I could stand as much as the miners.[24]

Not since student days had he concentrated on drawing the male body. This commission gave him a new interest, which was to lead to his *Warrior with Shield* 1953–54, *Falling Warrior* 1956–57, and the *Goslar Warrior* 1973–74, all of them conceived of in a context of war.

Bacon's fascination with violence can perhaps be traced back to his father's severity, but much of his childhood in Ireland was unpeaceful.

> The atmosphere of threat and violence, the fear of the sniper
> in the woods and the hidden bomb, made an indelible impres-
> sion.[25]

He belonged to the Country House set, the Protestant Ascendancy who, after 1919, were under threat from the Irish Republican Army, and guerrilla war.[26] When asked if he felt Irish he replied:

> You can't really say that I'm Irish. It's true that I was born

24 Berthould, *Henry Moore*, p.179.   25 Peppiatt, *Francis Bacon*, p.17.   26 A good account of growing up under these conditions may be found in the autobiography by T. R. Henn, *Five Arches*, Colin Smythe, 1980. See also T. R. Henn, *Last Essays*, Colin Smythe, 1976, Chapter 2 'The Weasel's Tooth'.

in Ireland and that there are some things that I like about Ireland, especially the way people construct their sentences. There are some very great Irish writers and poets such as Synge and Yeats. Perhaps I share with them a certain desperate enthusiasm.[27]

One of Bacon's most violent works, about which much has been written, is *Crucifixion* 1965, the triptych in Munich.[28] Bacon disliked narrative being deduced from his paintings, yet this, with its Nazi swastika armband, and rosettes on two battered victims, seems to invite interpretation. His biographer, amongst others, writes of the influence of 'Cimabue, whose Christ on the Cross Bacon had long admired' and 'perhaps photographs of Mussolini's inglorious hanging upside down (like the crucified Peter)'[29] as relevant.

A possible source (doubtless among many others) I have not seen mentioned is the painting attributed to Jan de Baen 1633–1702, portrait specialist at The Hague after his arrival there in 1660. Its subject is *The Mutilated Corpses of the de Witt brothers, Johan and Cornelis, hanging on the Groene Zoodje on the Vijverberg, The Hague, 1672.*

It hangs in the Rijksmuseum, Amsterdam, and Bacon showed me a reproduction. So strong was its effect on me, an upside down double 'crucifixion' with the most extreme of sexual mutilation painted in loving detail, that it haunted me for decades until, incorporated into a play on Rembrandt in 1999, something of its impact was exorcised.[30] Like Bacon's *Crucifixion* 1965 it, too, has a detached spectator viewing the scene.

A spectator also views the reclining female nude in *Study of a Nude with Figure in a Mirror* 1969. He sits on a metal chair in tie, suited, with trilby hat on head, his right ankle resting on his left thigh, his gaze anything but detached. As he is seen in a mirror, the viewer of Bacon's painting becomes implicated.

---

27 M. Archimbaud, *Francis Bacon: In Conversation with Michel Archimbaud*, Paris 1992; trans. London 1993, p.116.
28 *Crucifixion* 1965, oil and acrylic on canvas, Triptych, 197.5 x 147 cm each, Bayerische Staatsgemäldesammlungen Pinakothek der Moderne, Munich.   29 Peppiatt, *Francis Bacon*, p.234.
30 Francis Warner, *Rembrandt's Mirror*, 2000, Colin Smythe, p.128 (also illustration).

Another *Lying Figure* of the same year [31] shows a sprawled female nude on her back, a hypodermic syringe stuck in her right arm. Beside her bed is an ashtray showing the stubs of four cigarettes, with two more stubs beside it. A lit bulb hanging from the ceiling illuminates her spread legs.

The faces of both women are dehumanized, the first being a toothy African mask, the second unrecognizable pulp. It is not difficult to see what Bacon intends. He, clearly, is not attracted to the voyeurism of the mirrored man (and yet he paints the scene); and the bulb's illumination of the spread smoker is not for him.

In his *Triptych Inspired by T. S. Eliot's Poem 'Sweeney Agonistes'* 1967 there are four nude lying figures, two women on their backs in the viewer's left-hand panel, and a couple in congress in the right. The centre panel has clearly recently held another 'lying figure', but although the railway carriage compartment and discarded clothes are splattered with blood, no body is now to be seen.

On the outer edge of the right hand panel, in a curved mirror image, a clothed man wearing glasses looking like T. S. Eliot is making a telephone call, apparently communicating the scene. We remember two lines from Eliot's poem *Sweeney Agonistes*:

> Any man has to, needs to, wants to
> Once in a lifetime, do a girl in.

Bacon's lying or reclining figures are at the opposite pole from those of Henry Moore. Moore's do not belong in viewing booths or private rooms but in the open air. They are seen as a part of the natural world, reminding the viewer that he or she is also a part.

He frequently enlisted the names and works of the greatest artists to throw light on his own works, not to assert his ego but as a teacher wishing the pupil to judge by the highest criteria. According to Irina, soon after their wedding – anxious that his young French-speaking Russian bride should not be ignorant of our greatest poet – Henry started to read with her the works of Shakespeare. Later she came to know the plays well through seeing so

31 *Lying Figure* 1969, oil on canvas, 198 x 147.5 cm, Riehen-Basel, Fondation Beyeler.

many of them with her husband, but their honeymoon reading did not
proceed beyond a few sonnets and Shakespeare's first published poem *Venus
and Adonis*, 1593.

Involved as Moore was in creating reclining female figures, one can see
why this poem appealed. Titian's amusing painting of a well-coiffured naked
Venus trying her best to prevent a fully clothed Adonis leaving her by clinging
round his chest was known to them both.[32] Shakespeare's word-painting uses
the metaphor of Venus's body as landscape. His Venus, however, is more on
the scale of Titian's *Venus Anadyomene*.[33] C. S. Lewis writes of Shakespeare's
predatory nude:

> Shakespeare's Venus is a very ill-conceived temptress. She is
> made so much larger than her victim that she can throw his
> horse's reins over one arm and tuck him under the other, and
> knows her own art so badly that she threatens, almost in her
> first words, to 'smother' him with kisses.[34]

Here she is.

> Sometime her arms infold him like a band:
> She would, he will not in her arms be bound . . .

> 'Fondling,' she saith, 'since I have hemm'd thee here
> Within the circuit of this ivory pale, [her bare arms]
> I'll be a park, and thou shalt be my deer:
> Feed where thou wilt, on mountain or in dale;
>   Graze on my lips, and if those hills be dry,
>   Stray lower, where the pleasant fountains lie.

> 'Within this limit is relief enough,
> Sweet bottom grass and high delightful plain,
> Round rising hillocks, brakes obscure and rough,
> To shelter thee from tempest and from rain:

32 Titian, *Venus and Adonis* 1553–54, 186 x 207 cm, Madrid, Prado.
33 Titian, *Venus Anadyomene* 1518/25, 76 x 57.3 cm, Edinburgh, National Gallery of Scotland.
34 C. S. Lewis *English Literature in the Sixteenth Century, Excluding Drama*, Oxford, 1954, p 498.

> Then be my deer, since I am such a park,
>
> No dog shall rouse thee, though a thousand bark.'

Henry often referred to Shakespeare, not least to elicit comparative differences.

> If I compare Michelangelo's David with Giovanni Pisano's figure of David from the Siena façade, I find that although the David of Michelangelo is an unbelievable, superhuman achievement for a young man of twenty-five, it is very different as an expression of a philosophical outlook on life. . . The David of Giovanni Pisano has behind it an intensity of human understanding, of deep personality; it's like comparing Benedick and Hamlet.[35]

Irina would sometimes tease him by saying that he talked of Shakespeare when I turned up. He told her

> I think that people with a gift for words have had the biggest influence of all on our past, like Shakespeare . . . I admire literature and the gift for words in a person more than I do somebody who dances well, somebody who even does sculpture well.[36]
>
> At one time I thought I wanted to write, I wrote little plays and essays. I thought that poetry was the biggest and most marvellous of human activities. But actually they're all the same. Poetry and sculpture are both about people trying to express their feelings about life, about nature, about their response to the world.[37]

When I asked him about the poetry he had learned at school, he quoted one of Wordworth's Lucy poems:

> A slumber did my spirit seal;

35 Wilkinson (ed.) *Henry Moore*, p 170.   36 Ibid., p 39–40.
37 Ibid., p.38.

Warner teaching Moore poetic form in Dante's lyric poetry

> I had no human fears:
> She seemed a thing that could not feel
>   The touch of earthly years.
>
> No motion has she now, no force;
>   She neither hears nor sees,
> Rolled round in earth's diurnal course,
>   With rocks, and stones, and trees.

He went on:

> Wordsworth often personified objects in nature and gave them
> the human aspect, and personally I have done rather the
> reverse process in sculpture . . . I have, as it were, related a
> human figure to a mountain [as Wordsworth for once does in
> this poem], and so got the same effect as a metaphor . . .
>   I believe it's a question of metamorphosis. We must relate
> the human figure to animals, to clouds, to the landscape –

bring them all together . . . By using them like metaphors in
poetry, you give new meaning to things.[38]

An example from his own work that he used as illustration was the
bronze *Two Piece Reclining Figure No.2* 1960, 259 cm long:

> This particular sculpture is a mixture of the human figure and
> landscape, a metaphor of the relationship of humanity with
> the earth, just as a poem can be.[39]

So the Reclining Figure as a welcoming nude, such as the woman half
raised on her left elbow, knees parted, of 1926, 40.7 cm; or the Mother
with Child feeding, or burrowing into her – that enigmatically beautiful
terracotta (later large elmwood) *Reclining Figure* 1945 created while Moore
was awaiting the birth of his daughter Mary, these now yield at times to
Reclining Figures in two or three pieces, such as the bronze *Three Piece
Reclining Figure No.1* 1961-62, 287 cm long, which is half way between the
human form and protruding cliffs washed by the sea.

But the distances between the two or three pieces in the dismembered
figures are exact.

> If somebody moved one of those parts one inch, straightaway
> I'd know.[40]

In his *Memorial Figure* 1945–46, 142 cm long, in the grounds of Dartington
Hall, Devon, in memory of Christopher Martin, founder of its art school,
Moore tells us

> . . . the raised knee repeats or echoes the gentle roll of the landscape.[41]

In this analogy of answering motifs we catch perhaps a gentle echo of
Moore's love of music.

Some music (like Chopin's *Nocturnes*) is an escape from reality, it

---

38 Wilkinson (ed.) *Henry Moore*, pp.126–7, 222. Context, and words in square brackets, not in
Wilkinson. 39 Ibid., p.289. 40 Ibid., p.288. 41 Ibid., p.270.

makes one sit back and go 'soft and mushy'. I prefer the kind which keys one up, — the later quartets of Beethoven for example.[42]

Sometimes he used musical analogies when teaching:

> I would say that all young sculptors would be better if they were made to finish their early works to the very utmost. It's like a singer learning to sing higher than he can readily go, so that he can then sing within his own range.[43]

And this love of music has been reciprocated by the musicians.

A recent example is the organ work *Pebbles, Rocks, Shells, and Bones* composed by Ian Coleman[44] in 2011 for the virtuoso organist David Goode. In his introduction Coleman says:

> The piece takes two sources of inspiration – the theme of Bach's *The Art of the Fugue*, and the work of Henry Moore. The title comes from a quotation by Moore that I came across that speaks of his lifelong fascination with these objects in nature and how they influenced his sculpture . . . Out of this the piece tries to find some sense of form and thematic material, and various 'snippets' of ideas are heard. Eventually, the piece finds its thematic material and formal design in a fugue . . . in a grand, full manner before returning to the sound world of the beginning.

At the beginning the sound world is mysterious, tentative, creating a reflective mood of expectation before the music's embryonic and disparate forms cohere to bring forth the fully developed and contrasting fugal section, clear in its outline and majestic in its effect. When this is completed the music subsides back into the subdued delicacy of the opening, quietly climbing above a low pedal D sustained through the final seven bars to

---

42 Wilkinson (ed.) *Henry Moore*, p.190. 43 Ibid., p.157.
44 British born and educated composer Professor Ian Coleman B.A., M.M., D.M.A., Chair of Music Department, William Jewell College, Liberty, Missouri, USA.

resolve on a concluding chord of D major that has added to it a major seventh, implying that something new is to come in the future. Analogies with Henry Moore's Mother and Child sculptures, and his Internal/External Forms are not far to seek.

This musical homage is part of a tradition across the arts, another example being C. V. Stanford's symphony No.6 in E flat major, Op. 93, of 1905 dedicated *In Memoriam G. F. Watts* (1817–1904). Watts' powerful equestrian sculpture in Kensington Gardens, London, called 'Physical Energy' is a major inspiration, not least in the energetic physicality of the *Allegro con brio* First Movement.

Physical energy is most certainly caught in Bacon's portraits. Writing of his *Study of George Dyer in a Mirror 1968*, 198 x 147.5 cm, Michael Peppiatt pointed out that:

> Dyer swings round to look at himself with such violence
> that his features are thrown into the mirror like a torn mask,
> leaving only the stump of a head behind on his shoulders.[45]

Bacon's *Head VI* 1949, 93.2 x 76.5 cm, the last of the series of six *Heads* painted for his first one-man exhibition,[46] is a variation on Velázquez's portrait of Pope Innocent X reduced to a purple satin-caped scream in a transparent cube, the upper part of the head missing save for two ghostly eyes between which hangs the tassel of a blind.

By 1955 he was driving visceral animality of the scream to extreme by making the subject of his portrait a *Chimpanzee*, 152.5 x 117 cm. Bacon concentrates all his ferocity of focus on the open teeth scream of rage up to the non-existent sky of the ape's cage as our tormented cousin grips its rail while, with its other arm, it punches the black void.

With the 1960s such pictures gave way to portraits of his friends, but these are not the still meditations of patient sitters in gorgeous clothes that Van Dyck, Reynolds and Gainsborough provide. Bacon's most extraordinary is of his dead and absent lover as no more than a large black rectangle. Its title is *Self-Portrait with a Watch* 1973, 198 x 147.5 cm.

45 Peppiatt, *Francis Bacon*, p. 261.   46 Hanover Gallery, London, 8 November–10 December 1949.

George Dyer had been found dead, Bacon's sleeping pills strewn around him, in the bathroom of their shared room in the Hôtel des Saint-Pères the day before the opening of Bacon's exhibition at the Grand Palais, Paris, October 25 1971. The autopsy gave the cause of death as 'either suicide, or accidental overdose of barbiturates due to alcohol-induced confusion'. Bacon blamed himself for being so preoccupied with the exhibition that he had neglected Dyer. Their violence, when he had finally come in at nights, had disturbed the other guests. At Bacon's invitation I attended the Preview the night before the opening. We waited among the pictures, but uncharacteristically our courteous, punctual and genially enthusiastic host did not appear. We found this strange, until we learned next day that he had been detained to help the French police with their enquiries.[47]

In this *Self-Portrait with a Watch* Bacon sits on a round wooden chair with his feet together and knees tightly gripping his right arm while his left hand clings to his left ankle, and in the process shows the time on his watch. Beside him on a table is propped up a large rectangular canvas completely black with

absence – a 'colour' also appearing on the side of Bacon's head nearest to it, like black light. Below is a torn newspaper cutting.

The picture's raw emotion captures the painter's struggle to look at, and at least in paint face up to, using all his art, his experience, his memory, his intellect, to comprehend the grief and guilt. The contortion of his body is summed up in the bleakness of his one eye.

Another *Self-Portrait* of the same year and size is its twin. The watch, on his right wrist now,

Self-Portrait with a Watch 1973. Oil on canvas 198 x 147.5 cm

47 See Notes.

shows the same time as he holds the top of his head as he leans on a basin. The grief's anguish can perhaps be fought by painting it; a precarious battle he only just wins: hence the enormous power of these two self-portraits.

The impact of his *Triptych May–June 1973* (each panel 198 x 147.5 cm) is – by Bacon or anyone else – unrivalled. Here he directly faces what he believes are the consequences of his actions. Each black panel unflinchingly records Dyer's final moments. It is unadorned narrative; it reads from right to left.

In the viewer's right hand panel the naked, nose-bleeding George Dyer leans urgently over a basin vomiting. The centre panel shows, under a bare bulb giving scarcely any light, Dyer's shoulder and head red and bruised above a waste pipe, his shadow forming a horned and spread-winged silhouette. By the third, his life has drained away, and his hunched, naked corpse slumps on a lavatory pan, its head fallen between the knees.

Triptych May–June 1973. Oil on canvas, each panel 198 x 147.5 cm

It is the ultimate Bacon subject: the painter as model's murderer. The devilish shadow cast in the centre panel seeps from the waste pipe as well as from Dyer's body, and appears to be leaving the dying man to fly at the painter – or his substitute, the viewer. Death will claim us. Here is truth unequivocal.

In May 1985, at the opening of Bacon's second retrospective Tate exhibition, my seventeen-year-old daughter Lucy – later to become an artist not uninfluenced by Lucian Freud – accompanied me. Not having seen the label, she asked Francis whether his *Triptych — Studies of a Human Body 1979*, 198 x 147.5 cm had a title. He replied mischievously with a quotation from T. S. Eliot's 'Sweeney Agonistes':

> Birth, and copulation and death.
> That's all, that's all.

and reading the triptych from viewer's right to left it is true that the right panel shows a nude reclining male from the front, and the last with a new bullet-wound bleeding through his back. The quotation also suits Bacon's final *Triptych 1991*, 198.1 x 147.6 cm, where the right panel shows the nude bottom half of a male body stepping towards us out of the darkness into light, and on the left the same half body (both are surmounted by portrait photos) steps out of the light into the dark, genitals prominent. The centre panel of each of the two triptychs shows two entwined lying nude bodies.

It was his final distillation of his view of life.

'Unaccommodated man' had been Bacon's theme since before his first painting of George Dyer – a triptych – in 1964: *Three Figures in a Room*, each panel 198 x 147 cm, but here it is on a large scale. In all three panels Dyer is naked in a room empty save for one seat.

On the viewer's right, balancing on a bar stool, he steadies himself with

Triptych. Three Figures in a Room 1964. Oil on canvas, each panel 198 x 147 cm

his right leg on the floor whilst his left knee covers his genitals. Twisting his body his left arm bends over his head. He could not look more awkward or precarious.

The centre panel displays him on a large, soft armchair, his right knee hiding his genitals. He appears to be resting his left cheek on his hand in a parody of relaxation, while his pose is hunched and vulnerable. The left of the triptych is Dyer seen from behind, his spine emphasised, sitting on the lavatory.

What gives this early triptych its unnerving poignance is that this penetrating study of a man intellectually and socially out of his depth, inarticulate, following a hero supremely fluent and intelligent; Dyer's impressive physique and thin veneer of London's East End gangland menace belying the fact that he was far too gentle for Bacon's pain-seeking pleasures; by a terrifying intuition this painting seems to forecast in what state and where he is to die.

No wonder Bacon returned to this panel in *Triptych, May – June 1973*, and recreated the then–imagined scene here in stark fact, with Dyer's corpse on the lavatory against a black background seen now through an open door, rather than in the same room as the painter. The ultimate masochism is to choose a partner who is too lost, too nervous and withdrawn to be cruel enough: but that reverses into destruction.

Less clear is why Bacon returned to his early masterpiece *Three Studies for Figures at the Base of a Crucifixion 1944*, in 1988 with *Second Version of Triptych 1944*. When asked he gave a *faux-naïf* answer. The second is brilliant in technique, more classical and uncluttered in design, more considered, but – tellingly – set further back, more distanced, in its space. It has all of his mature skill and none of his genius. What it lacks is the rawness of immediacy.

A third revisiting of the past is *Painting 1946 (Second Version) 1971*, 198 x 147.5 cm, which evokes *Painting 1946*, 198 x 132 cm. This was the first painting that bought him public recognition, and meant a great deal to him. The *Second Version* changes the dominant colour, is more formal, calculated, and tidier. The row of bottom teeth in the half-head under the dark umbrella

Above: Painting 1946.
Oil on canvas 198 x 132 cm

Below: Second Version of Painting 1946,
1971. Oil on canvas 198 x 147.5 cm

is played down – the umbrella itself lightened in colour – and the slabs of meat behind and before the sitting figure have clearly been washed and trimmed. The first version's 'one continuous accident mounting on top of another' as he put it is vertiginous in its impact, not emotion recollected in tranquillity quarter of a century later.

It is just possible that I had a small part in provoking him to paint the *Second Version 1971*. In 1970 three one-act plays of mine, collectively titled *Maquettes* as they were small experiments for three larger plays, opened at the Oxford Playhouse, then later at the Edinburgh Festival on the Fringe.[48]

One, named *Lumen*, was a direct result of our conversations about the juxtapositioning of two carcasses of meat (as in *Painting 1946*) with – in my case – two human beings, in a context that sought to adapt cubism to the stage.[49] It is not true to say Bacon designed our stage set, but he did encourage my experiment seeing it for what it was: a tribute to him. He was intrigued.

48 See review by Harold Hobson in *The Sunday Times* (a lengthy article) on August 2, 1970.
49 See page 278.

I was, in fact, drawing on my friendships with both artists, hoping to blend aspects of each into one stage metaphor. Moore's mastery of the archetypes extended to archetypal gestures. His bronze *Family Group* 1948–49, height 152 cm, has had a mixed reception, but to me the view from behind, with its inexplicable tenderness of touch as the Father places his hand on the Mother's near shoulder, a gesture hidden from sight by their baby unless one walks round the back, is haunting. Is she supporting his heavy arm? Her neck shows no strain.

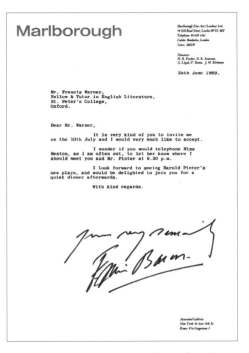

Letter from Bacon

Or is he lovingly supporting her? The ambiguity is perfectly balanced, and concentrates the power of Moore over our emotions at his greatest. It is not Michelangelo's spark of life across the fingertips of God and Adam but something more mundane, understated, scarcely noticed.

I tried to capture these two influences in the close of *Lumen*, the last play of the smaller trilogy.

Two are sitting a little apart, bodies bare except for minimal underclothes, in front of the two carcasses of meat.

ACTOR	(*Holding lighted candle*) Come, to bed.
ACTRESS	It is late.
ACTOR	Weariness brings compulsion. (*Blows out candle.*)
	Lights dimming
ACTRESS	Are you there?
ACTOR	(*Pause*) I'm here.

Jeremy Treglown and Jennifer Earl in Lumen, *1970*

	Lights continue dimming.
ACTRESS	Hold my hand. I'm afraid.
	ACTOR raises his left hand, ACTRESS *her right and they reach out, but their fingertips are not quite able to touch. Then their arms slowly, and together, decline.*
ACTOR	We have left it too late.
ACTRESS	We shouldn't have joked.
ACTOR	Darken our lightness.
ACTRESS	Bear with our weakness.
	Dark

An act of kindness to me by Henry was unexpectedly to benefit him, and had far-reaching consequences for good in my life. In 1970 Betty Tinsley sent a message to my Oxford college to say that Mr Moore had a visitor arriving from Canada. Would I be free and like to come to Perry Green to help entertain him? In retrospect I can see this was a friendly way of showing appreciation for the fact that I was dedicating the last of the trilogy of full-length plays, *Meeting Ends*, to him. (Henry was to create its poster.)[50]

The visitor was a Canadian in his early forties who from humblest Russian-immigrant origins had built up a booming property empire in Toronto. His name was Albert Latner, the youngest and most brilliant of those 'merchant princes' of Prime Minister Pierre Trudeau's[51] years turning Toronto from 'a hick town into a great metropolis' as its Mayor, Philip Givens, put it.

I knew two of Albert Latner's older mentors: Sam Zacks, financier, property developer and – with Ayala his wife – legendary art collectors. Each had the dedication of a play in *Maquettes*.

Sam and Ayala, together with Albert Latner, Signy Eaton and her husband John of the department store chain, Edmund Bovey – President of the Northern and Central Gas Corporation, and a few others were to bring into being the Henry Moore extension of the Art Gallery of Ontario in Toronto four years later in October 1974. Henry invited both me and my daughter Georgina aged eleven to the opening. At the dinner he sat this youngest member at our party by the great Canadian photographer 'Karsh of Ottawa', who memorably told her how he had managed to capture the famous photograph of Churchill with fierce, bull-dog expression by suddenly pulling the cigar out of his mouth and photographing.

Albert Latner

On that original Perry Green afternoon in 1970, Albert Latner bought a bronze of *Three Motifs Against a Wall, 1958*, 20 x 43 inches, 8 x 17 inches, followed later by the bronze *Reclining Figure: Angles* 1979, 43 inches x 90 inches, to add to his and his wife Temmy's rapidly expanding collection of modern

50 See Francis Warner, *Requiem*, a trilogy comprising *Lying Figures, Killing Time,* and *Meeting Ends*, together with its *Maquettes*, with an introduction by Tim Prentki, Colin Smythe, 1980.
51 Pierre Trudeau, 1919–2000. Prime Minster of Canada April 1968–June 1979 and March 1980–June 1984.

art. He also bought my production of *Maquettes*, and flew the whole company to Toronto for the North American première at Hart House Theatre in November, Samuel Beckett contributing his two tiny plays *Come and Go*, and *Breath*.[52] Alan Schneider, Beckett's North American stage director, directed all the plays. The Press was favourable: Toronto was buzzing. Alan Schneider wrote to Beckett:

> The *Maquettes* I tried to make as simple and clear as possible, and the audience was most attentive. Mrs Zacks most pleased, and our friend Al Latner radiant in his first venture as producer.[53]

On June 15, 1975 Henry gave my daughter Georgina a lesson in drawing sheep, and showed us his *Sheep Book*:

> I went on drawing, because the lambing season had begun, and there in front of me was the mother-and-child theme. This is one of the favourite themes in my work: the large form related to the small form and protecting it, or complete dependence of the small form on the large form. I tried to express the way lambs suckled with real energy and violence. There is something biblical about sheep. You don't hear of horses and cows in the Bible in the same way; you hear of sheep and shepherds.[54]

The large form protecting the small is there in the Helmet Heads that go back to the outbreak of World War II:

> . . . like a face peering out from inside a prison. There are two versions, one in bronze and one in lead. The lead version, I think, is more expressive because lead has a kind of poisonous quality; you feel if you licked it you might die.[55]

By 1964 this had evolved into *Maquette for Atom Piece*, which when cast in

52 See p. 263   53 Ed. Maurice Harmon, *No author better served: the correspondence of Samuel Beckett and Alan Schneider*, Harvard University Press, 1988, pp. 236–240.
54 Henry Moore *Sheep Book*, London, Thomas and Hudson, 1980, penultimate page.
55 John Hedgecoe, *A Monumental Vision: The Sculpture of Henry Moore*, London, Collins and Brown, 1998, p 96.

bronze combined the idea of the atomic mushroom cloud with the human skull. Over 3.5 metres high, it stands at the University of Chicago to commemorate the twenty-fifth anniversary of the first self-sustaining nuclear chain reaction achieved there, and was re-named *Nuclear Energy*, lest people should misunderstand the spoken word 'Piece'. Moore's concept, though, came before this commission.

Later, as his health began to fail we talked, as so often before, of Michelangelo. Moore wanted to beat his hero's age of eighty-nine, though that was not to be. In the end eighty-eight proved an honour-

Georgina, Warner and Henry with Sheep, 1975

able try. He wrestled intellectually with understanding Buonarrotti's genius. Speaking of his *Rondanini Pietà* (1552–4) in Milan he asked:

> Why should that hand, which scarcely exists, be so expressive? Why should Michelangelo, out of nothing, achieve that feeling of somebody touching another body with such tenderness? I don't know. But it comes, I think, from the spirit. And it seems to me to have something of the same quality as the late *Crucifixion* drawings.[56]

My Christian belief began to come into his conversations.

> Although I was baptised and confirmed and made to go to church as a boy, I am not a practising Christian. But I still respect people's beliefs. . .[57]

56 Wilkinson (ed.) *Henry Moore*, pp. 158–9.   57 Ibid., p. 269.

Perhaps the single period in past art which I love most is the Romanesque – when sculpture and architecture had such complete unity and religious sincerity.[58]

I asked whether he had chosen to be buried in the little churchyard of Perry Green, where, with Irina beside him, his body lies today, and he suddenly became alert and excited when I quoted words from Edmund Blunden's poem 'The Deeper Friendship':

> I would sue for peace where the rats and mice have gnawed,
> And well content that Nature should bury me.

'Sue for peace! Now there was a soldier poet! You know, don't you, he won the Military Cross?'

He beamed.

Henry knew I would be there to see him committed to the earth. Nine months before his death Penelope and I brought our baby Miranda to see him who had for so long been a Grandfather figure to my two elder daughters, my own father having died in 1955 at the age of 51. Now for a few moments, as of old, a living Mother and Child was with him. As he looked down at the small face, his arm, his hands, protected our future; he had glimpsed a tremor of bliss, wide-eyed and contentedly sucking her thumb, and he wanted this happiness photographed. His last letter to me begins:

> Your book arrived safety and the photographs of Miranda with
> me – what a lovely baby she is, you must be very proud of her.

For his Memorial Service I wrote the Bidding Prayer of thanksgiving for his gifts,[59] and asked that it be followed by the 'Introit' and 'Kyrie Eleison' from Mozart's *Requiem*. To evoke the skill with which Henry could elicit from stone a vulnerable human form, with his daughter Mary we chose Gerald Finzi's setting of Thomas Traherne's poem that opens:

---

58 Ibid., p. 111. 59 This was based on the suffrages from Warner's father's London Memorial Service in St Martin-in-the-Fields gathered by Francis's mother. See Nancy Le Plastrier Warner, *Hugh Warner: The Story of a Vocation*, London, S.P.C.K., 1958, p. 203.

Penelope Warner, Miranda and Henry

These little Limbs,
    These Eys and Hands which here I find,
This panting Heart wherewith my Life begins;
    Where have ye been? Behind
What Curtain were ye from me hid so long!
Where was, in what Abyss, my new-made Tongue?

When we look more closely at one of the last great bronzes, *Mother and Child: Block Seat*, height 244 cm, we realize that instead of a nipple on the Mother's breast there is a hole. Opposite is the baby, not with open mouth but with a protuberance to enter the hole. One day their roles will be reversed, the child will nurse the mother, and insert the feeding tube into *her* boneless gums: Moore's added major seventh to his final tonic chord.

Mother and Child: Block Seat, 1983–84.
244 cm high. Photo: Michael Muller

HENRY MOORE, O.M., C.H.   HOGLANDS,
Telephone: Much Hadham 2566/3194   PERRY GREEN,
                                           MUCH HADHAM,
                                           HERTS.

                                    2 December 1985

Dear Francis,

    Your book arrived safely and the
photographs of Miranda with me - what
a lovely baby she is, you must be very
proud of her.

    I have not had time to look through
the book, but I am looking forward to
doing so this week.

    Irina and I would like to send you
all best wishes for Christmas and 1986.

                        love
                        Henry

'The Sorceress'
A hitherto unknown poem by Samuel Palmer

As August of 1838 opened Vesuvius began to erupt. The rumbling, 'sometimes a noise like the incessant discharge of cannon', and the 'brilliant and highly finished white cloud issuing from the crater' were witnessed by an English honeymoon couple, the painter Samuel Palmer, aged thirty-three, and his nineteen-year-old bride Hannah, daughter of the painter John Linnell. Their vivid letters home convey their excitement as 'our papers were sprinkled with little black particles of ashes'. 'As I sit writing 10 p.m.' (says Samuel Palmer) 'the door is again shaken, two or three times more violently than before – and now I hear the giant begin to growl – which in the stillness of night is rather awful.'[1] During these days, Palmer painted a series of water-colour sketches of the spectacular event.

Though it cannot be proved, it seems likely that it was at this time that Samuel Palmer wrote the unfinished draft of the poem which we have for convenience called 'The Sorceress', tentatively deciphered here. The single sheet of paper, both sides of which are entirely in Palmer's hand, I found amongst the honeymoon letters, and it belongs – as they do – to Joan Linnell Ivimy, John Linnell's great-granddaughter, for whose kind permission to print we are grateful.

The honeymooners had come south to the Bay of Luxury from Rome, where they had been greatly helped on their arrival by Joseph Severn, another painter, who some eighteen years earlier had devotedly cared for the dying Keats, even hiring a piano on which to play arrangements of Haydn's symphonies (Haydn being Keats's favourite composer) to rally him. Keats meant much to Palmer. We have a letter, written in September 1851 to George Richmond,[2] which playfully quotes 'Provençal song and sun-burnt

---

1 *The Letters of Samuel Palmer*, ed. Raymond Lister, Oxford, 1974, pp.169–170. See also Edward Malins, *Samuel Palmer's Italian Honeymoon*, Oxford, 1968. 2 *Letters*, p.485.

Samuel Palmer
self-portrait
c. 1824–5
Ashmolean
Museum, Oxford

mirth' from the *Ode to a Nightingale*; and many years later Palmer was to draw 'The Burial-place of Keats' for Keats's *Poetical Works and Other Writings,* edited by H. Buxton Forman in 1883. In 'The Sorceress' it seems that Palmer is trying to capture something of the opening of 'Hyperion':

> But where the dead leaf fell, there did it rest   (line 10)

with

> And not a leaf did move upon the trees
> > *(The Sorceress*, full transcript, line 15)

and other lines and images in this poem remind the reader of Keats.

An equally powerful influence on Palmer as he wrote this poem was

Coleridge. In an undated letter, probably written to Frederick Tatham a few months earlier, he writes:

> Meanwhile the cranium becomes stuffed with gallipots and varnishes; the blessed winter-evening talks are curtailed; and with the exceptions, now and then, of a whole play of Shakespeare at a gulp and now and then your favourite *Christabel*, matters go on much more prosily and orderly.[3]

'Christabel' did indeed appeal to the more gothic side of Palmer's imagination, and its influence throughout 'The Sorceress' is pervasive. In addition to Keats's 'Hyperion', we may also hear behind the above line 15 Coleridge's lines from 'Christabel':

> There is not wind enough to twirl
> The one red leaf, the last of its clan,
> That dances as often as dance it can,
> Hanging so light. and hanging so high,
> On the topmost twig that looks up at the sky.   (lines 48–52)

The Geraldine of 'Christabel' who refuses to pray, who drives away the guardian spirit (the spirit of Christabel's dead mother), who is described as 'the worker of these harms'; together with the castle bell that will 'Strike twelve upon [Christabel's] wedding-day' (eleven strokes, not twelve, and of an Abbey bell, in line 61 of Palmer's poem, but the final stroke is expected) and much of the atmosphere leading up to:

> Her bridal peal rung with the flames and fiend of Hell (line 52)

all seem echoes from Coleridge's poem.

These and other memories are set in a framework that has parentage in Marlowe's *Dr Faustus*, and probably the Ambrosio of Matthew G. Lewis's *The Monk* (1796). Both Marlowe's scholar and Lewis's monk sell their souls to the devil, only to discover that the devil expects his bond to be honoured.

3 Ibid., p.84.

The Romantic poets, the gothic novelist, the Elizabethan dramatist: we should not forget the book that Samuel and Hannah were reading as the 'thick, sulphurous closeness stifled everything' (line 14), the anticipation

> That oft devoted cities hath o'erhung   (line 22)
>
> Ere earthquakes   (line 24)

was felt by the attentive couple, their minds filled with Milton:

>   I fly
> These wicked tents devoted, lest the wrath
> Impendent, raging into sudden flame
> Distinguish not [4]   (*Paradise Lost* V. 889–892)

> I used to stand and watch it at night (writes Hannah to her parents) sending up flames and bright stones, while the noise was fearful . . . The noise kept me awake some nights before I left Pompeii, and gave me a headache; but I am now quite well.[5]

The book was, of course, Edward Bulwer-Lytton's historical novel, published four years earlier, before he became Lord Lytton. Samuel wrote to John Linnell:

> I think it is worth while to skim the 'Last Days of Pompeii' . . . as he has woven into his tale . . . almost all that history and a residence on the spot with careful investigation can give.[6]

These experiences, and something like this combination of influences, fired Samuel's poetic imagination.

Palmer had written poetry before. In his 1824 sketch-book[7] he left two

---

4 Ibid., p.701, where Palmer writes to Leonard Rowe Valpy, August 1864: 'I am never in a 'lull' about Milton in the abstract, nor can tell how many times I have read his poems, his prose, his biographers. He never tires. He seems to me to be one of the few who have come to full maturity of manhood; not however to infallibility, which is superhuman . . .'

5 Ibid., p.168.   6 Ibid., p.171.

7 Palmer's 1824 Sketch-book, British Museum. Facsimile, with an introduction and commentary by Martin Butlin, William Blake Trust, 1962. 'Twilight Time' is printed in full in *Garland*, ed. Francis Warner, Cambridge, Golden Head Press, 1968.

completed poems, 'Twilight Time', and a draft of a poem with emendations in ink and pencil, to be entitled either 'The Shepherd's home' or 'The old Churchyard'. There is a second draft of the final verse of 'The old Churchyard' on page 184 of the sketch-book. Both poems are Christian and didactic. Each in its different way is of great interest.

'Twilight Time' is strongly indebted to the Milton of 'Il Penseroso', and to such seventeenth century poets as Vaughan and Crashaw:

> All is safe, and all is still
> Save what noise the watch-dog makes
> Or the shrill cock the silence breaks ... (*Twilight Time*, lines 13–15)

> While angel music haunts the air
> Heard dispersed, here, and there,
> Or in distant choral swell
> As they take the spirit to dwell
> Ever, ever, ever, ever
> Fast by his spear-pierced side
> Who pitied, pardoned, loved, and Died
> There to tell (though griefs no more)
> What did here once vex him sore ...   (lines 83–91)

The second poem takes Gray's *Elegy*, and tries to make it more convincingly Christian. In Gray's stoic poem, the only false rhyme is the last, on 'God'. In 'The old Churchyard' the shepherds, rather than the plowman, 'wind their homeward way'.

> Low lies their home 'mongst many a hill,
>   In fruitful and deep delved womb;
> A little village, safe, and still,
>   Where pain and vice full seldom come,
>   Nor horrid noise of warlike drum.   (stanza 2)

Where Gray's 'rude forefathers of the hamlet sleep' 'Where heaves the turf in many a mouldering heap', Palmer tells us that:

> . . . there's a church-yard something raised
>   Above the more unholier gound,
> Where swains unnoted, and unpraised,
>   In innocent sleep lay sound.   (stanza 5)

The poem closes with stanza 8:

> For I 'though base believe that Thou for me
> Hast better things prepared than village gardens be:
> By streams of life, and th' ever blooming tree,
> To walk, and sing with antique saints, & see
> Bliss above all, dear Lord, thy face eternally.

There has been, before this conclusion, a gothic touch:

> Free from press of stony tomb
> Or gloomy vault, shall they from earth's kind womb
>   Joyous at the last trump rise
>   Light of heart and win the skies
> While many more in sculptured marble bound
> Shall wake with sudden horrid shriek . . .   (stanza 6)

Gray, too, when not elegiac, could close 'The Bard' with

> 'Be thine despair and sceptered care;
> To triumph and to die, are mine.'
> He spoke, and headlong from the mountain's height
> Deep in the roaring tide he plunged to endless night.

At least Gray's Bard was spared the lingeringly described torments that await 'Monk' Lewis's Ambrosio, when

> darting his talons into the monk's shaven crown, he sprang with him from the rock. The caves and mountains rang with Ambrosio's shrieks. The daemon continued to soar aloft, till reaching a dreadful height, he released the sufferer. Headlong fell the monk . . . [8]

The landscapes of the gothic novels fascinated Palmer. 'Mrs Radcliffe far exceeds Sir Walter Scott in descriptions of scenery', he was to write to Laura Richmond.[9]

In the end, though, it was to be the classical side of Gray, the classical side of Palmer, that was to flower. From schooldays to his deathbed, Palmer was to love the early poetry of Virgil. In his late teens he was to write:

> I sat down with Mr Blake's Thornton's *Virgil* woodcuts before me, thinking to give to their merits my feeble testimony. I happened first to think of their sentiment. They are visions of little dells, and nooks, and corners of Paradise; models of the exquisitest pitch of intense poetry. I thought of their light and shade, and looking upon them I found no word to describe it. Intense depth, solemnity, and vivid brilliancy only coldly and partially describe them. There is in all such a mystic and dreamy glimmer as penetrates and kindles the inmost soul, and gives complete and unreserved delight, unlike the gaudy daylight of this world. They are like all that wonderful artist's works the drawing aside of the fleshly curtain, and the glimpse which all the most holy, studious saints and sages have enjoyed, of that rest which remaineth to the people of God.[10]

In 1883, posthumously, his translation of Virgil's *Eclogues* was published. Though we may raise our classical eyebrows at some of the liberties he takes with the Latin, the translation does convey, beautifully, what Palmer found in Virgil. He had little formal education, and the translation is the fruit of a lifetime's devotion. To it was prefaced Palmer's essay 'Some Observations on the Country and on Rural Poetry', in which he defined and defended his view of poetry. He sets poetry against war:

> By night, on the St Lawrence, General Wolfe, having repeated Gray's *Elegy* to some of the officers of his staff. told them he

8 M. G. Lewis, *The Monk*, London, 1796, end.
9 *Letters*, p.672.
10 A. H. Palmer, *The Life and Letters of Samuel Palmer*, London, 1892, pp.15–16.

would rather have written that poem, than achieve the victory for which, a few hours later, he was content to have given his life . . .

against politics:

It was shrewdly said, 'Let anyone make the laws of a country, if I may make the songs'; for its national lyrics are the animal spirits of the body politic. Its graver verse tempers public morals and even the established faith . . . The influence of poetry pervades all civilized life; the more so from its point and brevity and because metre and rhyme are easily remembered . . .

beside reason and religion:

A bird deprived of her wings is not more incomplete than the human mind without imagination, a faculty distinct from the spiritual and rational, yet having a common language; for the language of imagination is poetry, and it is in poetry that both sacred aspiration and secular wisdom have found their noblest utterance.

And, as if subconsciously justifying his use in the nineteenth century of a gothic past in his poem 'The Sorceress', he writes:

The mind of a great poet is thrown back into antiquity, whence he symbolizes the present: sometimes, in various mood, refreshing attention or awakening sympathy by allusion to passing affairs; adding mystery by these flashes of the hour, to the twilight of an ideal past: but he who lays his story in the present, is little likely to grasp it, for contact is not vision, and he has no vantage ground of observation; but is himself an atom of his subject, a fly upon the axle.[11]

11 Samuel Palmer, *The Eclogues of Virgil*, London, 1883, note to 'Eclogue VIII', p.102.

In Samuel Palmer's poetry he tries to evoke the Christian faith of the age of the cathedrals, to depaganize the Augustan and yet retain its idyllic pastoral serenity. In his poetry he failed: but that failure was the cause, in etching, sketch and paint, of his lasting triumph.

A selective outline of the poem, edited and punctuated but by no means definitive, may help the reader approaching this complicated text to appreciate Palmer's intentions.

A sorceress has made a Faustian pact with the devil, and this poem describes her emotions on the last evening of her life before she descends into hell, or is saved through confession and repentance.

> Thus sat the thin red woman and the cat,
> Her fierce familiar. Twilight's dunnest pall
> With clouds and hovering cloudlings hung around
> Her dusky banner, and a death hush sat
> Upon the forest. Not the smallest sound . . .
> Broke the death hush of nature . . .
> Flitted not the bat . . .
> The low'ring clouds had long been gathering
> Without a noise of wind or moving breeze.
> A sulphurous closeness stifled everything
> And not a leaf did move upon the trees.
> Such is a stifled conscience, not at ease,
> Like the dull heart that feels not any sting
> Within the breast when it has cause to speak
> But mars the quietness it will not break.
> Like this dread evening is the ominous calm
> That oft devoted cities hath o'ercast,
> Though on that morn the bells have rung their last,
> Ere the grim earthquake takes his dread repast.
> The owl whooped not, the wolf was not abroad;
> Only the sorceress seemed wakeful then,
> And black remorse the vulture in her breast.

A murderess she, and Vengeance from his den
With stealthy steps was moving to inherit
Body and soul . . .
Helpless and hopeless the vile creature lay
Counting the hours till she be taken away.
That night, that dreadful night, the bond expired,
Sealed with her hand, and written in her blood,
And yet not prayer for heavenly ruth she saith.
All was corrupt, and nothing left of good
Which she so many a year had still withstood.
Prayer came not forth but as a stifled breath
Amidst unconfined darkness left to grope –
No outlet.
A wilderness of horror without hope.
O, who can paint — O who can sing the horror
With which she counts the distant abbey bell
Which was her soul's and body's knell,
Her bridal peal rung with the flames and fiend of Hell.

So ends Phase I. Phase II reveals the prayer that does, finally, find an outlet:

O, suddenly she arose, and bursting forth
Into a bitter, lamentable cry:
'Is there no mercy – mercy for the worst?
Or cannot the blood-guilty spirit die
And live no more? Cannot some angel thrust
The fatal bond aside? O tears of [sorrow] burst
Forth from this flint, and cool my burning heart
And quench the fierce, intolerable smart!
I cannot pray, cannot repent, in guilt . . .
But is not Mercy made for blackest guilt
If penetential tears be spent? . . .

The murderer's hand is cleansed if he repent!
But O, this bosom knows not to repent –
Iron shall melt in dew ere the soft rain
Of Bliss cools my scorched heart again.
The hard, unpitying eye can not distil
Tears even for its own calamity . . .
Harden thyself at once. Prepare . . .
The fire! . . '
Then flung upon the ground, writhed did she lie . . .
And groaneth . . .
'Hell is my bed, my horror nigh to hell! . . .'
With hollow gaze fixed on the hour glass still,
The running sand relentless she doth measure . . .
The golden train.
'Bid it run quick that thou may'st know the worst!'
In horrible surmisings more accurst
Then stares . . .
Upon the hollow monitor . . .
So fixed she seems like terror carved in stone.
Only when sudden a quick glance is thrown
To corner of the cell, she, frightened, shivers
Expecting the foul fury to be near . . .
The Abbey bell now struck, she shrieked and rose
She shrieked and rose and then in frantic mind
In spite of pain and the long fear:
'I will, I will confess!' Then rushed she forth
Into the darkness . . .
If she might gain the Abbey gate
Before it should forever be too late,
And all convulse.

In this outline much has been omitted, as the reader may see from the following transcript.

Transcript, by R. E. Alton and Francis Warner

The poem survives in draft on both sides of a single sheet of paper measuring 228 x 182 mm. It was apparently composed in two main bursts of activity. Palmer wrote what must be the earliest phase (hereafter 'Phase I') in light brown ink down the left-hand column of the recto, and continued in the same ink for four lines at the top of the left-hand column of the verso. Phase I totals 52 lines. At the head of the right-hand column of the recto Palmer, in a smaller and in the main less cursive hand, has recorded in four narrow columns fourteen groups of words which he has used or might use as rhymes. There are ten groups of three words, one of four, two of seven, and one of eight. Immediately to the right of lines 1 and 2 of Phase I there appear again three monosyllables identical with the first three in a group of seven, and related to the final words of lines 1, 3, and 4 of Phase I. In the right-hand column of the recto and in the left-hand column of the verso, in a smaller hand and darker ink than Phase I, Palmer subsequently added a further 75 lines or parts of lines (hereafter 'Phase II''). The track followed by the left-hand margin of Phase II on the recto side is dictated by the line lengths of Phase I and must therefore be later. Some additions and amendments to the early phase are, however, in the smaller hand and darker ink of the second phase of composition, and at some time Phase II has been separated by rules from the groups of words, and from the concluding lines of Phase I on the verso.

The draft provides many alternative readings, some written above the line and some below. There are, however, few cancellations such as are found in the opening line of Phase II, and even here the choice between 'aloud', 'at last', and 'forth' as the adverb to modify 'bursting' has been left quite open. Throughout, Palmer has not made up his mind about the way a line or series of lines should develop. Sometimes he has left a gap in a line or at the end of a line intending to complete it later (e.g. Phase I, lines 7 and 8); sometimes a dash indicates that composition is still in progress (Phase I, line 20); sometimes a rule joins an alternative reading to the word which seems to be intended to follow it in a reorganization of the line. In Phase II, line 3, for example, Palmer seems first to have written 'Is there no mercy in the heavens', then added slightly below the line and in a different ink 'for the worst', with 'accurst' interlined above as an alternative to 'the worst'. Presumably uneasy about the metre of these two possibilities he next wrote in a second 'mercy' below the line, and joined it by a rule to the first, thus producing a more acceptable version:

> Is there no mercy – mercy for the worst

But none of the other words is deleted. Similarly in line 25 of Phase II a short double rule angled from the lower interlineation and followed by a single 'o' may indicate that the line could read either

> Tears for its own – its own calamity

or, if we give weight to the careful placing of the interlineation,

> Tears even for its own calamity.

Again, we cannot be sure whether Palmer would have left the last line of Phase I with twelve syllables, or what he would have omitted to compensate for the insertion of 'rang' above the line and of 'the' below it. Phase I, lines 5, 6, and 7 present another kind of problem. It is likely, but by no means sure, that the jumble of words inserted at the end of lines 5 and 6 is intended to form an additional line between lines 7 and 8, so that the passage may read:

> not the smallest sound
> broke the death hush of nature of all things
> which stillness the senses might astound
> more fearfully than thunder.

At the end of the poem Palmer seems to indicate by a caret and a short rule that 'And all convulse' should appear above the longer rule with which he had closed the draft.

Because of the impossibility of being secure of Palmer's intentions we

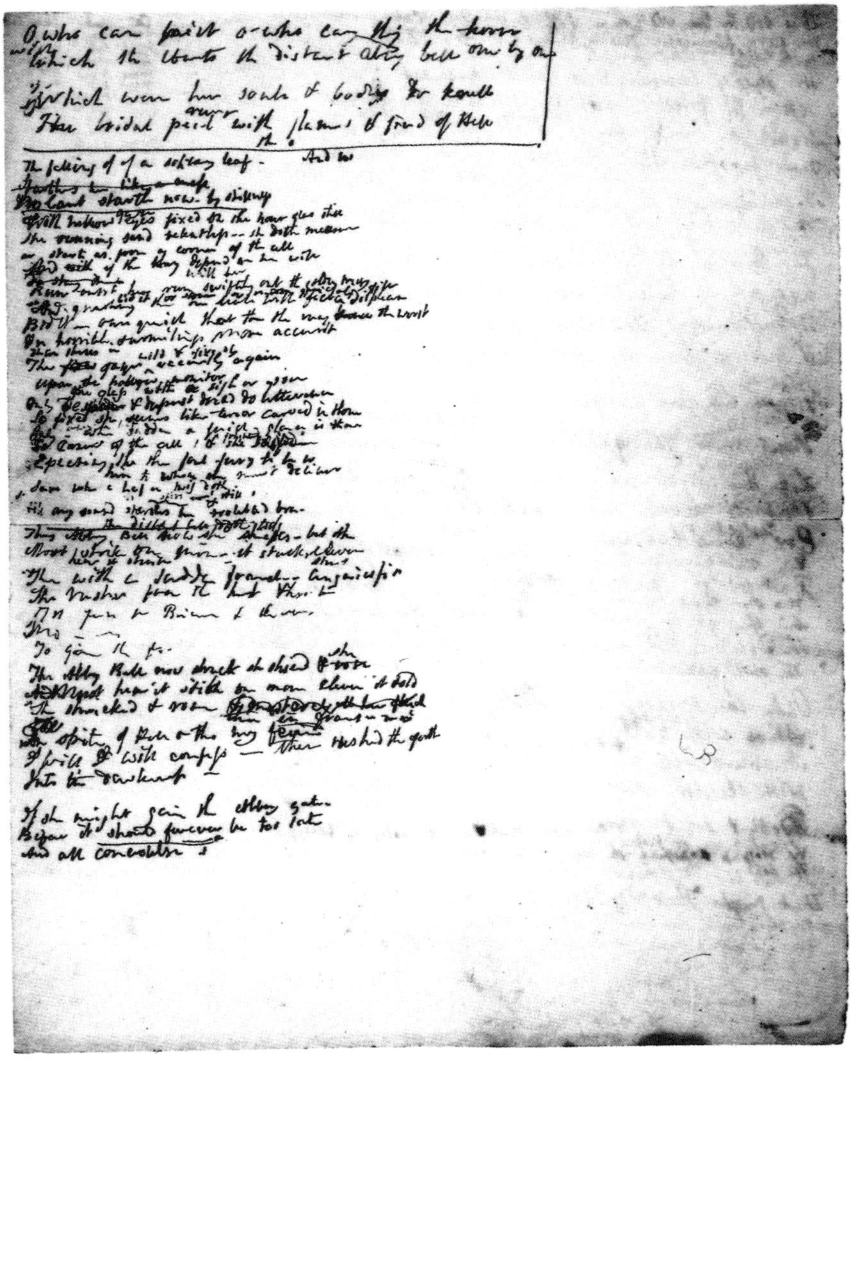
O who can paint o who can tell the horror
With which she heard the distant abbey bell one by one
Which were her souls & bodies dire knell
Her bridal peal with flames & fiend of Hell

The falling of a solitary leaf -

If she might gain the abbey gate
Before it shuts forever be too late

have provided a transcript which tries to indicate in type the marks on the manuscript and their placing. We have, however, not distinguished between the size of the hands in Phase I and Phase II, and, since normally Palmer does not use a smaller hand for interlineations than he does for text, we have used the same size of type throughout, with words lined and placed as in the manuscript.

We have numbered what we take to be separate lines or what were intended to be separate lines, whether completed or not, and whether they are first thoughts or afterthoughts. The spacing shows where Palmer has inserted a new line.

Palmer's writing is very hurried: letters are omitted, especially at the ends of words; final *ing* is usually represented by no more than a couple of minims and a descender; final *m* and *n* are frequently merely a flourish; medial vowels are often suggested by undulations in a horizontal line. So that the transcript can be read, therefore, without more difficulties than Palmer's layout imposes, we have normalized all expansions of what is a sort of short-hand, without indication by pointed brackets or other means. Where we are convinced that we are faced by an idiosyncratic or metrical spelling by Palmer we have retained it (e.g. *equathquaqes*, *earquaques*, in line 24 of Phase I; *takn*, Phase I, line 40). After the full point in line 2 of Phase I punctuation is minimal. We have made no attempt to supply it.

We have employed the following conventions: square brackets denote deletions, thus:

aloud

[Form rises] O suddenly she arose & bursting [out] forth

at last   (Phase II, line 1)

Where a word has been cancelled by writing the substitution directly over it we again use square brackets, thus:

It seemed as [if <u>cancelled by</u>] all the world within the graves —

(Phase I, line 8)

Where a reading is no more than a conjecture we precede it by a question
mark in pointed brackets, thus: <?>

    A few words seem not to be recoverable and are indicated by: <?>


```
          PHASE  I

⟨Recto⟩  Thus sat the thin red woman & the Cat beast      Cat
                                                          round
     2   Her fierce familiar. Twilights dunnest pall      sat
              & hovering
     3   With clouds    cloudlings_      hung around

     4   Her dusky banner & a death hush sat

     5   Upon the forest _ not the smallest sound    the senses
      6                  of nature       which stillness
     7   broke the death hush of all things      might astound

     8   more fearfully than thunder              profound

     9                         flitted not the bat

    10   It seemed as [if cancelled by] all the world within the graves-

    11   And echo dead within her stony caves

    12   The lowring clouds had long been gathering
                                            breeze
    13   without a noise of wind    -   or moving breath
            thick
    14   A  sulphurous closeness - stiflêd every thing
                           qu
    15   & not a leaf did move  upon the trees

    16   Such is :a -a stifled conscience not at ease
       17   Like the dull heart that feels not any sting   speak
    18   Within  the  breast  when   it   has   cause  to
         19                    from the hushed conscience
    20   [The cancelled by]But mars the quietness it will not break
                                ominous    calm,
    21   Like this dread evening is the sultry [hush]
                                     oercast
    22   That oft devoted cities hath oerhung
         23   Quiet &    --        [ & calm]
         Ere  equathquaqes =
    24                          dreaming naught of harm
         Ere  earquaques -

    25   But in the fullness of their

    26   Tho on that morn the bells have rung their last;

    27   And the grim earthquake takes his dread repast
                    birds          on this night abough
    28   The doleful owl [was] whoop not -the nights shrouded ⟨?⟩deaths

    29   The owl whooped not the wolf was not abroad
                           seemed wakeful
    30   Only the sorceress was then   - then
                     wakeful    ravening on her brest brest
    31   Alive with vultures feeding on her heart
       32          & black remorse the vulture in her breast
```

33   A murderess she - & Vengeance from his den
                                          & the smart
34   With stealthy steps was moving -on- [blood] & apart
                                      to inherit   the dart
   35   without rest   no rest
                                      small delay
36   [A cancelled by]Body & soul was aim [that] & in the solitary den

37   From help or hope
   38 w Helpless & hopeless the vile creature [stood] lay
39   In bond -
40   Counting the hours till she be takn away
                                          death
41   That   night that dreadful night the bond expired
                                                    in
42   [With cancelled by]Sealed with her hand & written with her blood

43   And yet not prayer for heavenly ruth she saith

44   All was corrupt & nothing left of good
                  a year
45   Which she so many years had still withstood

46   Prayer came not forth but as a stifled Breath
                  died with her lips as —

47   Amidst unconfined Darkness left to grope

48   No outlet — A wilderness of horror without hope -

⟨Verso⟩ O, who can paint o - who can sing the horror
        with   one by one
   50   which she counts the distant abbey bell

51   Which was her souls & bodys [Tr] knell
                  rung
52   Her bridal peal with flames & fiend of Hell
                  the

PHASE   II

                                          aloud
⟨Recto⟩ [Form rises] o suddenly she arose & bursting [out] forth
                                            at last
2   Into a bitter lamentable cry —
                                  accurst
3   Is there no mercy in the heavens
                  ———— mercy   for the worst

4   [And cannot] [by th] the blood guilty spirit die
            Or cannot
5   And live no more [O tares of pi] cannot some angel thrust

6   The fatal bond aside. [Flint] O tears of sory burst

7   Forth from this flint & cool my burning heart

8   And quench the fierce intolerable smart

9   I cannot cannot pray cannot repent
                           in guilt
10   Is not soever mercy for the guilty
                           dares repent
11   Who saves the vilest that will yet respond

12   But what is that to me the blood I spilt

13   The murderers hand is cleaner if 'tis red

14   But long ago was all compunction sped

15   From out my spirit all

16   But how shall I relent

17   But is not Mercy made for blackest guilt

18   If penetential tears be spent

19   What if the sea of hardship should be spilt

20   The murderers hand is cleansed if he repent

21   But O this bosom knows not to repent

22   Iron shall melt in dew ere the soft
                         rain
23   of Bliss cool my scorchd heart again
           s
24   The hard unpitying eye can not [distil] shed

25   Tears for its own   o
          even for its own calamity —
                   on
26   all is sulphurous blue & red
27   all all is stench &   [loathly cancelled by] deathly dry

28   Harden thyself at once   Prepare here

29   The fire O- now I have
                 might I should
        This thirst of death
30   assuage

                                           lie
                                    writhed did
31   Then flung upon the ground she

32   with with⟨sic⟩ not - no sound Is my inmost Hope
                                                    This
33   And groaneth [until hid so] she

34   Hell Is my bed my horror nigh to hell

35   Then stifled her big groanings in dust

⟨Verso⟩   The falling of a solitary leaf -   And her

37   [Startles her like a mass]

38   [Bo] Cant startle now - by stillness
      ─────────────────────────────────
                        gaze
39   With hollow eyes fixed on the hour glass still

40   The running sand relentless -- she doth measure

41   or starts as from a corner of the cell

42   And [with] if the Way depend on her will

43   [do stay]   with her

44   Run out at her run swiftly out the golden train
  45   bid it or slow or as some quick false gift
46   And gnashing then her teeth with fierce displeasure

47   Bid it - run quick that thou then may know the worst

48   In horrible surmisings more accurst
             Then stares in   wild & fixedly
49   Then [fixes] gazes accurstly again

50   Upon the hollow monitor
             the glass with [a] sigh or groan

51   Only Despair & deepest dread do utterance

52   So fixed she seems like terror carved in stone
                  when a last
53   Only - when sudden a quick glance is thrown
                                   frightened
54   To Corner of the cell, & she [⟨ ? ⟩cancelled by] shivers

55   Expecting the the ⟨sic⟩ foul fury to be near
    56   him to whom she must deliver

57   Same like a leaf on twig doth
                  it stirs   & still

58   till any sound startles her troubled brain
      ─────────────────────────────────

59   the distant bell doth toll

60   This Abbey Bell now str   strikes - but then

61   Must strike one more - it struck eleven
          hear it strike   strokes

62   Then with a sudden frantic anguishing

63   She rushes from the hut & hearth

64   Yes from her Brain & Nerves

65   This - -

66   To gain the Ab --
                                        she
67   The Abbey Bell now struck   she shrieked & [rose]

68   [And] Must hear it [still cancelled by]strike once more eleven it told

69   She shrieked & rose [& mastered all her flesh]
     [She]   then in frantic ⟨?⟩mind

70   In spite of Pain & the   long fear

71   I will I will confess — then rushed she forth

72   Into the darkness —

73   If she might gain the Abbey gate -

74   Before it should forever be too late
                         ⸻ ⌄
75   And all convulse   ⟋

James Joyce's Poetry

The wonderful measure and smack of Joyce's prose is not to be found in his poems; nevertheless, they make a fascinating study. Echoing his artificer, Stephen Dedalus explains to Cranly that

> The lyrical form is in fact the simplest verbal vesture of an instant of emotion

a 'cry or a cadence or a mood'.

> He who utters it is more conscious of the instant of emotion than of himself as feeling emotion.

When Joyce comes to write prose,

> The narrative is no longer purely personal. The personality of the artist passes into the narration itself, flowing round and round the persons and the action like a vital sea.[1]

It also fills them out from inside, as Keats knew, and could certainly operate through narrative verse. Consider John Donne's growing mandrake root:

> His right arme he thrust out towards the East
> Westward his left; th'ends did themselves digest
> Into ten lesser strings, these fingers were:
> And as a slumberer stretching on his bed,
> This way he this, and that way scattered
> His other legge, which feet with toes upbeare.
> Grew on his middle parts, the first day, haire,

---

1 James Joyce, *A Portrait of the Artist as a Young Man*, London, Granada, 1977, p.194.

> To show, that in love's business hee should still
> A dealer bee . . .[2]

One scarcely goes to Joyce for verse of this kind. However, a glance at 'A Memory of the Players in a Mirror at Midnight' shows something of the same gritty delight. The difference is that in Donne's poem we are aware above all of the feelings of the mandrake; in Joyce's of the poet:

> They mouth love's language. Gnash
> The thirteen teeth
> Your lean jaws grin with. Lash
> Your itch and quailing, nude greed of the flesh.
> Love's breath in you is stale, worded or sung,
> As sour as cat's breath,
> Harsh of tongue.
>
> This grey that stares
> Lies not, stark skin and bone.
> Leave greasy lips their kissing. None
> Will choose her what you see to mouth upon.
> Dire hunger holds his hour.
> Pluck forth your heart, saltblood, a fruit of tears.
> Pluck and devour![3]

Joyce peers at Donne 'despoyl'd of fallacies' through Yeats's spectacles. We remember Yeats's letter to Donne's editor, Sir Herbert Grierson, in 1912:

> [I] find that at last I can understand Donne . . . I notice that the more precise and learned the thought, the greater the beauty, the passion.

and letters to Lady Gregory from Yeats about Pound:

> Ezra never shrinks from work . . . A learned companion, and a

2 H. Grierson, *Poems of John Donne*, OUP 1951, p.300.
3 James Joyce, *Pomes Penyeach*, London, Faber and Faber, 1966, p.23.

James Joyce: portrait in oils 11 x 9 inches, painted by Joyce's friend Frank Budgen, who gave it to Warner in June 1968. It is the portrait referred to in the letter from Samuel Beckett on p.291

pleasant one . . . He . . . helps me get back to the definite and the concrete, away from modern abstractions.[4]

By which, presumably, he means the Celtic Twilight. The result was the Yeatsean style already foreshadowed in 'The fascination of what's difficult'.

> There's something ails our colt
> That must, as if it had not holy blood
> Nor on Olympus leaped from cloud to cloud,
> Shiver under the lash, strain, sweat and jolt
> As though it dragged road metal.

The same 'verbigracious bigtimer', having left behind modern abstractions, can now write a marvellous, jaw-breaking line such as

Where we wrought that shall break the teeth of Time

4 The letters are dated 1 January 1915, and 3 January 1913.

in that finest of all his poems of friendship, 'The New Faces'.

Joyce is aware of all this happening between *Chamber Music* (1907) and *Pomes Penyeach* (1927). Hence the difference in style between 'Lean out of the window/Goldenhair' and 'They mouth love's language. Gnash'. During this period Joyce learns to plump out, Hopkinslike but in prose, the human mouth from inside, instead of describing it as in the first three lines of 'A Memory of the Players' like an irritated dentist. The words now tongue the cheeks, and touch inside the teeth:

> Wine soaked and softened rolled pith of bread mustard a moment mawkish cheese.[5]

In Joyce's poem above (from *Pomes Penyeach)* we know the poet feels betrayed (hence the Judas number thirteen); prefers, like Caesar, a 'warm human plumpness' near him, such as Molly's ('Your lean jaws'); and has Lear's lashing beadle (or is it the flagellating God of Francis Thompson's 'Hound of Heaven'? 'Naked I wait Thy love's uplifted stroke!') on literary mind. Oddly, the rare side of Donne, and more particularly the familiar side of Donne's Elizabethan fellow-singers, whispers from the wings through the second verse; not least of the anonymous author of 'I saw my lady weep'.

> Leave off in time to grieve

Becomes

> Leave greasy lips their kissing

bringing greasy Joan from her pot in *Love's Labour's Lost.* After Yeats, he can now risk a jaw-breaker:

> Will choose her what you see to mouth upon

and with a nod to Swinburne ('a fruit of tears'), end with a flourish playing Prometheus with Dedalus:

> Pluck and devour!

5 James Joyce, *Ulysses*, London, Bodley Head, 1960, p 222.

It is not the Donne of the *Satires* that fathers most of Joyce's poems: rather is it Donne and Dowland's

> Stay, O sweet, and do not rise,
> The light that shines comes from thine eyes;
> The day breaks not, it is my heart,
> Because that you and I must part.
> Stay, or else my joys will die,
> And perish in their infancie.   (Grierson, p.432)

> Of that so sweet. imprisonment
>   My soul, dearest, is fain –
> Soft arms that woo me to relent
>   And woo me to detain.
> Ah, could they ever hold me there,
> Gladly were I a prisoner!   *Chamber Music* XXII

and we must return to the earlier book of poems. Many critics have drawn attention to the links with 'the asphodel fields of Fulke Greville and Sir Philip Sidney' (Horace Reynolds),[6] Rochester (Arthur Symons)[7] Waller and Herrick *(Manchester Guardian)* [8] and noted 'a deliberate archaism and a kind of fawning studiousness' (Morton D. Zabel).[9] What strikes us though today in the nineteen-eighties, surely, is the splendidly jarring technique Joyce cultivates of placing an askew word exactly where one might have expected the traditional lyric resolution.

> What counsel has the hooded moon
>   Put in thy heart, my shyly sweet,
> Of Love in ancient *plenilune*,
>   Glory and stars beneath his feet –
> A sage that is but kith and kin
> With the comedian *capuchin?*   *Chamber Music* XII

---

6 See *James Joyce: The Critical Heritage*, edited by Robert H. Deming, New York, Barnes and Noble, 2 vols, 1970, Vol. II, p.649.   7 Ibid., vol. I, p.38.   8 Ibid., vol. I, p.41.   9 Ibid., vol. I, p.46.

Why should the critic italicize? Let the words speak for themselves, and not only those from *Chamber Music*.

> The sly reeds whisper to the night
> A name – her name –
> And all my soul is a delight
> A swoon of shame.   'Alone' (1916)

Back to the earlier volume:

> How sweet to lie there,
> Sweet to kiss,
> Where the great pine forest
> Enaisled is!   *Chamber Music* XX

Many of the words that provide this effect are indeed 'antique' but the effect of their use in this way is most modern.

> Happy Love is come to woo
>   Thee and woo thy girlish ways –
> The zone that doth become thee fair,
> The snood upon thy yellow hair.   XI

> Go seek her out all courteously
> And say I come,
> Wind of spices whose song is ever
> Epithalamium.   XIII

and better still, remembering 'the more precise and learned the thought, the greater the beauty, the passion',

> That mood of thine, O timorous,
>   Is his, if thou but scan it well,
> Who a mad tale bequeaths to us
>   At ghosting hour conjurable –
> And all for some strange name he read
> In Purchas or in Holinshed.   XXVI

Now this is splendid. Far from ruining the delicate lyrics, this is what makes them worth re-reading. We soon forget that the lady's mood was timorous, but happily remember unexpectedly meeting once more the inspirers of Shakespeare and Coleridge. We are astonished to find cherubs like boy scouts using their bugles as loud-speakers:

> When thou hast heard his name upon
>   The bugles of the cherubim
> Begin thou softly to unzone
> Thy girlish bosom . . .   XI

still more to find this a summons to nuptials. But nuptials they are. For this consummation nothing less than the greatest, the *Song of Songs*, must be versified (XIV). He can crack Yeats's Celtic bells with a grammarian's googly (no, he does not write 'innumerable' and follow Keats):

> While sweetly, gently, secretly,
>   The flowery bells of morn are stirred
> And the wise choirs of faery
>   Begin (innumerous!) to be heard.   XV

He can call up Greensleeves from the grave:

> Dear heart, why will you use me so?
>   Dear eyes that gently me upbraid
> Still are you beautiful – but O,
>   How is your beauty raimented!   XXIX

He can even disturb "The Blessed Damozel" once more:

> His hand is under
>   Her smooth round breast.   XVIII

But by the last poem in the book he is doing something different. For Pound, 'I hear an army charging' was one of 'the few beautiful poems that still ring in my head' – and how well Pound writes on *Chamber Music*![10] Horace

10 *The Literary Essays of Ezra Pound*, ed. T. S. Eliot, London, Faber, 1963. p 413.

Reynolds listens for Yeats's 'Hosting of the Sidhe' as he reads this poem. We should do better to remember Yeats's 'Valley of the Black Pig':

> . . . the clash of fallen horsemen and the cries
> Of unknown perishing armies beat about my ears.

when we read

> I hear an army charging upon the land
> And the thunder of horses plunging, foam about their knees.

Morton D. Zabel welcomes 'Suckling and the Cavaliers' and 'the minor work of Crashaw' to aid our appreciation of the early poems; but the pressure of sensuous thinking in Crashaw is unlike anything in the poems of Joyce, and Joyce is best when he is furthest from the only Suckling he resembles, the coy one.

Joyce may indeed be, in *Chamber Music*, as he confesses, a 'sweet sentimentalist' (XII), but the sentimentality is redeemed not only by the overall theme and shape of the book, to which we shall come in a moment, but also by many incidental felicities over and above those mentioned, not least Joyce's ability to capture 'a gesture and a pose' or (to exchange Eliot for Pound) a medallion:

> Firmness,
> Not the full smile,
> His art, but an art
> In profile.

If medallion is too strong a word, then Joyce's still moments are at least clear-cut snapshots.

> All softly playing
>   With head to music bent,
> And fingers straying
>   Upon an instrument.   I

We hear much about his musicality, but should also note how visual many of the songs are.

> The old piano plays an air,
>> Sedate and slow and gay;
> She bends upon the yellow keys,
>> Her head inclines this way.   II

> My love goes slowly, bending to
>> Her shadow on the grass   VII

(We are in the world of Bonnard rather than the Pre-Raphaelites.)

> The sun is in the willow leaves
>> And on the dappled grass
> And still she's combing her long hair
>> Before the lookingglass.   XXIV

This is not to deny his ear. He can fill a line with every open vowel:

> For lo! the trees are full of sighs

'the verse with its black vowels and its opening sound, rich and lutelike', as Dedalus says, misquoting Nashe; and indeed Joyce wrote to Gogarty as early as 1900:

> my idea for July and August is this — to get Dolmetsch to make a lute and to coast the south of England from Falmouth to Margate, singing old English songs.

The musicality, and the visual awareness, the ability to evoke mood with 'the cross run of the beat and the word, as of a stiff wind cutting the ripple-tops of bright water' as Pound notes,[11] all draw us back to these poems, but there is a deeper music, of the intellect beyond the senses, that lifts *Chamber Music* above slightness, and to bring this into focus we must go back to Joyce's own words on the book.

11 *Literary Essays of Ezra Pound*, p.413.

On 19th July, 1909, he wrote to G. Molyneux Palmer from Trieste:

> I hope you may set all of *Chamber Music* in time. This was
> indeed partly my idea in writing it. The book is in fact a suite of
> songs and if I were a musician I suppose I should have set them
> to music myself. The central song is XIV after which the move-
> ment is all downwards until XXXIV which is vitally the end of
> the book. XXXV and XXXVI are tailpieces just as I and II are
> preludes.

We are now in a position to see the work whole. The central climax of the
suite is the *Song of Songs,* greatest of all love-poems and neatly versified by
Joyce. At the centre of this (thirty-five words before it in a poem of seventy
words) is the upstanding and timeless cedar of Lebanon. The poem immediately preceding this one urges

> Go seek her out all courteously
>   And say I come,
> Wind of spices whose song is ever
>   Epithalamium.

In other words, as was hinted earlier in this note and in later words of this
poem, a 'bridal wind is blowing'. *Chamber Music* is a book that presupposes
marriage at its centre. The poem following XIV (the climax) begins

> From dewy dreams, my soul, arise,
>   From love's deep slumber and from death,
> For lo! the trees are full of sighs
>   Whose leaves the morn admonisheth.

We can now see that those poems leading up to the *Song of Songs* are all of
hopeful expectancy. But by XXX

> We were grave lovers. Love is past . . .

'the movement is all downwards' after the cedared celebration, and XXXIV
'which is vitally the end of the book' lays a gentle tombstone on the memory

of the romance:

> Sleep now, O sleep now,
>> O you unquiet heart!
> A voice crying 'Sleep now'
>> Is heard in my heart.

The tailpiece, the final line of the book, simply reads

> My love, my love, my love, why have you left me alone?

So the whole process, from wooing, proposal, eager anticipation of marriage, fulfilment (either real or imagined), betrayal and desertion by the woman is complete, and the poet is left alone, rueful, in despair, exchanging

> those treasures I possessed
> Ere that mine eyes had learned to weep   XXIII

for a new outward emblem of an inner state, the whirling laughter of a charging army of horsemen, clanging upon his heart as upon an anvil, fighting bitterness with an anguished rhetorical question.

The book survives because, over and above the individual qualities of single poems, the sequence is not only (as many critics have implied) more than the sum of its parts, but that sum is the archetypal theme of the depth and intensity of male devotion measured against the playfulness and 'slydynge corage' of a female who is unable to sustain a love involving those highest stakes we call marriage. Joyce may at times be sentimental in this book, but we do not feel he is insincere; and in the end we grieve with him (or his poet in the verse-narrative) and remember the woman as beautiful, sweet-bosomed, musical, goldenhaired, but girlish and spiritually inadequate to cope with the poet's intensity and the integrity of a serious relationship.

Pomes Penyeach does not make this claim on us. 'You don't think they're worth printing at any time?' asked Joyce? 'No, I don't.' replied Pound. 'Read Ralph Cheever Dunning. They belong in the Bible or the family album with the portraits.'[12] Not so. We have already enjoyed 'A Memory of the Players in a Mirror at Midnight', and the last poem in the book brings back Hopkins's (and Thompson's)

> I did say yes
> O at lightning and lashed rod

with a vengeance:

> *Come!* I yield. Bend deeper upon me! I am here.
> Subduer, do not leave me! Only joy, only anguish,
> Take me, save me, soothe me, O spare me!

The childhood carol 'Star of wonder' is briskly turned insideout in 'Bahnhofstrasse':

> Ah star of evil! star of pain

(Swinburne's to blame, not Baudelaire), and he can both bring on the earlier techniques:

> Uplift and sway, O golden vine,
> Your clustered fruits to love's full flood,
> Lambent and vast and ruthless as is thine
> Incertitude!   'Flood'

and send them up with a straight face in 'Simples':

> Be mine, I pray, a waxen ear
> To shield me from her childish croon.

'Simples', opines Morton D. Zabel, 'must rank as one of the purest lyrics of our time.'[13]

Joyce has changed since the earlier volume. We have word-coinage that looks forward beyond *Ulysses:*

> And long and loud,
> To night's nave upsoaring,
> A starknell tolls

---

12 See Richard Ellmann, *James Joyce*, New York, Oxford University Press, 1959, p.603, for the full anecdote. 13 Deming, vol. I, p.48.

> As the bleak incense surges, cloud on cloud,
> Voidward from the adoring
> Waste of souls.   'Nightpiece' (1915)

The puns on 'tonight' and '(k)nave' scarcely succeed; 'voidward' passes; 'starknell' is good and the pun on 'Waste' excellent. In the first verse of this same poem Francis Thompson's 'fled him down the arches of the years' reappears (perhaps) in

> Ghostfires from heaven's far verges faint illume,
> Arches on soaring arches,
> Night's sindark nave.

but we read this today with added relish recalling Joyce's later pliant girls and knavish priests after dark in Phoenix Park: 'bidimetoloves sinduced by what tegotetabsolvers'.[14] Richard Ellmann has skilfully unfolded the biographical mystery within 'She weeps over Rahoon':

> Still trying to penetrate [Nora's] soul, he wrote a poem to express what he felt to be her thoughts about her dead lover and her living one. He shifted Bodkin's grave from Oughterard, seventeen miles from Galway, to the Galway cemetery at Rahoon with its more sonorous name . . . The dead sweetheart was brought into a mortuary triangle with the two living lovers. With a sense of sacred coincidence Joyce found a headstone at Rahoon with the name J. Joyce upon it.[15]

Ellmann also explains why the first poem in the book is called 'Tilly:

> The word 'tilly' means the thirteenth in a baker's dozen; Joyce had thirteen (instead of twelve) poems in *Pomes Penyeach*, which sold for a shilling[16]

and points out that it was written as early as 1904, some months after his mother had died, and James had found and read a packet of love-letters from his father to his mother.

14 James Joyce, *Finnegans Wake*, London, Faber & Faber, 1966, p.4.   15 Ellmann, pp.335–6.
16 Ibid., p.142.

Boor, bond of the herd,
Tonight stretch full by the fire!
I bleed by the black stream
For my torn bough!

None of them are in the same league as that perfect poem "*Ecce Puer*", written after Helen Joyce's difficult pregnancy and on the day of the birth of Stephen James Joyce, his grandson. The deep joy is set in perspective by the recollection in the last verse that Joyce's own father had died only forty-nine days before. It is superb. As in a different context Samuel Beckett wrote of Jack Yeats's achievement, so here: we will not criticize; 'simply bow in wonder'.[17]

Of the dark past
A child is born;
With joy and grief
My heart is torn.

Calm in his cradle
The living lies.
May love and mercy.
Unclose his eyes!

Young life is breathed
On the glass;
The world that was not
Comes to pass.

A child is sleeping:
An old man gone.
O, father forsaken,
Forgive your son!

17 'Hommage à Jack B. Yeats', *Les Lettres Nouvelles*, 2e année (Avril 1954).

J. M. Synge's Poetry

Synge's editors differ widely in their estimation of his poems. At one in appreciating the achievement of his plays, their verdicts are not so unanimous when his non-dramatic poetry is under consideration. Indeed, one could scarcely find two more opposite evaluations, by well-disposed editors, of one slight body of poetry. Robin Skelton, editor of the *Poems* volume in the Oxford University Press edition of the *Collected Works*[1] of J. M. Synge, states his considered judgement in the opening paragraph of his Introduction:

> The verses which were published in 1909 and 1910 are not only admirable, but also important from an historical point of view, in that they had a considerable influence upon W. B. Yeats, and also upon much English and Irish poetry of the twentieth century. It is high time that as complete a collection of Synge's poems as is reasonable should be published in order both to document his 'poetic progress' and to bring into the light many good poems which have not previously been available for consideration.

The verses published in 1909 and 1910 include all those that Synge wished published. The proofs were corrected by him, and the book was published by the Cuala Press just fifteen days after his death. There were sixteen poems and eleven translations, together with a brief Preface by Synge of five paragraphs. It is on this corpus that Synge wished to be judged as a poet, and on an augmented edition of which T.R. Henn, in *The Plays and Poems of J. M. Synge*[2], bases his critical appreciation:

---

1 *Collected Works.*, I, p.xi.
2 *The Plays and Poems of J.M. Synge*, ed. T. R. Henn, London, Methuen, 1963, pp.274–275, 278.

*Portrait photograph of
J. M. Synge circa 1906
by W. James Patterson
R. S. A.*

It is just to say that at nearly every point the breakdown is
caused by sheer failure of technique; a lack of desire to shape
and re-shape until a poem becomes a unity . . .

The achievement of the Poems, then, is slight . . . They are
valuable for the light they throw on Synge's personality, and
on the plays; as well as for some rough vigorous balladry.

In such a case as this, where critical opinions diverge so sharply, it may
be as well for a fresh investigator to avoid any generalizations at this stage,
and confine himself to a reading of one poem that may not be dismissed as
wholly incompetent. One, moreover, that is not 'rough vigorous balladry',
and perhaps – to alter the traditional angle of vision – one that has remained
unpublished until Mr Skelton's publication of it in 1962. Mr Skelton has
given it the title 'The Masque of May', and it consists of two verses of six
lines each. There is no punctuation. The first verse reads:

The chiffchaff and the celandine
The blackbird and the bee
The chestnut branches topped with green
Have met my love and me
And we have played the masque of May
So sweet and commonplace and gay.[3]

The emotion is clear, nature has come to meet the poet and his love in the garb of May; there are two birds, a flower, a bee and the first shoots of leaves on a chestnut tree. Whether the 'we' refers merely to 'my love and me', or includes the personified manifestations of nature is not clear, though the general feeling, thanks to the three adjectives of the last line, is. There are two rhymes, no contortions of syntax such as we find on other occasions, usually for the sake of rhyme; and the placing of the longer word, whose meaning is in direct contrast to its individuality in this stanza, 'commonplace', is effective, coming as it does to separate the adjectives 'sweet' and 'gay'. The atmosphere is not allowed to become too serious, and a touch of self-mockery reins back a tendency to sentimentality, to hold it in the realm of the charming.

Verse two, using the same technique, is not so successful:

The sea's first miracle of blue
Bare trees that glitter near the sky
Grow with a love and longing new
Where went my love and I
And there we played the masque of May
So old and infinite and gay.[4]

The syntax is less clear – we are not sure where they went, if not under the trees beside the sea – and the emotion generated by the lovers is projected on to the sea and bare trees in a pair of poetic exaggerations that do not seem earned by the quality of the poetic emotion involved in creating them. The sea's first 'miracle' of blue may be the first light of morning or a

3 C.W., I, p.54.   4 Ibid.

dozen other visual experiences, and the trees glittering 'near the sky' only serve to reveal the inadequate vision of the spectators beneath. Indeed, this may be true of the poem as a whole. Synge is so close to his subject that he can no more detach the poem from its emotional source in a delivered birth than he can see that though the trees are high, to say that they glitter near the sky is to ask for too willing a suspension of disbelief.

The last line relies on our recollection of the rhythmic pattern of the last line of stanza one. To achieve the effect at which he is aiming, his penultimate adjective must be more than we are anticipating, and so delight by surprising expectation. It does not. Indeed, it is so clearly the geometric opposite of the word in the same place in stanza one, and so vague, containing neither music, shape, colour nor concept, that we fail to be either sensually or metaphysically pleased. In stanza two the charm of the first stanza has been lost owing to inadequacy of invention and a failure of common technique.

Something may be learned from this. The subject matter is that of many of the poems — love in a natural, usually Irish, context. Relaxed pressure of imagination and modesty of technical achievement, content as it is to remain within the realm of the easily attainable, is common to the greater number. He may be meditating on age:

> I've thirty months, and that's my pride,
> Before my age's a double score,
> Though many lively men have died
> At twenty-nine or little more.
>
> I've left a long and famous set
> Behind some seven years or three,
> But there are millions I'd forget
> Will have their laugh at passing me.[5]

but the quality of thought remains the same. In view of the fact that this was a poem he chose for his volume, it is hard to understand why he permitted

5 Ibid., p.59.

the obvious awkwardness of the sixth line to remain unrevised. Or he may turn to a given moment in a love experience, real or imagined:

> In a nook
> That opened south,
> You and I
> Lay mouth to mouth.
>
> A snowy gull
> And sooty daw
> Came and looked
> With many a caw;
>
> 'Such,' I said,
> 'Are I and you,
> When you've kissed me
> Black and blue!'[6]

Whether the image of two lovers, having completed their embraces, looking the one like a white gull and the other a sooty daw (or each a mixture of both) is worth an entire poem depends on the treatment. The irregular word order of the second line of the last stanza may be defended as being the opposite of the same line in stanza one; but as it is also — and more importantly — there to gain a rhyme for 'blue', the reader is uneasy. Does it matter, save for the rhyme's sake, that the nook opened south?

On the other hand, when his emotion is less lyrical, we may expect something with a harder edge. Such is promised on first reading 'A Wish':

> May seven tears in every week:
> Touch the hollow of your cheek,
> That I – signed with such a dew –
> For a lion's share may sue
> Of the roses ever curled
> Round the May-pole of the world.

6 Ibid., p 53.

> Heavy riddles lie in this,
> Sorrow's sauce for every kiss.[7]

The style is familiar. May-poles range from Herrick to Yeats's Yggdrasil, riddles are most familiar to us perhaps in Campion and his colleagues and Anglo-Saxon poetry, and tears, cheeks, dew, lions, roses and global imagery are all over-familiar from poets such as A. E.. What is lacking here in the reader's mind is a conviction that the virtuosity of the technique compels curiosity enough to disentangle the riddle. The familiar connotations of 'lion's share' militate against an over-serious acceptance of the problem posed, and the concept of Synge suing for a lion's share of all the roses that ever curled round the May-pole of the world is not immediately arresting.

Synge can do better than this, as in 'The Curse: To a sister of an enemy of the author's who disapproved of "The Playboy"':

> Lord, confound this surly sister,
> Blight her brow with blotch and blister,
> Cramp her larynx, lung, and liver,
> In her guts a galling give her.
> Let her live to earn her dinners
> In Mountjoy with seedy sinners:
> Lord, this judgment quickly bring,
> And, I'm Your servant, J. M. Synge.[8]

Humour redeems the insincerity of the exuberance, as it does in 'On An Island', which ends

> You've cooped the pullets, wound the clock,
> And rinsed the young men's drinking crock;
> And now we'll dance to jigs and reels,
> Nailed boots chasing girls' naked heels.
> Until your father 'll start to snore,
> And Jude, now you're married, will stretch on the floor.[9]

7 Ibid., p.51. 8 Ibid., p.49. 9 Ibid., p.35.

and fails to in 'To the Oaks of Glencree':

> My arms are round you, and I lean
> Against you, while the lark
> Sings over us, and golden lights, and green
> Shadows are on your bark.
>
> There'll come a season when you'll stretch
> Black boards to cover me:
> Then in Mount Jerome I will lie, poor wretch,
> With worms eternally.[10]

It would be tempting to quote from Synge's Preface for justification,

> In these days poetry is usually a flower of evil or good; but it is
> the timber of poetry that wears most surely, and there is no
> timber that has not strong roots among the clay and worms.[11]

were it not that Synge wrote just two paragraphs later in that same Preface a partial disclaimer:

> The poems which follow were written at different times
> during the last sixteen or seventeen years, most of them before
> the views just stated, with which they have little to do, had
> come into my head.[12]

Even the clay and worms of Mount Jerome fail to save this crude juxtapositioning of warm human embracing a tree and talking to it of birdsong and shadows, and the same man thinking ahead to the time when the tree will become boards for his decomposing corpse.

All the same, juxtapositioning of a more effective kind lies behind the success of 'Dread'. The contrast drawn between the ceremonial formalities of the Church's ritualization of human love, and the warm immediacy of two lovers under a window out of sight is startling and effective.

10 Ibid., p 47.   11 Ibid., p.xxxvi.   12 Ibid.

Beside a chapel I'd a room looked down,
Where all the women from the farms and town,
On Holy-days and Sundays used to pass
To marriages, and christenings, and to Mass.

Then I sat lonely watching score and score,
Till I turned jealous of the Lord next door . . .
Now by this window, where there's none can see,
The Lord God's jealous of yourself and me.[13]

Whereas the contrast in 'To the Oaks of Glencree' is trite, and we leave the poem no wiser than we came, 'Dread' creates an atmosphere of farm and townswomen coming on Sundays and Holy-days to Catholic services and observes it from a vantage-point above them; by inference Synge implies his own warm woman in his arms is preferable to the chaste piety of the religious people below, even if his is unsanctified: indeed the Lord God Himself is jealous of Synge's present-tense predicament.

So the main themes of Synge's poetry can be seen, together with their stronger and weaker forms of expression. Most deal with the contrast between love and death, some with death alone – whether his own or that of such as 'Danny'. A few with drinking, such as the 'Epitaph: After reading Ronsard's lines from Rabelais', or dancing and conviviality such as 'Beg-Innish'. A third group create the feeling of aloneness, in 'Winter: With little money in a great city', and a fourth are pastoral of memory or song after the manner of Wordsworth, 'In Glencullen', 'Epitaph', 'Prelude' and – not so Wordsworthian – 'On A Birthday'.

Throughout, the diction is simple, the rhyme-schemes are elementary. Those that deal with death are violent unless they involve his own decease, when they tend to become morose; in comparison with the objective violence of

But seven tripped him up behind,
And seven kicked before,

13 *C.W.*, I, p.40.

> And seven squeezed around his throat
> Till Danny kicked no more.
>
> Then some destroyed him with their heels,
> Some tramped him in the mud,
> Some stole his purse and timber pipe,
> And some washed off his blood.[14]

The odds were twenty-nine to one, and the cause of Danny's death the fact that

> He's left two pairs of female twins
> Beyond in Killacreest,
> And twice in Crossmolina fair
> He's struck the parish priest.[15]

The 'rough, vigorous balladry' of which Henn speaks is well illustrated by this poem. Not so successful, perhaps, is 'Patch-Shaneen', a poem on a subject that had also been treated by Coventry Patmore with great success, that of a husband waking to find his wife dead beside him. Synge's

> Till on one windy Samhain night,
> When there's stir among the dead,
> He found her perished, stiff and stark,
> Beside him in the bed . . .
>
> And when the grey cocks crow and flap
> And winds are in the sky,
> 'Oh, Maurya, Maurya, are you dead?'
> You'll hear Patch-Shaneen cry.[16]

seems no more than a pale imitation of the Scottish ballad 'Sweet William's Ghost':

> Then up and crew the red, red cock,
>   And up then crew the gray:

14 Ibid., p.57.   15 Ibid., p.56.   16 Ibid., p.36.

> 'Tis time, 'tis time, my dear Margret,
> That you were going away.'[17]

and set beside Patmore's hesitant strength in 'The Azalea', Synge's poem is seen to be no more than unremarkable verse.

When Synge's own death is the subject the tone is either whimsical:

> And so when all my little work is done
> They'll say I came in Eighteen-seventy-one,
> And died in Dublin . . . What year will they write
> For my poor passage to the stall of Night?[18]

where the half-memory of Ovid's cry from his mistress' arms strengthens the final line in a way that is not typical of the rest of Synge's poetry; or, much more frequently, it is contrasted with his living love, as in 'A Question':

> I asked if I got sick and died, would you
> With my black funeral go walking too,
> If you'd stand close to hear them talk or pray
> While I'm let down in that steep bank of clay.
>
> And, No, you said, for if you saw a crew
> Of living idiots pressing round that new
> Oak coffin, – they alive, I dead beneath
> That board – you'd rave and rend them with your teeth.[19]

The emotion is clear, the final image of a distraught woman gnawing the idiots perhaps rather overdrawn. It is emotion as Synge would like it to be rather than as it is, and as a result self-indulgent. Preferable, in spite of the grossness of its rhymes, is the 'healthy violence' of 'The 'Mergency Man':

> 'We'll wash our hands of your bloody job.'
> 'Wash and welcome,' says he, 'begob.'

17 *English & Scottish Popular Ballads*, ed. H. C. Sargent and G. C. Kittredge, Cambridge, Mass. 1904, p.165. 18 *C.W.*, I, p.33. 19 Ibid., p.64.

He made two leps with a run and dash,
Then the peelers heard a yell and splash.

And the 'mergency man in two days and a bit
Was found in the ebb tide stuck in a net.[20]

The love poems use traditional devices of hyperbole and contrast – Synge's mistress is 'the Queen/Of all are living, or have been'. All those he names –

Judith of Scripture, and Gloriana,
Queens who wasted the East by proxy,
Or drove the ass-cart, a tinker's doxy.
Yet these are rotten – I ask their pardon –
And we've the sun on rock and garden;[21]

and 'In Kerry' he takes the emotion to a deeper level, recording

What change you'd wrought in graveyard, rock and sea,
This new wild paradise to wake for me . . .[22]

and then remembering that just such sexual excitement had brought the previous generations to birth, now buried:

Yet know no more than knew those merry sins
Had built this stack of thigh-bones, jaws and shins.[23]

This emotion is also created with gentle effect in the beautiful two-verse poem 'In Glencullen', where for once the subject is exactly appropriate to Synge's unambitious technique:

Thrush, linnet, stare, and wren,
Brown lark beside the sun,
Take thought of kestrel, sparrow-hawk,
Birdlime and roving gun.

20 Ibid., p.58.   21 Ibid., p.34.   22 Ibid., p.55.   23 Ibid.

You great-great-grand-children
Of birds I've listened to,
I think I robbed your ancestors
When I was young as you.[24]

Again, as in the first verse of 'The Masque of May', the humour places the emotion for us and prevents it becoming over-rich.

So, too, with the drinking poems. Dr. Henn's detailed analysis of the translations, and especially of the 'Epitaph: After reading Ronsard's lines from Rabelais' should be studied, and needs no recapitulation here. But the cheerful mockery of 'Beg-Innish', another drinking song, may be seen to have affinities with the macaronic poems of the Scots poet Dunbar:

We'll have no priest or peeler in
To dance in Beg-Innish;
But we'll have drink from M'riarty Jim
Rowed round while gannets fish . . .[25]   (Synge's 'Beg-Innish')

I will na preistis for me sing,
Dies illa, dies ire;
Na yit na bellis for me ring,
Sicut semper solet fieri;
Bot a bag pipe to play a spryng,
Et unum ail wosp [inn sign] ante me.[26]

(Dunbar's 'Testament of Mr Andro Kennedy')

In each, a robust affirmation of the pleasures of life, set against the restraints of religion as represented by its ministers, is achieved, though in this example it is Dunbar who brings in the theme of death, not Synge. The contrast, however, between the thinness of abstract 'poetic' beauty, and the robustness of earthy life spiced with a hint of the illegal, is amply illustrated – rather as Wordsworth had done in a milder way in 'The Tables Turned' without the masculine bravado –

24 Ibid., p.48.   25 Ibid., p.37.   26 *The Poems of William Dunbar*, ed. By W. Mackay MacKenzie, Edinburgh, The Porpoise Press, 1932, p.74.

> Books! 'tis a dull and endless strife:
> Come, hear the woodland Linnet,
> How sweet his music! on my life,
> There's more of wisdom in it.[27]

Synge, in his turn, breaks with the poetry of the Celtic twilight to recapture a hint of the tone of a poet he admired a great deal, and indeed translated, François Villon:

> Adieu, sweet Angus, Maeve, and Fand,
> Ye plumed yet skinny Shee,
> That poets played with hand in hand
> To learn their ecstasy.
>
> We'll stretch in Red Dan Sally's ditch,
> And drink in Tubber fair,
> Or poach with Red Dan Philly's bitch
> The badger and the hare.[28]

The eight-line 'Epitaph' draws on Wordsworth, emphasising rather the solitariness of the 'silent sinner' against a backcloth of nature and the seasons:

> A silent sinner, nights and days,
> No human heart to him drew nigh,
> Alone he wound his wonted ways,
> Alone and little loved did die.
>
> And autumn Death for him did choose,
> A season dank with mists and rain,
> And took him, while the evening dews
> Were settling o'er the fields again.[29]

and the theme of 'aloneness' forms the central emotion of two other poems, one urban, 'Winter: With little money in a great city', ending

27 *The Poetical Works of William Wordsworth*, IV, ed. by E. De Selincourt and Helen Darbishire, Oxford, Clarendon Press 1947, p.57.   28 *C.W.*, I., p.38.   29 Ibid., p.31.

> For I go walking night and noon
> To spare my sack of coals.[30]

and the other rural ('Prelude'):

> I knew the stars, the flowers, and the birds,
> The grey and wintry sides of many glens,
> And did but half remember human words,
> In converse with the mountains, moors, and fens.[31]

'On A Birthday' takes the lark of springtime as his emblem, to welcome in Lady-day, and to serve as the pretext for a roll-call of proper nouns that recall in different ways Marlowe, Herrick and Flecker:

> Friend of Ronsard, Nashe, and Beaumont,
> Lark of Ulster, Meath, and Thomond,
> Heard from Smyrna and Sahara
> To the surf of Connemara,
> Lark of April, June, and May,
> Sing loudly this my Lady-day.[32]

We remember Jaques' instructions to Amiens, 'Sing it: 'tis no matter how it be in tune, so it make noise enough',[33] forgiving the ornithological inaccuracy and the patently manufactured rhyme (and hence the third line) for 'Connemara'.

Mr Skelton's edition of the *Poems* unearths some thirty-five or so unpublished poems, most of which Synge wisely decided to omit from his own selection. They fall into the same categories as those so far mentioned, and one or two deserve a second reading. 'In Spring', for instance, combines the loneliness of the solitary with the season of love:

> Buds are opening their lips to the South
> Sparrows are pluming their mates on the sill
> Lovers are laying red mouth to mouth
> Maidens are marging their smocks with a frill

30 Ibid., p.63.   31 Ibid., p.32.   32 Ibid., p.60.   33 *As You Like It*, iv, 2, 9.

Yet I lie alone with my depth of desire
No daughter of men would I choose for my mate
I have learned loving and lived to require
A woman the Lord had not strength to create[34]

It is a strange poem. The four centre-rhyme present participles of stanza one create a curiously languid air which is built on in stanza two when we find that this is not a love poem in the ordinary sense of the word at all, but an account of an erotic urge without an object. In 'The Meeting' Synge has an object for his emotion, and celebrates it in such extreme terms that the poem's final line breaks off in our hands, both metrically and in view of its metaphysical weight:

Then in the hush of plots with shining trees
We lay like gods disguised in shabby dress,
Making with birches, bracken, stars and seas,
Green courts of pleasure for each long caress;
Till there I found in you and you in me
The crowns of Christ and Eros — all divinity.[35]

Nothing has prepared us for this Crashaw-like merging of Eros and Christ. Indeed, if the art of the love poem is to make appreciable and freshly imaginative what is intimate, then in very few cases can Synge be said to be a fine love poet. The disproportion at the heart of his own articulation of his feelings topples poem after poem into sentiment or banality. Some simply remain intimate and no more, such as 'The Omission':

Today you have tutored and healed my head
Have taught me to see you and love you apart
But you have not forgiven the words I said
You have not renewed me the life of my heart.[36]

There is scarcely enough here to claim our attention, and technical achievement is minimal. So it is with so many of the tiny poems that it is with a

34 *C.W.*, I p.27.   35 Ibid., p.43.   36 Ibid., p.25.

measure of relief that we watch him – albeit in Job-like and literary stance – curse:

> I curse my bearing, childhood, youth
> I curse the sea, sun, mountains, moon,
> I curse my learning, search for truth,
> I curse the dawning, night, and noon.
>
> Cold, joyless I will live, though clean,
> Nor, by my marriage, mould to earth
> Young lives to see what I have seen,
> To curse – as I have cursed – their birth.[37]

Though we scarcely believe him, we admire the tension between energy and, for once, poetic control in the second stanza, and also the overall shape of the poem.

Synge was a fine dramatist who was not a good poet. The translations from Petrarch and Villon are better than his own original verses, and it is significant that these translations are into English prose. The mannered prose of the plays, coming as it does in a realm somewhere between prose and verse, a kind of liturgical mandarin, employing both Gaelic and Elizabethan syntax and homely, down-to-earth imagery of a striking and dramatically effective kind, this prose was Synge's great stylistic achievement. The poems add nothing to it, and may be regarded as the occasional memorials of private romances; verses written when ear, mind and imagination were not fused into bright focus as they were when he created *Riders To The Sea* and *The Playboy*, but rather one or other working independently. The verses are not vehicles for deep thought so much as occasional fancy. We read them as an act of homage to the man, but turn to the plays to appreciate his genius.

37 Ibid., p.14.

Edmund Blunden's Pastoral Poetry

Centennial celebrations at Christ's Hospital,
8 November 1996

Edmund Blunden shared my rooms in St Peter's College, Oxford, during the time that he was Oxford's Professor of Poetry.[1] In May, 1967, he and I visited Christ's Hospital, our old school, *incognito,* sharing many memories of our different times at Housie. It was a secret detour taken while I was driving him on to a reunion of the Royal Sussex Regiment – 'Lowther's Lambs' – through the countryside that had moulded each of us, and both of us loved; countryside of which he had written so feelingly in *The Country Round Christ's Hospital:*

> . . . now passes
> None but the bee's, the rook's, the reaper's traffic . . .

Yalding, and our countryside here – Doctor's Lake, Sharpenhurst, Shelley Wood – were to give a firm pastoral basis to his poetry from earliest days

> Names are vanished, save the few
>   In the old brown Bible scrawled;
> These were men of pith and thew,
>   Whom the city never called;
> Scarce could read or hold a quill,
> Built the barn, the forge, the mill.
>
> On the green they watched their sons
>   Playing till too dark to see,
> As their fathers watched them once,
>   As my father once watched me . . .

'Forefathers'

1   See Barry Webb, *Edmund Blunden: A Biography*, London, Yale University Press 1990, p.xi.

Edmund Blunden as Oxford's
Professor of Poetry, 1966

and for this brief celebration we may look at five different modes of pastoral poetry in which Edmund excelled.

First, there was his ability to describe nature with his eye on the object – and his eye was absolutely sure, like a musician's perfect pitch: his 'Barn':

> The light pales at the spider's lust,
> The wind tangs through the shattered pane:
> An empty hop-poke spreads across
> The gaping frame to mend the loss
> And keeps out sun as well as rain,
>   Mildewed with clammy dust.

This extends to fish: 'The Pike'; plants, and all sorts of animals, not least those 'Malefactors' stoat, kite and snake:

> Nailed to these green laths long ago,
> You cramp and shrivel into dross,
> Blotched with mildews, gnawed with moss,
> And now the eye can scarcely know

The snake among you from the kite,
So sharp does Death's fang bite.

Whether it's a 'Poor Man's Pig' 'nuzzling the dog', or 'The Watermill', or just 'The Last of Autumn' with its 'shorn, empty fields', his awareness of the detail, and his truth to nature is evident.

Second is the landscape with figures. These are the most numerous, perhaps; most wide in their range:

Beneath that hawthorn shade the grass will hardly grow,
So many babes have played and kept the bare clay so,
So many loves delayed in the moonlight's ebb and flow –
Daisy-chains and May beginnings
Fail not till I pass below.

'Hawthorn'

or 'Sheet Lightning':

When on the green the rag-tag game had stopt
And red the light through alehouse curtains glowed,
The clambering brake drove out and took the road.
Then on the stern moors all the babble dropt
Among our merry men, who felt the dew
Sweet to the soul and saw the southern blue
Thronged with heat lightning miles and miles abroad,
Working and whickering, snakish, winged and clawed . . .
The night drooped oven-hot . . .

Third, there is this as it were reversed: landscape with figures indeed, but at war – Blunden's unique war-pastorals:

I have seen a green country, useful to the race,
Knocked silly with guns and mines, its villages vanished,
Even the last rat and last kestrel banished –
God bless us all, this was peculiar grace.

'Report on Experience'

or

> Some found an owl's nest in the hollow skull
> Of the first pollard from the malthouse wall . . .
>
> 'Battalion in Rest'

Often, of course, these last two categories are blended, as in that subtle and deceptive poem 'Come on My Lucky Lads' (also called 'Zero'). It may seem, on first reading, that dawn is being described; on second it dawns on us that it is an artillery burst, before dawn, lighting up the sky:

> O rosy red, O torrent splendour
>> Staining all the Orient gloom,
> O celestial work of wonder –
>> A million mornings in one bloom!
>
> What, does the artist of creation
>> Try some new plethora of flame,
> For his eye's fresh fascination?
>> Has the old cosmic fire grown tame?

This method of using pastoral for late-flowering, fragrant grenades of hidden meaning, is highly effective. 'The Pike', for instance, seems on initial reading to be an anecdote. Later, the multiple meanings – like the predator – reveal themselves: the end of the feudal system, for example, with its images of murderous patriarch, vassals, glutted tyrant, gorgon eyes, and rule by intense terror from the shadows of rich oaks with their mossgreen bastions – a power enforced throughout by killing. Why should the miller that opens the hatch stand amazed at the whirl in the water when the diction has been describing nothing less than his own decaying society? But it is tactfully, gracefully, lethally done.

At the other end of the emotional range – fourthly – is the mystical pastoral:

> From love's wide-flowering mountain-side I chose

This sprig of green, in which an angel shows.

'Values'

or

Over the skeleton the grass comes creeping,
And life's too short for wondering, too aflame for weeping.

'From Age to Age'

Love transfigures 'Late Light':

Come to me where the swelling wind assails the wood
    with a sea-like roar,
While the yellow west is still afire; come borne by the
    wind up the hillside track;
There is quiet yet, and brightness more
Than day's clear fountains to noon rayed back
    If you will come . . .

Lastly, there are the poems with literary pastoral orientation; full of his love – though he knew his Theocritus, and Virgil's *Pastorals* well – of the English poets: 'Milton in his young prime' – even of German:

Doubt might cloud dense upon me, but I hear
    Goethe and Shelley, Melville and poor Clare
With many another whose track from spring to sere
    Now flushed with May, now glinted flintily bare,
I hear them answering that same morning song,
And heavenly silence more than belfry-strong.

'Change and Song'

One of his loveliest is that tribute to those early romantic landscape poets he so loved, such as the Wartons:

Mild hearts! and modest as the evening bell
    That rings so often through your meadow rhyme,
May there be elms and belfries where you dwell,

And the last streaks of day still gild old time!. . .

Nor shall the shades of poets not be seen
   Whom you have loved. Milton in his young prime,
Spenser and Chaucer on the daisied green
   Shall join with you and hear May-morning chime.

'The Wartons'

Nature observed, mankind in the natural setting, war-pastoral, mystical pastoral, and literary pastoral. I'll end, if I may, with one exquisite literary pastoral that I myself urged him to publish near the end of his life. It is a translation, by Edmund, of Andrew Marvell's Latin poem 'Hortus'. The tone, the craftsmanship, the technique touch perfection. With its close I bend my head, and honour our friendship:

Nor shall you, Gardener, modestly depart
Before my verse pays homage to your art;
With short-lived plants and ever pleasant flowers
You have marked the times of day and growing hours.
The clearer sun there rides through fragrant signs,
Nor in the angry Bull nor Crab's claw shines,
But slides to rose and violet's harmless sphere.
See, the bees too on honeyed work appear
To measure it with Thyme, their dial here.

O smoothly passing time, O gracious hours
Of peace told truly by your herbs and flowers.

Richard Wall's Rondeau Cycle *In Aliquot Parts*

In May 1976 Richard Wall's rondeau cycle *In Aliquot Parts* was published. Elegant, lyrical, perfectly made, the book achieved what Wall had intended; which was, by means of a series of poems written after Marot[1] according to the strictest rules of tradition – in which microcosm reflects macrocosm and the number and length of lines within the rondeau are reflected in the number and length of poems in the cycle – to body forth a series of emotional states arising from a love-affair.

In this tradition a rondeau is either a decasyllabic or an octosyllabic poem of fifteen lines in which the ninth and fifteenth lines are a refrain, and this refrain is the same as the first half of the opening line. So the fifteen poems of this book are arranged in the same way, the 'refrain' poems being nonasyllabic, half-way between the other two line-lengths.

This particular cycle may perhaps best be seen as a triptych, poems one to five forming the left panel, poems six to eight the centre, and ten to fourteen the right; with two refrains, poems nine and fifteen.

The first five poems in the cycle treat the theme of unhappy love. We are not told whether it springs from rejection or from loss, though some measure of each is implied by the book taken as whole. Emphasis in the first five is thrown on to the emotion itself rather than its source.

In the centre three poems the poet tackles the question of why he writes about experiences in poetry. Can the magic of poetry in any way alter the situation? The middle poem of the centre panel of the triptych, flanked by matching but contrasting poems 'Doubt and Hope' (6) and 'Doubt and Despair' (8), is in fact a magical spell to the recalcitrant lady:

Take these my words and bind them in your hair,

1 For Warner's presentation of Clément Marot on stage see Francis Warner, *King Francis I*, Oxford Theatre Texts 12, Gerrards Cross, Colin Smythe, 1995.

Richard Wall in 1976

> Or, gently crushed, inhale their heady air,
> Then dream . . .

But the centre section closes on a note of despair as the poet realises that though words can record, they can change nothing.

The last five poems or right hand panel show a mingling or intertwining of the personalised consciousness of the three that make up the centre section, and of the images of the first group of five and the middle three.

The two refrains are direct addresses to the lady, one in each of her two aspects:

> Lady Despair
> I'll drink to you
> Phantom of Care,
> Till drink and the sun bring snowdrops anew
> Lady Despair.   (9)

the cycle closing on a note of hope:

> Lady Delight
> In fantasy I'll enmantle you,

Vision of Night,
For fantasy's spells make memories true,
Lady Delight.   (15)

To look more closely at the grouping, and the individual poems, is to see more clearly the assurance and mastery with which the book is constructed. The first two poems work from a static, literary situation; it might be a tapestry or an old painting of a Minstrel and a Lady that he is expounding upon. The next two poems (3) 'The Moon' and (4) 'The Sun' are a more generalised lyrical situation, timeless rather than of the Middle Ages or Marot's time. The whole first section culminates in the powerful and romantic (for we remember Coleridge's 'Dejection Ode') image of 'The Wind' (5), which is established here as memory, more potent than sun or moon.

In the sixth poem the poet evokes archetypal witnesses

Galatea, Euridice shall bear
Witness

to the fact that

gods and the Muses answer prayer.

and that he has a charm

to conjure love from hate

in fact the magical spell of the following poem.

This poem, (7) 'A Spell,' is the centrepiece, and appropriately an acrostic on the name of the beloved. Within the cycle are no fewer than five acrostic poems, arranged around this centrepiece to set it in relief. Poem (2) 'The Lady' gives the name of an alternative lady with whom he hoped to fall in love to drive out the memory of the loss; but failed, defeated by the memory of the subject of poem (7). Poem (6) 'Doubt and Hope' asserts the identity of the poet amid the turmoil of conflicting emotions

I, Richard G. Wall.

Poem (8), 'Doubt and Despair' is an acrostic on an older poet who has been with him throughout the writing, a friend and encourager, a brooding presence whose own poetry, meditated on in this poem, is directly answered in poem (12):

> I too have danced with the seasons and turned
> With the tide. . . But the dance is a cheat.

Poem (11) 'Pygmalion on Galatea: a documentary' takes the names of two of the poet's closest friends who have fallen in love with each other, this acrostic bringing into the cycle the magic of a perfect love-match, in compensation for his own state of mind, and as the goal to which his hopes aspire.

In Poem (10) 'The Minstrel and the Lady recalled: two interviews', we are presented with an interview with a soldier who had been present at the Battle of Hastings (Richard Wall's home town). There is a legend that the Song of Roland was sung to the Norman troops on the eve of the Battle of Hastings. The Minstrel is supposed to have sung at this battle, and the soldier recalls having seen him there. The second interview is with the maid-servant of the Lady celebrated in the second poem. What is discussed is the part that art plays in our emotions. Art that is based on a previous historical experience (the Minstrel's song being based on the battle of Roncevaux) turns out to predict the future, the grief of the battle of Hastings. The tapestry, which in this poem and poem (2) is being stitched by the maid and the Lady, predicts the coming deaths; as though we are mentally disposed from birth to sing notes of anguish.

> Disposed to language means disposed to woes

Because we are disposed to think in such patterns, those patterns come into being in our lives.

In the next poem 'Pygmalion on Galatea : a documentary' we are asked to look at a case in which it seemed that art triumphed over life

> Defined in form, the ideal stays

True, but art is too static for life.

> The trouble is, Time intervenes,
> Our visions . . . change

Earlier, in (6) 'Doubt and Hope' he had for a while believed

> gods and the muses answer prayer

as had been the case with Galatea and Euridice. Now, at this stage of the cycle, after the views on art expressed in the two interviews, the poet goes back to the examples where art had seemed to triumph over life to check them – but poem (6) is answered by poem (11): Pygmalion's idea of beauty changes in a way that the statue-become-woman cannot accommodate.

We have now an interlude, before going on to the other witness (Euridice), an interlude in which the poet, in a pure lyric outburst, contrasts the state of flux in Nature with the mental stagnation with which memory burdens us. Then we return to (13) 'Euridice and Orpheus'. There is an implied contrast between these two, and Pygmalion and Galatea, in that Pygmalion was attempting to hold the present in art, whereas Orpheus is trying to tame the future.

> Love, can your music tame the days
> Which lie behind the hill-top haze . . . ?

So Orpheus, amongst these dreams of permanence, is also found wanting. This leaves us, then, at the point reached in (10), the poem on the Battle of Hastings, the belief that art can only celebrate and predict pain. So we end with (14) 'The Aeolian Harp', and the final 'Refrain'.

It is here than an understanding of the title of the book is essential. The epigraph of the book is a quotation from the *Encyclopaedia Britannica* of 1910.

> 'The aeolian harp is placed across a window so that the wind
> blows obliquely across the strings, causing them to vibrate in
> aliquot parts, i.e. (the fundamental note not being heard) the
> half or octave, the third or interval of the twelfth, the second
> octave, and the third above it, in fact the upper partials of

the strings in regular succession. With the increased pressure of the wind, the dissonances of the 11th and 13th overtones are heard in shrill discords, only to give place to beautiful harmonies as the force of the wind abates.'

So the wind which has blown throughout the cycle is seen as the spirit of grief, the bringer of change, which continually tears us from our positions of rest and tranquillity, but refuses to let us forget what we have lost.

> And I? – A harp, nerves strung for your sport, to
> Spawn cynic discords, mock all I sought to
> Love. Spirit of Grief, Bringer of Change, oh
> Now, wind, I know you.

However, if the poet is to shriek discordantly like an aeolian harp caught in its wind of grief, we must also remember that when the wind abates, the discords give way to delicate harmonies. These harmonies are these rondeaux that make up the cycle – order crafted from chaos: and so the final poem, the 'Refrain: Lady Delight', closes the book.

> For fantasy's spells make memories true,
> Lady Delight.

Japanese Noh Plays and W. B. Yeats, Benjamin Britten and Samuel Beckett

It is a great honour for me to address you at the invitation of Professor Yasuo Tamaizumi and Professor Yuichi Midzunoe. To think about the Noh Theatre in the very country that gave it birth is, for one who has loved it for more than thirty years, a humbling honour. I lack your language, and you all know your own tradition better than I can begin to understand it. So, with your generous consent, and your pardon for my poor pronunciation, I shall, if I may, say a few words about what the Noh plays have meant to one or two of us back home.

It is thirty years since Professor Shotaro Oshima, my friend from Waseda University, gave me a boxed copy of his beautifully printed book *W. B. Yeats and Japan* after he had attended a lecture by me on the subject. He himself had been to see W.B. Yeats and his wife George (she preferred being called George and protested against the name so many used: 'Georgia'), when they were living at Riversdale, their house at Rathfarnham, near Dublin, Ireland, just five months before Yeats died. As a result, both of this visit, and of the correspondence Professor Oshima had enjoyed with Yeats for more than twenty years, his perception of what Yeats had found attractive in the Noh theatre is unrivalled, and I commend his book to those of you who are interested. I myself did not know Yeats, so will be placing before you simply some of the facts, and thoughts, that have struck me during my study of his work.

First, some facts. Yeats published his little Macmillan volume *Four Plays for Dancers* in 1921. It was illustrated, and notes were added to each of the four plays, along with music for two of them written by Edmund Dulac. The four plays by Yeats in this book are *At the Hawk's Well, The Only Jealousy of Emer, The Dreaming of the Bones,* and *Calvary.* The book is very rare now, but I have brought a rather fragile copy here today for you to look at.

Behind this publication, however, lies another book; published five years earlier on Yeats's sisters' hand press, The Cuala Press, at Churchtown, Dundrum (Ireland) in 1916. This book is called *Certain Noble Plays of Japan: From the manuscripts of Ernest Fenollosa, chosen and finished by Ezra Pound. With an introduction by W.B. Yeats.*

This book included translations of four Japanese Noh plays: *Nishikigi, Hagoromo, Kumasaka,* and *Kagekiyo.* Note that Yeats wrote the introduction. As this book's publication pre-dates the first of the *Four Plays for Dancers (At the Hawk's Well),* we can therefore say with some confidence that before Yeats began to write Noh plays, adapting the Japanese form to his Western idiom, he first studied the four Japanese plays I've just mentioned.

Fenollosa, who did not live to complete his translations, nevertheless wrote passionately about the Noh form:

W. B. Yeats: a portrait in pastel 15¼ x 4¾ inches, by Harry Kernoff, R.H.A., who gave it to Warner 9 June 1965

> The beauty and power of Noh lie in the concentration. All elements – costume, motion, verse, and music – unite to produce a single clarified impression. Each drama embodies some primary human relation or emotion; and the poetic sweetness or poignancy of this is carried to its highest degree by carefully excluding all such obtrusive elements as a mimetic realism or vulgar sensation might demand. The emotion is always fixed upon idea, not upon personality. The solo parts express great types of human character, derived from Japanese history. Now it is brotherly love, now love to a parent, now loyalty to a

master, love of husband and wife, of mother for a dead child, or of jealousy or anger, of self-mastery in battle, of the battle passion itself, of the clinging of a ghost to the scene of its sin, of the infinite compassion of Buddha, of the sorrow of unrequited love. Some one of those intense emotions is chosen for a piece, and, in it, elevated to the plane of universality by the intensity and purity of treatment.[1]

When Pound introduced Yeats to this tradition, dating from 15th century Japan, and sanctioned by aristocratic tradition, written for some learned Shogun and his friends, Yeats knew that he had found what he had been seeking for in his drama.

> I have found my first model. . . in the 'Noh' stage of aristocratic Japan . . . It has been a great gain to get rid of scenery, to substitute for a crude landscape painted upon canvas three performers who, sitting before a wall or patterned screen, describe landscape or event, and accompany movement with drum & gong, or deepen the emotion of the words with zither or flute . . . Our imagination kept living by the arts can imagine a mountain covered with thorn trees in a drawing-room without any great trouble . . . We are a learned people, and we remember how the Roman theatre, when it became more intellectual, abandoned 'make-up' and used the mask instead, and that the most famous artists of Japan modelled masks that are still in use after hundreds of years.[2]

Yeats took over many suggestions, beyond the mask and the absence of scenery. He followed his Japanese examples by having, in a play such as *The Only Jealousy of Emer,* a ghost, clinging to the scene of its departure, by the dead body of the *Sch'te* (the chief character), into which the evil *Hannya* has entered, while the *Sch'te's* wife, and his mistress, try to drive out the *Hannya*

---

1 Ezra Pound and Ernest Fenollosa, *The Classical Noh Theatre of Japan,* 1959, pp.69–70.
2 *Four Plays,* pp.86–87.

by bringing the ghost back into the body. In *The Dreaming of the Bones* Yeats has, following his prototype *Nishikigi*, a pair of unrequited lovers as ghosts, come back to speak to the *Sch'te*, who is a young man.

Tsure (follower, or companion of the *Sch'te*), *Waki* (the one at the side, guest – perhaps a wandering priest), *Kyogenshi* (servant, sometimes a sailor), *Kogata* (a young boy) and others are taken over by writers in this tradition, following Yeats, be they Benjamin Britten in such a work as *Curlew River* or Samuel Beckett.

American criticism of the Noh plays has stressed the

> musical division of the play into three sections – *jo* (introduc-
> tion), *ha* (development), and *kyu* (climax),[3]

but this is not Yeats's approach. His was more subtle. Yeats adapted the form so that his Noh play might begin with verse, calling to 'the eye of the mind' the setting: *Utai*. Then came dialogue to carry the narrative, *Katari;* then central *Utai*, then more *Katari*, and then a final lyric *(Utai)* to close. He varied this, but it is this Noh form which Samuel Beckett takes over in his play called *Play*.

It is interesting to see how Yeats developed his adapted Noh form over the second half of his life. *At the Hawk's Well* was first performed in 1916 in Lady Cunard's drawing room in Cavendish Square, London, on Sunday, 2 April. Michio Ito played the Hawk, having practiced his 'Hawk Dance' outside the cages of birds of prey at the London Zoo, with Yeats beside him. The visitors to the zoo were mystified. Yeats and Ito tried hard to persuade a hawk to give a cry, even poking one when its keeper was not looking with an umbrella, but only a feeble murmur came out. At feeding time the noise of the other birds made the cry indistinguishable. The composer Edmund Dulac suggested on the way home that if the Japanese word for hawk was, as Mr Ito said, 'Taka', then 'Taka' was the cry he should use. And so it was.

In *At the Hawk's Well*, the hero or *Sch'te*, Cuchulain, is the young man who has come across the sea, led by a rumour, a story, told over the wine, towards dawn, to find a well which will give immortality to those who drink

3 D. Keene (editor): *20 Plays of the No Theatre*, Columbia University Press, 1970. p.13.

from it. After climbing the hillside he meets an old man who has been waiting all his lifetime for only a little cupful to bubble up. When the water,
briefly, flows, dampening the dried leaves, the old man has fallen asleep, and
Cuchulain has followed the hawk-woman of the place, 'half woman and half
bird of prey', a goddess named (we learn from later plays) Fand, and missed
his chance. He leaves to fight the wild women of the hills, and the play closes
with a bitter lyric.

The shape of the play is this: *Utai,* verse to

> . . . call to the eye of the mind
> A well long choked up and dry . . .

set the scene and launch the narrative of the young man's journey. Then
Katari, a dialogue between the Young Man and the Old Man. This culminates
in the dance of the Hawk-woman. There is *Utai* by the musicians who act as
chorus, then further dialogue between the Old Man and the Young Man, and
then a final *Utai,* by the musicians, the play closing with a lyric that sums
up the emotion, though not the plot, an 'emotion of winter' *(rangyoku?).*

This shape of verse, dialogue, dance, verse, dialogue verse is that of his
exquisite masterpiece *The Only Jealousy of Emer* (1919); in a more complex
arrangement in *The Dreaming of the Bones* (1919) (his play based in part on
Nishikigi, but using as its narrative the political conflict of 1916 in Ireland); in
Calvary (1920) with the dance moved to the penultimate place; in *The Cat
and the Moon* (1926) (a kyogen or farce) and in *The Resurrection* (1931), a play
dedicated to Junzo Sato.

In *The Words upon the Window-pane* (1934) Yeats brilliantly adapts this
technique to the form of contemporary realistic drawing-room drama. His
Noh of Ghosts here is set in a Dublin seance. Visitors gather in a lodging-
house room, talk, are settled, and then Mrs Henderson, the medium who is
to call up the spirits, enters, and after a verse of a hymn (the *Utai*) goes into
a trance and calls up the spirit of Jonathan Swift and his two female friends
Vanessa and Stella. The seance goes wrong; another verse from the hymn is
sung and the seance is over, save for a dramatic climax in the last line of the
play when the ghost of Swift inhabits Mrs Henderson's mouth again. There

is no dance, but the shape of the play is clearly that of the Noh of Ghosts.

In *Purgatory*, written at the end of his life, dated 1939 in the *Collected Plays*, he writes another masterpiece, this time violently crushing and re-shaping the Noh form he has used so many times. He cuts out the initial *Utai*, reduces the dance to a fight over a spilt bag of coins, brings in from the end the final *Utai*, reducing it to a mere two lines adapted from Sir Walter Scott's 'Lullaby of an Infant Chief':

> Hush-a-bye baby, thy father's a knight,
> Thy mother a lady, lovely and bright.

sung by the Old Man over the son he has just killed violently by stabbing. *Purgatory* is a Noh of Ghosts, as the spirits of his own mother and father return and are seen by the two characters (Boy and Old Man, as they are called); but the violence of the emotion is reflected in the violence Yeats does to the delicate form he has so long cherished and developed. In this Yeats is close to Picasso.

Not only the form was developed by Yeats from 1916 to 1939. He deepened its philosophical rationale. He wrote on two levels: the level of the sage and the level of the child, or of the Noh of the Eye and Ear, and the deeper Noh of the Mind for those who understood the symbols, the secret language of passion, as he called it. Yeats believed he could find forty or fifty people in any town of average size who could understand the 'learned speech' and 'agreed symbols' taken from the 'heterodox tradition' of Platonism, alchemy, the Eastern religions. So *The Cat and the Moon* on the surface level is farce, *kyogen*. At the deeper level it is tragic: time and reincarnation are cyclic, and there is little one can do, save go with Fate or define yourself against it.

Yeats's later plays – and I have by no means mentioned them all – are perhaps the best examples of the Noh form adapted to the Western mind in this century; but other Westerners have learned from the Noh.

In 1956 Benjamin Britten came to Japan.

> 'One thing', he wrote in a letter to Roger Duncan on 8 February,
> 'I unreservedly loved in Japan was the theatre. They have two

principal kinds – the Noh, and the Kabuki. The Noh is very
severe and classical . . .'[4]

Reg Close, who was British Council representative in Japan in 1956, writes
that he had 'asked Ben and Peter whether they would care to see a Noh play,
warning them that it might turn out to be as boring as a game of cricket'.

> They said they would just go along to see what it was like and
> we agreed that we would slip away at the first interval if they
> found it unbearable.[5]

At first they giggled, then as the play progressed and the strange Noh *yugen*
began to work they fell silent. It was *Sumidagawa,* and the power of the
emotion of the bereaved mother with her dead child was so great that, as Peg
Hesse writes:

> When . . . we asked if they wished to slip away, Ben started as if
> from a trance, and said, "What? Leave this? I couldn't possibly."[6]

Eight years later he wrote *Curlew River,* his adaptation of *Sumidagawa.* In
Curlew River the Mother is called the Madwoman, and the Japanese tragic
atmosphere is blended with a very different one: that of the medieval plainsong of the Catholic church. A letter from Britten to William Plomer dated
15 February 1964, just before Britten left Venice (where he had gone to have
peace to write *Curlew River,* his 'parable for church performance'), gives the
biographical key:

> When we arrived I was tireder than I thought . . . and honestly
> I still couldn't quite see the style of it all clearly enough. I was
> still very drawn towards the No, too close for comfort.
> However, a few days here, although Arctic in temperature, the
> Gothic beauty and warmth, and above all the occasional
> Masses one attended, began to make their effect.[7]

The 'occasional Masses' included those in San Giorgio Maggiore 'where the

4 Humphrey Carpenter: *Benjamin Britten: A Biography,* London, 1992, p.372.   5 Ibid.
6 Ibid., p.373.   7 Ibid., p.425.

monks still sang plainsong'. Colin Graham writes that he and Britten 'were impressed and moved by the ritual robing – the robes were unfolded from a linen chest with extreme delicacy and reverence.' This led Britten to follow 'the Abbot's address [in *Curlew River*] with a robing ceremony.'[8] The Madwoman was sung by a man, following the Noh tradition. *Sumidagawa* ends with the choric *Utai*. *Curlew River* closes with the disrobing, Abbot's Epilogue, and Te Lucis sung as a recessional. William Plomer who wrote the words brilliantly combines key passages of the Japanese, the

Benjamin Britten, 1954. Photo portrait by Yousuf Karsh, Camera Press, London, courtesy of Colin Smythe

atmosphere of the original, and his own cast of mind and effective changes and additions. As with Yeats, we see the fertile marriage between a powerful Western creative intellect (Britten's – and also Plomer's) and the Japanese Noh form which has cast the original spell.

Yeats had on the one hand carefully distinguished and juxtaposed *Utai* and *Katari,* while on the other intellectually and emotionally integrated the Noh of the Eye and Ear and the Noh of the Mind so that one deepened into the other or, without incongruity, reversed it, as in *The Cat and the Moon*.

What Benjamin Britten has done is build on this, but refract it through his own complex and divided personality so that the result, while certainly achieving the elusive, wistful Noh beauty of *yugen,* reveals tension, unreconciled contrasts, a reaching across between the two while still being unable to touch. Here Britten is doing far more than illustrate the desire of the living to reach out to the dearly-loved dead. He is embodying, though unlike Yeats

8 Ibid., p.426.

not resolving, the contrasting ways of thought of East and West, the Christian and the Buddhist – or if not Buddhist, that way of life the West cannot understand, and – as a result – fears.

To try to understand Britten's Noh play it is as well to hear, in Prince Ludwig of Hesse's words, how Britten met the form here in Tokyo in 1956, in the performance the Prince saw, with Britten, of *Sumidagawa*:

> The play which is hard to forget is the play about the Sumida river: the ferryman is waiting in his boat, a traveller turns up and tells him about a woman who will soon be coming to the river. The woman is mad, she is looking for her lost child. Then she appears and the ferryman does not wish to take a mad person, but in the end he lets her into his boat. On the way across the river the two passengers sit behind each other on the floor as if in a narrow boat, while the ferryman stands behind them, symbolically punting with a light stick. The ferryman tells the story of a little boy who came this way a year ago this very day. The child was very tired for he had escaped from robbers who had held him. He crossed the river in this boat, but he died from exhaustion on the other side. The woman starts crying. It was her son. The ferryman is sorry for her and takes her to the child's grave.
>
> The mother is acted by a tall man in woman's clothing with a small Woman's mask on his face. Accessories help you to understand what is going on: a bamboo branch in the hand indicates madness, a long stick is the ferryman's punting pole, a very small gong is beaten for the sorrowing at the grave side. As soon as these props are no longer necessary, stagehands who have brought them to the actors take them away again.
>
> The sorrowful declamations of the mother rising and subsiding in that oddly pressed voice, the movement of her hand to the brim of her hat as if to protect her sadness from the outside world, the small 'ping' of the little gong which she

beats at the child's grave, become as absorbing as does the sudden foot-stamping which emphasizes important passages. The play ends in the chanting of the chorus. We feel this is more than an interesting experience.[9]

Many have pointed out that the theme of 'innocence wronged', of a boy destroyed by adult evil, was one that again and again compelled Britten's creative attention. The emphasis in both *Sumidagawa* and *Curlew River* though is on the Mother: Britten calls her, as the West so often calls the Eastern visionary, the 'Madwoman'. Britten's musical phrase on the flute for the curlew, though, is the Madwoman's. She is much else musically, too, but the curlew's cry distils her finest element in a purified yet disturbing way. Musically the emotion called up, both orchestrally and vocally, seems to contradict the words being sung. Sorrow seems to be portrayed by orchestral excitement; and Carpenter has pointed out:

> The Madwoman's description of life with her boy before his kidnap is musically tense and disturbing . . . While the libretto gives a plain account of the child collapsing from exhaustion and dying by the wayside, the music suggests something quite different.[10]

So it is with the plainsong 'Te lucis ante terminum . . .'. Britten said 'from it the whole piece may be said to have grown'. Peter Evans has taken this programme note of Britten and demonstrated that the chant supplies nearly all the motifs of the work. (Peter Evans: *The Music of Benjamin Britten*, London, (revised edition) 1989.) Yet the effect is not of integration but of dislocation. The words close the *Katari* with the Spirit of the Boy offstage singing:

> Go your way in peace, mother:
> The dead shall rise again –
> And in that blessed day
> We shall meet in Heav'n.

9 Ibid., p.434.   10 Ibid., pp.436–7.

and the Abbot in a gathering crescendo commenting:

> At our Curlew River here
> A woman was heal'd by prayer and grace . . .

but that is not the message of the music. The liturgical plainsong at the beginning and end is counterpointed with the notes – though not the sound – of the Japanese *Sho* (mouth-blown instrument) which Britten had heard while in Tokyo.[11] Rather, Benjamin Britten has shown the gulf between the work-hungry Traveller – the restless, striving West, and the enigmatic, frightening self-sufficiency of the compassionate East:

> Curlew River, smoothly flowing
> Between the Lands of East and West,
> Dividing person from person!
> Ah! Ferryman, row your ferry boat!
> Bringing nearer, nearer
> Person to person
> By chance or misfortune
> Time, death or misfortune,
> Divided asunder!

The riddle of the curlew's cry is from a different world from that of the textual echoes of *The Dream of Gerontius*. It is the thimbles, the hard and soft sticks of the untuned, restless drums we hear still, though the Abbot sings:

> In hope, in peace ends our mystery.

The Noh of the Eye and Ear and the Noh of the Mind are a world apart.

Samuel Beckett, who was a friend of mine for over a quarter of a century, loved the Noh plays of Yeats, and read them every year. When Beckett was asked, by the Gaiety Theatre, Dublin, to send a tribute in celebration of the centenary of Shaw's birth, Samuel Beckett wrote back:

> You ask me for a tribute to G.B.S., in French, for your souvenir
> programme. This is too tall an order for me. I wouldn't write

11 Ibid., p.435.

in French for King Street. I wouldn't suggest that G.B.S. is not
a great playwright, whatever that is when it's at home. What
I would do is give the whole unupsettable apple-cart for a
sup of the Hawk's Well, or the Saints', or a wiff of Juno, to go
no further. Sorry.[12]

At the Hawk's Well, and *Purgatory,* were perhaps his favourites; and Beckett's
relationship with the Japanese Noh drama is a complex and subtle one.

At the end of each act of *Waiting for Godot* the *Kogata* (or very young
boy) enters. So, near the end of *Endgame:*

> Hamm: More complications! Not an underplot, I trust.
>
> Clov: (*Dismayed*) Looks like a small boy!
>
> Hamm: (*Sarcastic*) A small . . . boy!

Ghosts of the *Utai/Katari* relationship are frequent; for instance with the
song that opens Act Two of *Waiting for Godot,* and Winnie's musical-box
song that closes *Happy Days.* The sparse settings of the plays, on a road,
under a tree; or half-buried in a mound; the increasing limitation of plot to
one highly-charged moment such as in *Catastrophe,* the timeless nature of
the situations and emotions, all owe much to the Noh, as filtered through
Yeats's plays, and Beckett's own reading.

Beckett saw Yeats's plays in Dublin at the Abbey Theatre, and if we look
at his play called *Play,* mentioned earlier in this lecture, it is fascinating to
see what Beckett has done with Yeats's Noh form.

Yeats's play on the eternal triangle of husband, wife, mistress, *The
Only Jealousy of Emer,* treats of the immediate post-mortem condition of
Cuchulain (or so it seems until at the end he revives). Yeats's play *Purgatory*
explores the post-mortem 'dreaming-back' of the Old Man's parents, re-
enacting the 'sin' which led to the murder in the play.

In Samuel Beckett's *Play* a man, his wife and his mistress are in large urns
onstage, with only their heads sticking out. In the darkness a single spotlight
shines on each head in turn, and the head speaks on whom the light shines.
It is as though three tape-recorders were being switched on and off by the

---

12 *Samuel Beckett: an exhibition held at Reading University Library, May to July 1971,* p.14.

spotlight, the monologues running in broken parallel. Act Two is Act One over again, with the order of the solicitations reshuffled, if so wished. Act Two can be, if wished, slightly slower and dimmer.

The effect, as the subject matter is the affair the Man has had with the mistress (Woman 2) while still married to the wife (Woman 1), is of an eternal reliving back in a purgatorial state of the sin and the scene of the sin (if not exactly Fenollosa's 'unrequited love'). This Noh of Ghosts by figures totally incapable of moving, let alone dancing, is set in the strict Yeatsean Noh Framework: *Utai* (the chorus of the Man and the two women together); then *Katari*, as the three figures tell out the same story from their different perspectives; then *Utai* together; then *Katari* again, then final *Utai*. Interestingly, a third *Katari* seems to be starting at the very end, just as, in Yeats's play *Purgatory*, as the Old Man believes at the end he has released his mother's soul from her dreaming back, the hoofbeats begin again:

> Hoof-beats! Dear God,
> How quickly it returns – beat –beat – !
> Her mind cannot hold up that dream.
> Twice a murderer and all for nothing,
> And she must animate that dead night
> Not once but many times!
>   O God,
> Release my mother's soul from its dream!
> Mankind can do no more. Appease
> The misery of the living and the remorse of the dead.

So in Beckett's *Play*, after the final (or what we think is the final) *Utai*, the Man has one extra sentence, one we recognize as these were his first words at the beginning of the play:

> We were not long together – *(Spot off M. Blackout)*

and we realize that all three of them, Man, wife and mistress,

> must animate that dead night

of the dark stage

> Not once but many times

in theatrical performance after performance.

Early in 1970 I was staying with Mr Beckett in France and he showed considerable displeasure at the fact that Kenneth Tynan in New York had asked for a brief play from Beckett, and had used nude men and women in it. Tynan's dramatic anthology which included Beckett's piece was called *Oh! Calcutta!*. Beckett asked me to direct in Oxford what he had actually written for its first proper and authentic performance.[13] In fact he had been so angry he had screwed up the piece of paper (I still have it[14]) on which he had written the play, and thrown it into the waste paper basket. He picked it out when I came into the room and gave it to me. This is the briefest play ever written, and also the most widely seen ever, as, when Beckett was given the Nobel Prize, almost every television news station played it (because it is so brief), to illustrate the work of the prizewinner. It is called, simply, *Breath*.

Breath is the ultimate distillation of the Noh. There is faint light on a stage littered with miscellaneous rubbish (not nude bodies). Five second pause. Then a faint brief cry, a recorded instance of vagitus, the first cry a new-born baby entering this world; and immediately an intake of breath (amplified), and slow increase of light and inspiration together reaching maximum together in about ten seconds. Then a five second silence. Then expiration and slow decrease of light together reaching minimum together in about ten seconds and immediately the identical vagitus cry as before. Silence and hold for five seconds.

That is it.

We bring nothing into this world, and we take nothing out of it, except, perhaps, cries: as he says in *Waiting for Godot*: 'Down in the hole, lingeringly, the grave-digger puts on the forceps. We have time to grow old. The air is full of our cries.' As the human race still for a few years more seems intent on reproducing itself, instead of a death-rattle at the end Beckett has another cry of a new-born baby. Our whole life on earth beyond our birth, and

13 Oxford Playhouse, 8 March 1970.   14 See p.263.

departure having procreated, is summed up in five seconds' silence. That is the *Katari* between the two agonized infant *Utai*. No wonder Shakespeare, in a very Beckettian pun, brings Hamlet's life to a close with the words

'The rest is silence.'

Manuscript of Beckett's *Breath*

BREATH

Black. Then

1. Faint light on stage littered with miscellaneous unidentifiable rubbish. Hold about 5 seconds.

2. Faint cry and immediately inspiration and slow increase of light together reaching maximum together in about 10 seconds. Silence and hold about 5 seconds.

3. Expiration and slow decrease of light together reaching minimum together (light as in 1) in about 10 seconds. Silence and hold about 5 seconds. Then

Black.

———

Rubbish: no verticals, all scattered and lying.

Cry: instant of recorded vagitus. Important that two cries be identical, switching on and off strictly synchronized light and breath.

Breath: amplified recording.

Maximum light: not bright. If 0 = dark and 10 = bright, light should move from about 3 to 6 and back.

Samuel Beckett
1969

The Absence of Nationalism in the Work of Samuel Beckett (1971)

It is my pleasure, in this seminar on theatre and nationalism in twentieth-century Ireland, to give this final lecture, as an Englishman, on the absence of nationalism in the theatre of Samuel Beckett. After such tales as we have heard of heroism and self-sacrifice we may care to recall that Mr Beckett, too, in his earlier days received a knife through his body; but his assailant alas was not English but a Frenchman, and the cause a rather less romantic one, so the attacker told him when Beckett visited him in gaol, not nationalism but whim.

Beckett, indeed left Ireland for Paris in October 1928, and although he has made various return visits to his native country, has made Paris and the Marne district his home ever since. Influenced by James Joyce, his early mentor during these days, he decided that exile was appropriate for him also, and having tried the life of a don at Trinity chose to abdicate his scholastic ambitions and make his home abroad. As Mrs Rooney remarks in *All That Fall:* 'It is suicide to be abroad. But what is it to be at home, Mr Tyler, what is it to be at home? A lingering dissolution.'

But although Beckett settled in France, he has not become a Frenchman. We do not think of him, or indeed address him, as M. Beckett. He has kept, studiously up-to-date, his passport. On his walls hang reminders of Ireland, including a beautiful Jack Yeats oil painting of Trinity boathouse on the Liffey.[1] His country cottage overlooks what can only be described as the most Irish stretch of landscape in the whole of the region: 'Glorious prospect, but for the mist that blotted out everything, valleys, loughs, plain and sea.'[2] And when I saw him last he was once again greatly enjoying George Moore's *Hail and Farewell.*[3]

Oscar Wilde once said to Yeats, 'We Irish are too poetical to be poets';

1 'Regatta Evening' by Jack Yeats.   2 Beckett, *Texts for Nothing,* i.   3 See Notes, p.324.

*Portrait of Samuel Beckett
by Avigdor Arikha,
19 September 1965,
given to Warner by
the artist*

and Beckett might equally answer that he is too Irish to be a nationalist. Certainly he has never rejected Ireland in any save a bodily way, and before him not only Joyce but Shaw, Wilde, Goldsmith, Congreve, and a host of others had done the same. 'I am a typical Irishman,' said Shaw, 'my parents come from Hampshire.' Joyce might have replied 'But I am more typical, Mr Shaw, for my children were born in Trièste.'

Beckett, then, belongs to Ireland and is part of the long tradition that, thanks to many fine scholars such as Vivian Mercier, we know so well. But just how he belongs to it is the subject of my study; and perhaps we should begin by thinking of his relationship with James Joyce before moving back in time and to a wider perspective. James Joyce and Samuel Beckett make each an exactly complementary arc in their lifetime's experiment. They represent contrary but interdependent modes of vision, and each completes the other.

James Joyce wanted to make the soul of the commonest object radiant. He began by writing lyrics that were neo-Elizabethan or post-Pre-Raphaelite, graduated to what he called a style of 'scrupulous meanness' for *Dubliners,* began to evolve an organically growing prose style in which form exactly reflected content in *A Portrait of the Artist as a Young Man;* moved on to show his virtuosity with all English and many Gaelic styles in his mistress-piece *Ulysses,* and, his eyes failing, finally brought to birth his 'monster,' *Finnegans Wake,* the most comprehensive and densely-written book ever conceived, revealing in it a style that is at the opposite pole from that of the 'scrupulous meanness' of *Dubliners.* A rich, ever-shifting, punning, 'holy-caust' of a book vast in scope and infinite in depth; yet with a recognisable locale, a pub in Dublin on the banks of the Liffey, and a central core of a basic social unit, a family.

Joyce, then, moved from a position of almost Horatian chastity in his approach to language to the most extreme form of baroque – if we take that word to indicate an endlessly complex fantastification round a basically simple function or theme. Joyce progressed from brief and simple to massive and complex, and Beckett has done exactly the opposite.

For his earlier novels are full-length – *Murphy* (1938), *Watt* (1953), *Molloy* (1951). Scene and subject matter narrow in *Malone Dies* (1951), and from then on progressively through *The Unnamable* (1953) (these three last having been written, we should remember, as opposed to published, between 1946 and 1949), the *Texts for Nothing* (1955), and *How It Is* (1961) to *Imagination Dead Imagine* and *Ping,* recently published. So also with the plays; the longer ones such as *Godot* (1952) and *Endgame* (1957) come first, followed by *Krapp's Last Tape* (1959), *Happy Days* (1961), *Play* (1963), *Come and Go (1967),* and *Breath* (1970).[4]

We have to remember that the Beckett who is writing *Come and Go,* *Breath* and *Imagination Dead Imagine* – the shortest plays and the shortest novel in our language – is the man who in 1931 with friends published his translation into French of *Anna Livia Plurabelle* (a part of *Finnegans Wake);* and also the following year a prose fragment written in imitation of Joyce's

4 See p.263.

Work in Progress[5] seeking on his own account to discover what else might be discovered in the direction of the extreme baroque.

Beckett, then, quite literally, begins where Joyce left off, by translation and imitation of *Finnegans Wake*. The result was the only possible one – a commodius vicus of recirculation back to the utterly simple and plain, which was Joyce's starting-point. Beckett completes the circle begun by Joyce's elliptical experiment: from *Chamber Music* and *Dubliners* to *Finnegans Wake;* from translation and imitation of the *Wake* to *Imagination Dead Imagine, Come and Go,* and *Breath.*

The outline, then, is clear. But once this has been said, the differences are probably the really important things. Beckett probing the more negative emotions, horror, boredom, the comedy of hopelessness, the problem of speaking when there's nothing to say: and Joyce's gigantic affirmation of life in Molly's 'Yes,' and Kevin's seraphic ardour in his handbathtub and the cry 'Finn no more!'. Joyce's problem is rather the putting into a confining strait-jacket of words the torrents of an overflowing mind.

Beckett's attitude is in violent contrast. Speaking of Tal Coat in 1949 in the Duthuit dialogues he said:

> I speak of an art . . . weary of pretending to be able, of being able, of doing a little better the same old thing, of going a little further along a dreary road. . . [preferring] the expression that there is nothing to express, nothing with which to express, nothing from which to express, no power to express, no desire to express, together with the obligation to express.

Obviously the attitudes are remote from each other. Nevertheless, the more they are studied, the more the problems of one seem similar to the other's. Clearly Beckett is trying to pare language to the bone, even as his friend Giacometti pared the human form during the same years to its simplest concept, 'the shadow that is cast' and no more.

On the one hand, Joyce in his works is seeking to pack language full of meaning, make 'messes of mottage' many meanings deep, using the ammu-

5 *The New Review*, II 5 (April 1932).

nition of 'quashed quotatoes' and the setting of the Dublin 'gossipocracy' and its 'slipping beauties.' His challenge is in the very visual form of the word on the dreambookpage. Although much is gained when the *Wake* is read aloud, much also is lost, as Mary Ellen Bute discovered when she filmed parts of it. In the end she wisely chose to give quotations on the screen under each shot, and by this means considerably enriched the film. Oddly enough, in spite of the enormous musicality of the *Wake,* its full impact must finally be visual, the word on the page.

On the other hand Beckett, working more consciously from the visual arts (we should remember his friendship with artists such as Avigdor Arikha as well as his published criticism on the painting of Jack Yeats and Bram and Geer van Velde), writes a style that, although highly aware visually, does not belong on the written page, but lends itself eminently well to the spoken voice: so much so that he writes dramas, and expects his plays to be seen, acted, or heard on the radio, rather than read. Whereas for Joyce the dream-bookpage was the final deliverer, with Beckett the problem of the medium is rather more complex. In *Play* the man on the theatre spotlight is probably of equal importance with those actors whose voices he elicits to articulation, and silences; more especially as in rehearsal Beckett informed him that when the play was repeated for the second act, he could alter the order in which he called the voices from their dark. In *Film* the camera is our surrogate and co-stars with Buster Keaton. The human being perceived was, *Exiles* apart, of no interest to Joyce. For Beckett, at least for the filmscript, *esse est percipi.* But over and above this, in *How It Is* and the *Texts For Nothing* as well as the plays, if there is a final deliverer at all, and this is by no means certain, for him it 'lies' in the human voice.

If this is true, that except in his silent experiments Beckett relies on the human voice to an unmistakable degree, and that voice is also unmistakably Irish, may we not class him as a nationalist?

Artistically we may, as I hope this lecture will demonstrate, but politically we may not, as he 'takes no sides':

> I take no sides. I am interested in the shape of ideas. There is a

wonderful sentence in Augustine: 'Do not despair; one of the thieves was saved. Do not presume; one of the thieves was damned.' That sentence has a wonderful shape. It is the shape that matters.[6]

You remember how he rephrases this when he writes *Waiting For Godot*: 'One of the thieves was saved. It's a reasonable percentage.' And with this we begin to see how he belongs to that Irish tradition of expatriate and apolitical wits.

Leaving Joyce to one side now, and moving back in time, we may note that the sources of Oscar Wilde's wit (Wilde as you remember with his usual good taste died at the turn of the century in 1900) have several roots, but all depend on the spoken sentence, the conversational tone. When he says 'One's real life is so often the life that one does not lead,' or 'It is perfectly monstrous the way people go about, nowadays, saying things behind one's back that are absolutely and entirely true,' the art lies in part on the shaping tone of voice; and also, in this last, and 'the wages of sin is birth,' what strikes our ear is the substitution of exactly the opposite word for the one we were carefully led to expect. The scene between Lord Goring and his valet Phipps in Act Three of *An Ideal Husband* turns entirely on the common assumption on stage for the moment that the death of a relative is by no means as important as the aesthetic effect of the buttonhole when one is dressing for dinner. In other words, Wilde crosses the technique of comic rhythms of voice with abrupt and startling inversion of expected consequences and values.

Wilde could only do this because of the time in which he lived. Behind him lay the long reign of moral Victoria. Values, at least in public, were clear. He could make his audiences, in theatres and at dinner tables, laugh by leading them on to anticipate the platitude that they themselves would endorse and then turning it inside out. In so doing he acknowledged their morality by so geometrically inverting it.

6 Quoted by Harold Hobson, 'Samuel Beckett, Dramatist of the Year,' *International Theatre Annual*, I (London 1956), and by Alan Schneider, 'Waiting for Beckett,' *Chelsea Review* (Autumn 1958).

Beckett it seems can no longer see any system of values stable enough to overturn for his humour. What has happened is that he has taken the forms of diction and dislocated them, in the same way that Wilde took the values of the time and reversed them.

When Beckett writes 'One of the thieves was saved,' he accustoms our ears to the diction of a certain kind of utterance – that of the Bible, Augustine, the academic, the meditative piety. We do not usually associate such a style of diction with a stockbroker. So the second half of his sentence, 'It's a reasonable percentage,' comes as a shock as we recognise the rhythm in its own right, but from another walk of life so remote that its forced juxta-positioning like this, compelling us to align two classes of value-utterance, makes us laugh at the incongruity.

Again and again this is Beckett's humorous technique; not always to make us laugh, but at times to keep the fractured idiom of dictions present when a laugh is not essential. We remember the comments of the Man in *Play:*

> At home all heart to heart, new leaf and bygones bygones. I ran into your ex-doxy, she said one night, on the pillow, you're well out of that. Rather uncalled for, I thought. I am indeed, sweet-heart, I said, I am indeed. God what vermin women. Thanks to you, angel, I said.

But consider the later line of Woman I. 'She had means, I fancy, though she lived like a pig.' No obvious laugh is enjoined, yet middle-class feminine prevarication is immediately coupled with lower-class monosyllabic concrete directness. The art of the verbal unexpected has been taken over from Wilde by Beckett, but transferred from the realm of moral values and common assumptions to the common but amoral assumptions of contem-porary speech inflexions.

> I take no sides . . . That sentence has a wonderful shape. It is the shape that matters.

For Beckett it is also the incongruity of perfectly recognisable dictions.

From Joyce, if we may recall him for a moment, Beckett takes his ever present love of pun, but it is pun constructed on opposite principles to Joyce's. For Joyce, puns were constructed by combining many meanings and compressing them into one word. Beckett does something rather different. He strips syntax away from a word, leaving it naked and lonely on the page, so that, as the reader supplies many different contexts for the word, it takes on varieties of meaning. Oddly enough, one finds that the more language is stripped, the richer it becomes. His film is called *Film*, and as such this is the generic title. Yet one of the two objects of vision in the film is the camera representing our eyes, and this, at carefully defined moments, blurs, films over, so that we feel our eyes are, in both senses, being filmed.

So it was when he wanted to write a play with no words. The stage direction 'act without words' became the title, and soon by extension in rehearsal, a command. He calls one of his plays after the generic title *Play;* and then in the course of it the Man says 'All this, when will all this have been . . . just play?' But when we talk of Beckett belonging to the direct line of Anglo-Irish or Dublin Wits, we mean more than the fact that he took the art of moral incongruity and transferred it to the realm of diction, and that he learned from Joyce. Although it is impossible to isolate all that is incorporated by the term Irish Wit, we can note certain aspects that seem to be present, over and above those mentioned, in Beckett, Joyce, and Wilde.

Another is surely the use of imaginative flights upheld over extended metaphors or conceits by their own giddy logic. Wilde in *The Decay of Lying* wrote:

> Many a young man starts in life with a natural gift for exaggeration which, if nurtured in congenial and sympathetic surroundings, or by the imitation of the best models, might grow into something really great and wonderful. But, as a rule, he comes to nothing . . . He either falls into careless habits of accuracy, or takes to frequenting the society of the aged and the well-informed. Both things are equally fatal to his imagination, as indeed they would be fatal to the imagination of anybody, and

in a short time he develops a morbid and unhealthy faculty
of truthtelling, begins to verify all statements made in his presence, has no hesitation in contradicting people who are much
younger than himself, and often ends by writing novels which
are so life-like that no one can possibly believe in their proba-
bility.

Here are Wilde's familiar techniques: neatly inverting common assumptions about the wisdom of the old and the health of truthtelling, and pursu-
ing the theme on until it reaches a point which has more than a grain of truth
in it. The spectacular flight of irrational fancy is surely one of the marks of
the Irish playwrights of this tradition, and one thinks back in time perhaps
to Sheridan's Snake in *The School for Scandal:*

> LADY SNEERWELL Why, truly, Mrs Clackitt has a very pretty
>   talent and a great deal of industry.
> SNAKE True, madam, and has been tolerably successful in her
>   day. To my knowledge, she has been the cause of six
>   matches being broken off, and three sons disinherited; of
>   four forced elopements, and as many close confinements;
>   nine separate maintenances, and two divorces. Nay, I have
>   more than once traced her causing a *tête-à-tête* in the *Town
>   and Country Magazine,* when the parties, perhaps, had
>   never seen each other's face before in the course of their
>   lives.
> LADY SNEERWELL She certainly has talents, but her manner
>   is gross.

This last is pure Beckett, an eighteenth-century equivalent of 'She had
means, I fancy, though she lived like a pig.' And when we think of Arsene's
flights of macabrely rational fancy, with their Congrevean mock-heroics –
'and the duster, whose burden up till now she had so bravely borne, fell from
her fingers, to the dust, where having at once assumed the colour (grey) of its
surroundings it disappeared until the following Spring' – or indeed Beckett's

own, ruthlessly formalised so that geometry may impose some restraint on an otherwise uncontrolled variety of options, we see what Beckett has in common with predecessors such as Wilde and Sheridan, and all those in this tradition. We remember Lady Wishfort in Congreve's *Way of the World:*

> Well, and how shall I receive him? In what figure shall I give his Heart the first Impression? There is a great deal in the first Impression. Shall I sit? – No, I won't sit – I'll walk – ay I'll walk from the Door upon his Entrance; and then turn full upon him – No, that will be too sudden. I'll lye – ay, – I'll lye down – I'll receive him in my little Dressing-Room; there's a Couch – Yes, yes, I'll give the first Impression on a Couch – I won't lye neither, but loll and lean upon one Elbow; with one Foot a little dangling off, jogging in a thoughtful way – Yes – and then as soon as he appears, start, ay, start and be surpriz'd, and rise to meet him in a pretty Disorder – Yes – O nothing is more alluring than a Levee from a couch in some Confusion – It shews the Foot to advantage, and furnishes with Blushes, and re-composing Airs beyond Comparison. Hark! There's a Coach.

This is very close in mental process indeed to the great convolutions of self-examination that Beckett's 'heroes' in the dramas and the novels explore. What Beckett adds is the geometry. We think of Watt's way of advancing due east, or Molloy sucking the stones in his pockets turn and turn about, or Sam's

> To think, when one is no longer young, when one is not yet old, that one is no longer young, that one is not yet old, that is perhaps something. To pause, towards the close of one's three hour day, and consider: the darkening ease, the brightening trouble; the pleasure pleasure because it was, the pain pain because it shall be; the glad acts grown proud, the proud acts

grown stubborn; the panting the trembling towards a being gone, a being to come; and the true true no longer, and the false true not yet. And to decide not to smile after all, sitting in the shade, hearing the cicadas, wishing it were night, wishing it were morning, saying, No, it is not the heart, no it is not the liver, no, it is not the prostate, no, it is not the ovaries, no, it is muscular, it is nervous. Then the gnashing ends, or it goes on, and one is in the pit, in the hollow, the longing for longing gone, the horror of horror, and one is in the hollow, at the foot of all the hills at last, the ways down, the ways up, and free, free at last, for an instant free at last, nothing at last.

Even in the latest and most austere of the 'residual' novels the mannerism continues. 'Not count!' Mr Rooney exclaimed in the radio play of 1957 with yet another punning title, *All That Fall:* 'Not count! One of the few satisfactions in life!,' and the speaker in *Enough,* bent double in sympathy with her decayed companion whose 'trunk ran parallel with the ground' thinks over the possibilities of conversation:

> Immediate continuous communication with immediate redeparture. Same thing with delayed redeparture. Delayed continuous communication with immediate redeparture. Same thing with delayed redeparture. Immediate discontinuous communication with immediate redeparture. Same thing with delayed redeparture. Delayed discontinuous communication with immediate redeparture. Same thing with delayed redeparture.

But though Beckett has this in common with the Irish Comic Theatre, we should note a major difference. Sheridan's Maria says to Joseph Surface:

> If to raise malicious smiles at the infirmities or misfortunes of those who have never injured us be the province of wit or humour, Heaven grant me a double portion of dullness!

Against this we must set the famous words from Beckett's *Watt*:

Where were we. The bitter, the hollow and – Haw! Haw! – the
mirthless. The bitter laugh laughs at that which is not good, it
is the ethical laugh. The hollow laugh laughs at that which is
not true, it is the intellectual laugh. Not good! Not true! Well
well. But the mirthless laugh is the dianoetic laugh, down the
snout – Haw! – so. It is the laugh of laughs, the *risus purus*, the
laugh laughing at the laugh, the beholding, the saluting of the
highest joke, in a word the laugh that laughs – silence please –
at that which is unhappy.

In the end it is this that marks Beckett's theatre off from those other dramatists in the tradition to which, on so many other counts, he clearly belongs.

On the other hand it is important not to link him too closely with those
fellow-countrymen who may seem at first glance to be his obvious forebears
in the Abbey Theatre. With the plays of Synge, in spite of their humour and
tramps, his art has no connection. Yeats's tramps – not least in *The Cat and
the Moon* and *Purgatory*, where two are on an empty road, under a tree,
waiting – resemble Gogo and Didi in *Waiting For Godot* in their similar
predicament (though these are not specifically tramps). To one who is not
Irish, the similar idioms at times make the plays seem more closely related
than they are:

> ESTRAGON You gave me a fright.
> VLADIMIR I thought it was he.
> ESTRAGON Who?
> VLADIMIR Godot.
> ESTRAGON Pah! The wind in the reeds.

We remember the title of Yeats's book. But there is really little connection.
Beckett's preoccupations are different. As M. Arikha said to me in a recent
letter, 'The problem in Beckett is not the one of the symbol but the one of the
impact. *Godot* is not a presentation of tramps, in fact they are *not* tramps, but
a release of language in a process of self-reduction.' He is surely correct. The
most that can be claimed is that the form of the Noh play – which W. B. Yeats

took from Pound's edition of Fenollosa's manuscript translations, best artic-
ulated by Yeats in classical form in that play on the theme of Cuchulain,
Emer his wife, and Eithne his mistress, *The Only Jealousy of Emer;* and in
comedy in *The Cat and the Moon;* a structure built on opening lyric, followed
by a stretch of narrative to a brief midway lyric, in its turn followed again by
narrative, the whole rounded at the end by a lyric that bears some relation to
the opening and central ones —is almost exactly the form of Beckett's *Play.*
Play is, if you like, the sequel, set in purgatory, to any play on the eternal
triangle. If one takes it further than that, Murphy's will regarding the
disposal of his charred remains becomes apposite, and consideration of
Beckett's debts to the Abbey Dramatists should

> be burnt and placed in a paper bag and brought to the Abbey
> Theatre, Lr. Abbey Street, Dublin, and without pause into
> what the great and good Lord Chesterfield calls the necessary
> house, where their happiest hours have been spent. . . and I
> desire that the chain be there pulled upon them, if possible
> during the performance of a piece, the whole to be executed
> without ceremony or show of grief.

Much closer to the central situation in *Waiting For Godot* is the great picture
by W. B. Yeats's brother Jack, *The Two Travellers* (Tate Gallery), painted in
1942 when Beckett was living in hiding among the French farmers and peasants as a member of the Resistance. This two-year experience of being 'on
the run' seems to me by far the most important factor to bear in mind when
discussing Beckett's post-war writings. The feeling is well captured as the
Texts For Nothing open:

> Suddenly, no, at last, long last, I couldn't any more, I couldn't
> go on. Someone said, You can't stay here. I couldn't stay there
> and I couldn't go on.

It left its indelible mark; and the great picture painted at this time by his
close friend so much his senior, with its two figures perhaps about to part,
perhaps only just having met, on an empty road that disappears in the direc-

tion of a barren mountain and sky, is closer to *Godot* than anything the artist's brother wrote.

Beckett's love of painting is indisputable. In the *Irish Times* in August 1945 he wrote of Jack Yeats:

> He is with the great of our time, Kandinsky and Klee, Ballmer and Bram van Velde, Rouault and Braque, because he brings light, as only the great dare bring light, to the issueless predicament of existence, reduces the dark where there might have been, mathematically at least, a door.

Just before this he had carried a painting by Yeats in his possessions while working with the Red Cross on the front line. When Yeats exhibited in Paris in 1954, Beckett wrote:

> What is incomparable in this great solitary achievement is its insistence upon returning to the most secret part of the mind which originates it and upon letting itself be lighted only by the day of the mind . . . Simply bow in wonder.[7]

But Jack Yeats was not the only painter who, with the van Veldes, won Beckett's close attention. The names of Kandinsky, Klee, and Braque mentioned in his review of Yeats were not chosen at random. Braque had been introduced to Picasso by Apollinaire late in 1907, and in 1911, the year in which the friendship between the two painters was at its height, Picasso and Braque spent the summer together at Céret. These were the years in which they founded the cubist movement, and Braque was not only the first to show cubist works in public, but also probably painted the first cubist canvases. By the summer of 1911, the paintings in this manner of Picasso and Braque are virtually indistinguishable. The basic features are a linear grid, on which equal visual value is apportioned to both object and surroundings, the combination of several views of the object in a single image, and as a result a greater or lesser measure of abstraction.

---

7 'Hommage à Jack B. Yeats,' *Les Lettres Nouvelles*, 2e année (April 1954), pp.619–20, trans. Dr Marilyn Rose.

Dinner discussing theatrical cubism at La Closerie des Lilacs, Boulevard du Montparnasse, Paris 19 May 1969. Warner, Sam Zacks with back to camera, Sorel Etrog the sculptor and Beckett

In 1910 Robert Delaunay had become a member of the Cubist Group, only to move away soon after, like many others, to a more lyrical mode that Apollinaire dubbed 'Orphism'; a style that attempted to cultivate 'pure painting,' though obviously heavily indebted to and leaning on cubism. In 1911 Kandinsky invited Delaunay to exhibit with the artists of the *Blaue Reiter*. Klee came to Paris to see cubist works, and that autumn translated, as a result, some of Delaunay's notes on light for *Der Sturm*. Delaunay's 'Orphism' had taken to heart the austere lessons of analytic cubism, but substituted for its muted tones his own bright colours used in a more purely abstract way. For him, as for Jack Yeats, the principal elements were colour and light, and these were the elements that attracted both Klee and Kandinsky to him.

We can see perhaps the attraction that the formal clarity and use of light might have had for Beckett.[8] In *Come and Go* the three women, dressed in dull violet, dull red, and dull yellow, step in turn in and out of the stage's

8 *Cf*. Beckett, *Murphy* (London 1938), pp.111–12, 'There were three zones. . . states of peace.'For further information on Beckett's cubism see R. Pountney, *Theatre of Shadows*, Gerrards Cross, Colin Smythe, 1988, pp.236–239 where the manuscript of the grid page of *Sans/Lessness* that Beckett sent to Warner showing the cubist structure they had discussed is reproduced.See also R. Jeffrey, *Chess in the Mirror: A Study of Theatrical Cubism in Francis Warner's* Requiem *and its* Maquettes, Oxford, J.Thornton and Son, 1980.

pool of light. An opening stage direction in *Play* reads:

> Their speech is provoked by a spotlight projected on faces
> alone.
> The transfer of light from one face to another is immediate. No
> blackout, i.e. return to almost complete darkness of opening,
> except where indicated.
> The response to light is not quite immediate. At every solicita-
> tion a pause of about one second before utterance is achieved,
> except where a longer delay is indicated.

Indeed, as each of the three speaks directly ahead regardless of the other two
in a toneless voice, and only when provoked, like three continuous straight
lines of narration broken only by the cross-examination of the beam of light,
and never overlapping; and as the order of solicitations may be reshuffled
when the play is repeated, each fragment of each person's speech being self-
contained and the over-all picture of the events described, though built up in
an unfamiliar way, amounting to exactly the same once all have been
completed, we are presented with an experience that may perhaps be called
theatrical cubism, insofar as the emphasis is on muted colours, darkness and
light, a mental and visual grid on which the fragments of the three monologues are constructed, and the skill with which the narrative shape of Act
One is redistributed in Act Two with the same segments, is similar to cubist
theory.

*Warner, Ayala
Zacks, Sam Zacks
(art collectors),
Etrog and Beckett*

As for the value placed equally on objects and subjects, we remember among many such instances how Malone feels for the broken bowl of pipe he found:

> Perhaps I thought it pretty, or felt for it that foul feeling of pity
> I have so often felt in the presence of things.

If Beckett learned to appreciate painting from long walks round Dublin Bay with Jack Yeats, he developed his interest well beyond that one Irishman's work, without ever losing his admiration for it.

Colour, a sharp sense of the emotive power of theatrical darkness and a pool of light on stage, rigid formality imposed on the flux of human living, and juxtaposing of hermetically sealed sentences having no contact with another person or voice on stage, but merely running in broken parallel to it, as in *Krapp's Last Tape* and *Lessness,* all seem features better explained by comparison with the visual rather than the literary arts. But we must not forget that he is a dramatist, and the direction in which his dramas have increasingly progressed. Learning perhaps from Giacometti, whose work is somewhere between painting and drama, and who would work on a human form until ruthless pruning had reduced the life-size figure to one no bigger than a thumbnail, the direction of Beckett's later drama has been towards further and further austerity.

In his writings, we may trace the predicament of the unwilling will, the inarticulate voice, the croak in the mud, the hounded persona clarifying by careful negation his utterances, from the thirteen *Texts For Nothing* to the latest *Act Without Words*. It is only a short step from 'I'm a mere ventriloquist's dummy, I feel nothing, say nothing, he holds me in his arms and moves my lips . . . all is dark, there is no one, what's the matter with my head, I must have left it in Ireland,'[9] to Beckett's full-scale novel *How It Is:*

> in me that were without when the panting stops scraps of an
> ancient voice in me not mine

and the totally silent and crudely visual image of *Act Without Words II*, of a

9 *Texts for Nothing,* viii.

long pointed goad coming in from the wings of the stage and poking, hard, a sack from which a man emerges.

From whence comes the voice in *Eh Joe?* Who controls the goad? Who are the strangers who beat up Estragon before the play and during the interval? Who guards the guardians?

> How are the intervals filled between these apparitions? Do my keepers snatch a little rest and sleep before setting about me afresh, how would that be? That would be very natural, to enable them to get back their strength. Do they play cards, the odd rubber, bowls, to recruit their spirits, are they entitled to a little recreation? I would say no, if I had a say, no recreation, just a short break, with something cold, even though they should not feel inclined, in the interests of their health. They like their work, I feel it in my bones.[10]

Texts For Nothing is set in a first person *persona*, a solitary, who is speaking, if to anyone, to the reader, but certainly about himself. They all demonstrate a mind recording its feelings in a given context. To this extent they are dramatic monologues. Throughout them all we are reminded of the comment from the narrator of *From An Abandoned Work:*

> No, there's no accounting for it, there's no accounting for anything, with a mind like the one I always had, always on the alert against itself . . .

Throughout the *Texts For Nothing* we find the narrator's mind is continually 'on the alert against itself' – not to the point of silence, but often so that any word used has to be cancelled or withdrawn as soon as uttered. The first opens with the words 'Suddenly, no, at last, long last,' and we can see the narrator's refusal to use the dramatic word in place of the truthful one, the exact description of what happened. But how can anyone exactly describe what happened? This is the narrator's dilemma. The inclination towards truthful narration, and the impossibility of narrating the truth because

10 Ibid., vi.

one does not know what it is. 'Not good! Not true! Well well.' And so the narrator, after an attempt to describe his den. 'My den, I'll describe it, no, I can't' drags his body 'flat on my face in the dark earth' sustained by his own love for himself, which is a polite way of describing the instinct for self-preservation, until he has to sleep.

> That's how I've held out till now. And this evening again it seems to be working, I'm in my arms, I'm holding myself in my arms, without much tenderness, but faithfully, faithfully. Sleep now, as under that ancient lamp, all twined together, tired out with so much talking, so much listening, so much toil and play.

So the denial of an ability to understand through big words –

> I don't try to understand, I'll never try to understand any more, that's what you think, for the moment I'm here, always have been, always shall be, I won't be afraid of the big words any more, they are not big.

leads to the act of writing; the act of denial *is* the creative urge that sustains, be it toil or play, until sleep silences the conscious mind.

The mind 'always on the alert against itself,' rather like the contemporary heads of Picasso such as *Grande Tête* (linocut 1962) and *Tête De Femme* (linocut 1962) which comprise two interlocking profiles forming one overall face staring out at the viewer, splits into two equal and opposite aspects as Beckett moves from *Texts For Nothing* to write plays.

In *Endgame* we are asked to remember 'the solitary child who turns himself into children, two, three, so as to be together, and whisper together, in the dark.' In other words, the pairs in the plays, Vladimir and Estragon, Pozzo and Lucky, Hamm and Clov, Nagg and Nell, Krapp old and young, Bolton and Holloway, Winnie and Willie, Man and his two women in *Play*, are double or opposite projections of an anterior solitary made to face each other. Instead of the *persona* speaking in his own person as in *Texts For Nothing*, two characters are created so they can face each other, and breed, in spite of being diametrically opposed; and what they breed is company. The solitary loneliness of farcical despair gives place to the burden of intolerable companionship. And with this, as we approach the later drama, we carry with us the picture of hopeless farce, rueful impotence, of being blessed in attaining to consciousness, but also damned in having only enough to realise that it is insufficient; as, for instance, in the first *Act Without Words* (1957).

In this mime a man is flung on stage and shown to be unable to cope with the incomprehensible forces that surround him. In the second *Act Without Words*, two men emerge in turn from their respective sacks, one to spend his stage life religiously, praying, taking pills, brooding, and spitting out his carrot; the other with intolerable enthusiasm, doing exercises, combing his hair, and continually consulting his watch. Each goes through his motions without being in the least aware that the other exists except as an object of heavy weight that must be carried.

In *Krapp's Last Tape*, Krapp is at least aware of his own recorded voice of years ago, though the tape cannot be aware of him.

> Perhaps my best years are gone. When there was a chance of happiness. But I wouldn't want them back. Not with the fire in me now. No, I wouldn't want them back.
>
> *Krapp motionless staring before him. The tape runs on in silence.*

Would the present, much older Krapp, want them back? Little fire in him now. Sex has remained constant as a basis for pleasurable if transitory activity – but now his banana is kept locked in a drawer which he cannot always find; and when he does and eats it, he tosses the discarded skin into the pit with a vacuous stare.

With his white face and purple nose, this image of an old and weary man bathed in light listening to his tape-recorded youth seems, by the end, and especially in the final silence, like some Rembrandt portrait for a while come to life, now still. It is a moment of great theatrical poignance and power that can hold an audience silent for timeless minutes. Krapp, in common with some of the other narrators, has been able to prove to himself that he thinks, and therefore exists, by telling stories that he can listen to. Silence descends when he is more interested in listening to the stories than contributing his share. The uneasy partnership is broken when one refuses to play.

In *Happy Days*, Winnie has to take on herself three-quarters of the share. She is buried up to her waist in Act One, to her neck in Act Two, and her husband is uncommunicative.

> Oh I know you were never one to talk, I worship you Winnie be mine and then nothing from that day forth only titbits from *Reynolds' News.*

When on a rare occasion Willie does vouchsafe an answer to the immense monologue of his wife it is brief and succinct:

> What *is* a hog, Willie, please! *(Pause.)*
> WILLIE Castrated male swine. *(Happy expression appears on Winnie's face.)* Reared for slaughter.

To which Winnie replies 'Oh this *is* a happy day!' and the climax of Act One is reached.

It is true that among many other things in her long and varied speech Winnie does quote a line from one of Yeats's Noh plays, *At The Hawk's Well;* a line, indeed, that Yeats had taken from the Japanese, together with his form: 'I call to the eye of the mind,' but again the resemblances are only superficial. Much more important is the fact that the old Beckettian preoccupations with time and personality are yet again annotated, even in the *clichés* of Winnie's gossip to herself :

> I used to think . . . *(Pause)* . . . I say I used to think there was no difference between one fraction of a second and the next. *(Pause)* I used to say . . . *(Pause)* . . . I say I used to say, Winnie, you the changeless, there is never any difference between one fraction of a second and the next. *(Pause)* Why bring that up again? *(Pause)* There is so little one can bring up, one brings up all . . . Say no more. *(Pause)* But I must say more. *(Pause)* Problem here.

She is imprisoned not only in the flesh, not only in the ground, but above all in her own limitations of thought, which even communication with another can only alleviate by the temporary distraction which we call for convenience 'happiness,' and thus a day in which it has been assumed to have been achieved, probably by violence or a violent image, a 'Happy Day.'

The narrators must talk, even when there is nothing to say, whether it is a text for nothing or on stage in front of an audience of an unattending husband. The goad continues to exist, even when the external manifestations of it are removed. The spotlight in *Play* solicits speech. Should the person on whom the light shines answer? They have no choice: What should they do ?

> Bite off my tongue and swallow it? Spit it out? Would that placate you? How the mind works still to be sure!

This is the real problem. Not whether one speaks one's thoughts or not, but the fact that one has them. To comprehend without the ability to be comprehensive, this is 'hellish half-light'; hence the ever-recurring longing for silence and the dark.

In *Words and Music* non-visual, radio, drama is stripped to its basic essentials: Words awakened from silence in a dark box, only to find itself cooped up with Music:

> MUSIC *Small orchestra softly tuning up.*
> WORDS Please! *(Tuning. Louder.)* Please! *(Tuning dies away.)*
>   How much longer cooped up here in the dark? *(With*
>   *loathing.)* With you!

and having been woken to tyrannical loathing by Music is made humble by a second voice designated Croak.

> CROAK Joe.
> WORDS *(humble)* My Lord.

With violent thumps of a club and a musical baton Croak tries to coordinate Music and Words. 'Age Music' is called for by a rap of the baton. The Age Music is soon interrupted by a violent thump of the club.

CROAK Together. *(Pause. Thump.)* Together! *(Pause. Violent thump.)* Together, dogs!

Finally Words tries to sing, and between thumps and sighs the Pozzo-Lucky, tyrant-slave routine is enacted in that little dark portable box we call a radio set. This shotgun partnership is completed with the climax of the song that Words and Music achieve, on the final word which is a euphemism for the female sexual organ. But the tyrant Croak, having brought this about, indeed compelled it, now is powerless. His club falls, and the sound of shuffling slippers dies away.

The themes of master and slave, sexual gratification, the problems of communication, of the solitary, of the probing mind turned inwards against itself in spite of itself by some compulsion, are all here, and at the same time Beckett has stripped the form of the radio play as he was later to strip television down to its basic individuality; a live head in a box brought into one's living room, at whose agonised changes of expression one may stare undeterred.

In *Imagination Dead Imagine,* the novel form is treated to the same ruthless stripping. If the imagination lives by imagining, then it should be able to imagine itself dead and thus find oblivion. But the problem is, as this little novel tells us in its title, that as the imagination imagines its own death it in fact imagines. It lives. Consciousness, then, is an intolerable curse, but the 'ordering' of consciousness, in both senses, is one of the less intolerable pastimes.

We come and we go, and we imagine past, present, and future, being able to guarantee none of them. Beckett's latest playlet or 'Dramaticule' is really a kind of ballet. The extraordinary compression his style has now achieved makes it possible to gather these themes together in bright focus, extending the range of his experiments in media, even as it shrinks the bones of his intellectual preoccupations. When it is all form and as little content as possible, then, as he wrote of James Joyce's final experiment, there will be neither prize nor penalty: 'Simply a series of stimulants to enable the kitten to catch its tail.'

Come and Go has three characters, who are female, but their ages are 'undeterminable': Flo, dressed in dull yellow, Vi in dull red, and Ru in violet. They wear full-length coats, buttoned high, wear 'drab nondescript hats with enough brim to shade faces,' their hands are made up to be as visible as possible, and they speak 'as low as compatible with audibility.' Although they sit, it should not be clear what they are sitting on.

The three sit with their hands clasped in their laps, facing front, and there is a silence. Then Vi:

> When did we three last meet?

A cross between an old girls' reunion and the witches in Macbeth.[11] She receives the answer from Ru 'Let us not speak.' Vi goes off and Flo turns to Ru:

> FLO Ru.
> RU Yes
> FLO What do you think of Vi?

'I see little change,' Ru answers, and Flo moves to centre seat to whisper in Ru's ear. Appalled, Ru says 'Oh!' They look at each other, and Flo puts her finger to her lips, as Ru replies 'Does she not realise?' Flo answers 'God grant not,' and Vi returns and sits on the right.

After a silence Flo says 'Just sit together as we used to, in the playground at Miss Wade's.' And Ru answers 'On the log.'

With this 'Act One' ends, and after a silence Flo goes off left.

> RU Vi.
> VI Yes.
> RU How do you find Flo?

'She seems much the same,' Vi answers, and the same ritual of whisper and appalled response takes place.

> VI Oh! (*Ru put her finger to her lips.*) Has she not been told?

Ru answers 'God forbid,' and Flo returns to sit left.

11 *Cf.* The homage to Hamlet's predicament in *Endgame*: 'If I don't kill that rat he'll die.'

After a silence Ru says 'Holding hands . . . that way.'' and Flo comments 'Dreaming of . . . love.'

Then for Act Three it is Ru's turn to go out.

> VI Flo.
>
> FLO Yes.
>
> VI How do you think Ru is looking?
>
> FLO One sees little in this light. *(Vi moves to centre seat, whispers in Flo's ear. Appalled.)* Oh! *(They look at each other. Vi puts her finger to her lips.)* Does she not know?

and Vi answers 'Please God not.'

Ru comes back in and after a silence all three resume their front-facing pose. When they are still, Vi says

> May we not speak of the old days? *(Silence)* Of what came after? *(Silence)* Shall we hold hands in the old way?

They do, in a cat's-cradle circle, still facing front, and Flo says 'I can feel the rings.' The stage direction tells us that there are no rings apparent.

This dramaticule is the very quintessence of the familiar Beckettian preoccupations. The same conversation is repeated three times. It is a three-act, pretty well a well-made play. Each gossips and is gossiped about in turn. Two of the others always think they know more about the third than the third does herself. They ask when they last met, but Ru, like Estragon, would rather not speak.

Ru is prepared to remember the log on which they used to sit at Miss Wade's – and indeed they may be on one now, we cannot tell. The past is forgotten, perhaps by emotional command. It is Vi who twice asks after the old days, but she is answered by silence. The past, it seems, they may not speak of. Perhaps it is unspeakable. The future of each is dreaded by her friends on her account. It holds a clear though unknown menace. Does the potential victim realise? Flo prays 'God grant not,' Ru says 'God forbid,' and Vi 'Please God not.' God is seen as one who confers benefits, one who forbids – perhaps it is he who has forbidden them to speak of the past; they are religious women. And Vi mixes the random Irish colloquialism 'Please God not' with the penitent's prayer of desperation, 'PLEASE God *not!*' beautifully bringing into focus the two moods of the play: triviality of gossip about the past and friends' potential misfortunes, with the unanswered cry of anguish to a God who though unseen and absent must be placated. He can appear here no more than Godot can in *Godot;* but then, as in *Play,* Flo says 'One sees little in this light.' We see enough to know how little we can see. And together with a mandatory silence about the past, and proxy fears for the future, how do they spend the present? 'Dreaming of . . . love.' So Krapp. So nearly all the later solitaries.

Childhood at Miss Wade's, adulthood dreaming of love, all fearing the future, each leaving alone, in turn. We remember the little, happy things of the past, Miss Wade's inconsequential log, dream about love in the present, and for the future, each of us must part with our company alone,

 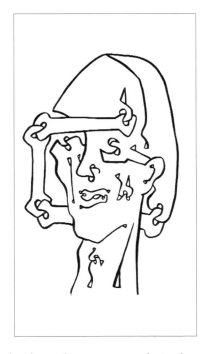

Twin portraits, each 19½ x 25½ inches, of Samuel Beckett and Francis Warner by Sorel Etrog. Lithographs, Atelier Art Paris, 1969. Warner collection

and step out of the light of the intellect into the waiting darkness and silence, while others fear and are appalled about us. As we become aware of the future of our fellows we become horrified. Better not to have prescience. Better a limited knowledge of the future. Perhaps that for which we grieve, our partial knowledge, should make us rejoice. So we laugh, down the snout – Haw! – so. And this *risus purus* springs from that split intellect, telling itself stories, even here where the burden of living is projected on to the immaculate and meticulous formality of Vi, Ru, and Flo; both horrified at and grateful for its limitations. We can merely pretend to ourselves that we feel the rings, pretend, even in the face of visible evidence, we are secure and happy; and meanwhile wait, hearing in the background the voices of courtesy, and encouragement, even praise:

> They said to me, Come now, you're not a brute beast, think upon these things and you'll see how all becomes clear. And simple! They said to me, What skilled attention they get, all these dying of their wounds.[12]

12 *Endgame.*

Manuscript of Beckett's *Sans*, and covering letter

MONTAGE

Sentences	I	Paragraphs
A3 B9 C9 A2		I
A9 D3 E9 B8 F2		II
F10 C6 D8		III
E6 D7 C1 F8 A5		IV
B4 C4 B1		V
F3 E4 C7 B7 F2 B6		VI
A4 C2 E3 C10 F5 E5 F4		VII
A1 C8 A6 B2 D5 A8		VIII
C5 F9 B5 D10 B3 D6		IX
F1 A10 E8 E9 E10		X
F6 B10 F9 A7		XI
D4 E7 E1 C3 D2		XII

Sentences	II	Paragraphs
C4 B6 A2		I
B8 B10 F2 F7		II
E6 B2 F8 B4		III
D1 B3 A9 A5 E2 E9		IV
A1 F4 D6 C9 F6 B5 D7		V
C3 C10 E5 F3 F5 E8		VI
A7 E1 D5 E3 D3		VII
A10 D9 F9 B1 B8 E4 C6		VIII
A3 E7 D2		IX
A4 B7 F1 C5 D10 B9		X
C2 A6 D10 D4		XI
C7 C1 C8 E10		XII

Effondrement du refuge

A

1. En quatre à la renverse vrai refuge
   Sans issue ruines répandues.

2. Eteint ouvert quatre pans à la renverse
   vrai refuge sans issue.

3. Ruines vrai refuge enfin vers lequel
   d'aussi loin par tant de faux.

4. Noir lent avec ruine vrai refuge quatre
   pans sans bruit à la renverse.

5. Cube vrai refuge enfin quatre pans
   sans bruit à la renverse.

6. Vrai refuge enfin sans issue répandu
   quatre pans sans bruit à la renverse.

7. Vrai refuge enfin ruines répandues
   même gris que les sables.

8. Ruines répandues gris cendre à la
   ronde vrai refuge enfin sans issue.

9. Ruines répandues confondues avec
   le sable gris cendre vrai refuge.

10. Eteint ouvert vrai refuge sans
    issue vers lequel d'aussi loin
    par tant de faux.

TERRE

B.

1. Gris cendre à la ronde terre ciel confondus lointains sans fin.

2. Lointains sans fin terre ciel confondus rien qui bouge pas un souffle.

3. Infini sans relief petit corps seul debout même gris partout terre ciel corps ruines.

4. Ciel gris sans nuage pas un bruit rien qui bouge terre sable gris cendre.

5. Terre sable même gris que l'air le ciel le corps les ruines sable fin gris cendre.

6. Silence pas un souffle même gris partout terre ciel corps ruines.

7. Terre ciel confondus infini sans relief petit corps seul debout.

8. Gris cendre ciel reflet de la terre reflet du ciel.

9. Lointains sans fin terre ciel confondus pas un bruit rien qui bouge.

10. Air gris sans temps terre ciel confondus même gris que les ruines lointains sans fin.

HOMME

C'

1. Petit corps soudé gris cendre coeur battant face aux lointains.

2. Jambes un seul bloc bras collés aux flancs petit corps face aux lointains.

3. Coeur battant seul debout petit corps face grise traits envahis deux bleu pâle.

4. Petit corps même gris que la terre le ciel les ruines seul debout.

5. Gris cendre petit corps seul debout coeur battant face aux lointains.

6. Petit corps face gris traits fente et petits trous deux bleu pâle.

7. Petit corps petit bloc coeur battant gris cendre seul debout.

8. Petit corps petit bloc parties envahies oue un seul bloc raie grise envahie.

9. Face grise deux bleu pâle petit corps coeur battant seul debout.

10. Seul debout petit corps gris lisse rien qui dépasse quelques trous.

REFUGE OUBLIÉ

D

1. Petit vide grande lumière cube tout
blancheur faces sans trace aucun souvenir.

2. Lumière blancheur proche à toucher tête
par l'oeil calme toute sa raison aucun souvenir.

3. Cube tout lumière blancheur rase faces
sans trace aucun souvenir.

4. Face à l'oeil calme proche à toucher calme
tout blancheur aucun souvenir.

5. Faces blanches sans trace oeil calme tête
sa raison aucun souvenir.

6. Face au calme blanc proche à toucher
oeil calme enfin aucun souvenir.

7. Faces sans trace proches à toucher
blancheur rase aucun souvenir.

8. Faces sans trace blancheur rase oeil
calme enfin aucun souvenir.

9. Tête par l'oeil calme toute blancheur
calme lumière aucun souvenir.

10. Lumière refuge blancheur rase
faces sans trace aucun souvenir.

PASSÉ-FUTUR NIÉ

E

1. Ne fut jamais qu'air gris sans
temps rien qui bouge pas un souffle.

2. Jamais ne fut que cet inchangeant
rêve l'heure qui passe.

3. Jamais qu'en rêve évanoui ne passa
l'heure longue brève.

4. Jamais qu'en rêve le beau rêve
n'avoir qu'un temps à faire.

5. Jamais que rêve jours et nuits
faits de rêves d'autres nuits jours
meilleurs.

6. Chimère lumière ne fut jamais
qu'air gris sans temps pas un bruit.

7. Jamais qu'imaginé le bleu dit
en poésie céleste qu'en imagination
folle.

8. Jamais que silence tel qu'en
imagination ces rires de folle
ces cris.

9. Jamais ne fut qu'air gris sans
temps chimère lumière qui passe.

10. Chimère ▓▓▓ l'aurore qui
dissipe les chimères et l'autre
dite brune.

(PASSÉ-FUTUR AFFIRMÉ)

F.

1. Encore un pas un seul tout seul
dans les sables sans prise il le fera.

2. Dans les sables sans prise encore
un pas vers les lointains il le fera.

3. Il bougera dans les sables ça
bougera au ciel dans l'air les sables.

4. Il hésitera le temps d'un pas il
se refera jour et nuit sur lui les
lointains.

5. Un pas dans les ruines les sables sur
le dos vers les lointains il le fera.

6. Il ira sur le dos face au ciel rouvert
sur lui les ruines les sables les lointains.

7. Il refera jour et nuit sur lui les lointains
l'air coeur rebattra.

8. Pleuvra sur lui comme au temps béni
du bleu la nuée passagère.

9. Tout beau tout nouveau comme au
temps béni régnera le malheur.

10. Il maudira Dieu comme au temps
béni face au ciel ouvert l'averse passagère.

A Cup of Coffee in Paris
By Penelope Warner

Monday, 13 February 1984, 11.00 – 12.30 p.m. Hotel PLM,
17 Boulevard St Jacques

We arrived at exactly 11 a.m. and Samuel Beckett was already waiting in the foyer. He was wearing a thin chocolate-brown polo-neck jumper under another thicker knitted one in grey/brown, over which he wore a brown donkey-jacket. On his head was a brown beret; on his feet light beige slipper-shoes. Folded newspapers were tucked into his jacket pocket.

He greeted us warmly, first shaking Francis's hand, then mine and touching me gently on the shoulder. He suggested we have a coffee, so we went to the hotel café following him as he chose a table. We sat down, he took off his beret and glasses and ordered coffee. Francis took our coats, and I said how happy I was to be in Paris.

Francis asked him how he was surviving, and he talked about the death of Roger Blin, of congenital heart trouble followed by pneumonia: 'He was incinerated a week ago last Friday.' Jean-Louis Barrault and his wife Madeleine (Renaud) were at the cremation. Francis had re-directed them both in Roger Blin's production of *Oh les beaux jours* at the Oxford Playhouse,[1] so Beckett reassured him that though Madeleine had recently had a replacement hip operation, she was now back on stage.

We in turn told Beckett of the hostile reception Barrault had received on his visit to the Barbican theatre in London, when a portion of the audience had turned nasty because Barrault was addressing them in French. Francis called it 'My most sickening experience ever in the theatre.'

Beckett asked if we were staying at L'Hotel, the small, left-bank hotel where Oscar Wilde had died. We were. His American publisher Barney

1 Performed on Sunday 14 March 1971. See review in *The Times*, 15 March, 1971, p.10.

Rosset of Grove Press always stays there, he said. 'He is on his fourth wife; has four children by different marriages. Christine, his third wife, knows Francis.'

He then became anxious that we should change tables, so that instead of sitting in a triangle, we faced him. He was smoking small cheroots. He told us of his planned visit to London on Sunday for two weeks and that he would be staying at the Hyde Park Hotel, and wanted a room overlooking the park. He was very concerned about this.

While there he has to go to the Riverside Studios to see Rick Cluchey, of the San Quentin Drama Workshop, direct three of his plays before they go on to the Adelaide Festival. Rick wanted to entitle the programme 'Beckett directs Beckett', but Beckett felt this wasn't right as he couldn't direct *Waiting for Godot* again; but he would go to oversee it. He said doing this would be awkward and embarrassing. The Riverside Studios had already informed the press, and he dreaded the publicity and the demands to be made on him. He was also anxious about his friends in England, as they would be hurt if he did not see them. I felt pleased we were meeting him quietly in Paris instead.

We spoke about our wedding seven months ago, and showed him Billett Potter's photographs of it. Early on in the conversation we spoke about my career as a therapeutic radiographer, and London's Royal Marsden Hospital

Jean-Louis Barrault and his Director during a break in rehearsals for Oh les beaux jours *at the Oxford Playhouse*

where I had been Superintendent; he referred back to this later when he was alone with Francis, and was clearly interested.

He talked about his new work *What Where* which was especially written for the Graz Festival last autumn, the English translation having been on in New York at the Harold Clurman Theatre with two other short plays – *Catastrophe* and *Ohio Impromptu*, directed by Alan Schneider. The last prose piece, *Worstward Ho*, had taken a lot

Samuel Beckett

out of him. 'I have at last written myself into a corner', he said with glee, and laughed. Francis asked if it were a longer piece he had cut down; Beckett replied 'No, but does it look like it?' Francis said 'No, it doesn't – but I remember you showing me how you wrote *Imagination Dead Imagine*' and he replied 'Ah, yes; but that was different.' It was touching because I felt he wanted Francis's approval – and also to know that he had read it.

There was more theatre talk: of Beckett's planned visit to Stuttgart for a television production of *What Where*. He moved on to the Schiller Theatre's production of *Warten Auf Godot* which he directed. His assistant on this was now directing Rick Cluchey's productions of *Endgame* and *Krapp's Last Tape*, but as Rick was playing Krapp *and* Hamm Beckett felt it was too much for any one actor to perform.

He said he had given up directing because it was so exhausting, not least because of the preparation time. 'You have to be able to visualise it all in your head, and in order to do this you have to learn the play by heart. This is more exhausting than the ten weeks of rehearsal time. When I wrote *Godot* I wasn't clear where each actor should be on stage. I can see its faults now.'

We talked of the war, he of his time in the Resistance; of the betrayal of his group. 'Suzanne had friends who were Communists. They were very well organized; we were hopelessly organized.' He talked of his escape with

Suzanne in 1940. It was the last time he saw James Joyce, who had eventually managed to procure papers to get out to Switzerland with Nora and Giorgio, but Joyce was unhappy at having to leave Lucia his daughter behind.

He told how Joyce had had stomach cramps and was taken to hospital early one Saturday, to die 'quite unnecessarily' 48 hours later. Beckett had spoken to the doctor who talked of a burst ulcer, peritonitis . . . 'Bad diagnosis, bad treatment. He would have survived nowadays.'

During the war Beckett had carried a little box in which to store tobacco poured out of cigarette ends, which he could then re-roll. 'Tobacco hunger – that was the worst!' he laughed. Francis asked if he could find enough to eat. 'I had to work with the peasants on the land for food.' He had had to spend three weeks in hiding, whilst waiting for the false papers needed to escape Paris, in a room just round the corner from there by the Madeleine.

Paul Léon, Joyce's secretary, left Paris but returned against advice for the baccalaureate of his son. The Nazis arrested him. When his wife tried to visit him and bring food parcels she was forbidden to see him and could only look up at the window where he was being manacled to be transferred into the cattle trucks. On arrival he was dead of exhaustion. 'I knew him well. He was a friend.'

Because Beckett had mentioned food parcels we spoke of my father. He had been a bomber pilot, shot down on his second mission, confined to the prison camps for three years and eight months. Beckett asked whether he had been treated badly, where he was imprisoned, and whether my parents were still alive. They were.

Francis asked if his father had lived until the war. 'No. He died of a heart attack on 26 June 1933. His parting words to me were "What a morning." My mother survived him seventeen years, and she smiled perhaps four times (pause) in that time. She always wore black.' Francis asked if they were close. 'Yes. I have been present at all three deaths – my father's, my mother's and my brother Frank's.'

They talked about Beckett's Uncle Jim and Aunt Peggy, whom Francis had just visited in Dublin. The door had been wide open to the street when Francis knocked, and Peggy's voice had called from upstairs 'Come on up!', not knowing who it was. In the bedroom Francis found a legless man devot-edly being cared for by his wife. (Francis learned from them that it was Sam's financial help that enabled Peggy to keep Jim at home. He did not mention this over coffee, but told me privately afterwards.)

Beckett wanted to know all about the visit; so Francis told him how he had left Jim and Peggy to find the young Irish-language ballad singer Treasa O'Driscoll, who had been acting in one of Francis's plays. She came and sat on the edge of Jim's bed in her green dress, with her long golden hair falling down; and in her clear innocent soprano voice sang 'Una Bhan', Thomas Laidir Costelloe's cry from the heart, as tears rolled down Jim's cheeks.

Dr James Beckett, to give him his full name, had according to Sam not only been a well-known anaesthetist, but also 'Champion Swimmer of Ireland and a great walker on the mountains'. Now 'this stump of a man', may have to lose his arms as well. Jim's brother, Beckett's Uncle Gerald, had also had to have a leg amputated 'due to poor circulation problems and gangrene'. Appropriately the conversation moved to *Endgame*; and from that to chess.

Jack MacGowran played Clov in the first production of *Endgame* that Beckett had not directed. George Devine played Hamm as well as directing the play. 'I was too nervous to be in the audience so I watched it on a video in Jacky's dressing room: and when he left the stage to go into the kitchen he came back to the dressing room and just had time for a quick one (Beckett mimed the drinking action) before (he chuckled) going back on again.'

Francis asked how he had got on with Patrick Magee. He had had to direct Paddie in W.B. Yeats's *Purgatory*, and found it nearly impossible. Magee, however, had been very good on stage in the part of Old Man. Beckett replied that he had written the part of Krapp for him before he met him, having heard his extraordinary Irish voice on the B.B.C. Third Programme.

Beckett's chess-set, a Staunton – a family heirloom – had been stolen from his two-roomed country retreat at Ussy-sur-Marne. Francis had described to me the heavy pieces and leather board on which the two of them had played when Francis was his guest. Beckett told us that he and

Suzanne had bought an empty plot of land there in the early fifties and helped the local mason to build their cottage.

Francis asked if he still used that piano, 'the Schimmel', that they had played Haydn on. 'Look at my hands' he said. The tendons in his fingers pulled inwards deforming the ring finger on his right hand and the ring and middle finger on his left. 'I don't play now. I don't walk as much as I used to.' I said I knew he had taken Francis on long walks, across Paris – sometimes to see the cemeteries – and in the Marne Valley. 'I can't manage it now.' He sighed.

Francis asked if Sam still had the old car, the one in which he had met him at Ussy station when Francis had gone there to write *Emblems* (the play in which Treasa O'Driscoll had acted). Beckett's eyes twinkled. 'Twenty years old'.

They talked of that creative visit, which had clearly been a happy one for them both, with affectionate amusement and quiet banter – mostly about whiskey, a subject on which Francis had made a character speak at length in another play. 'Don't get out there much – not as much as I would like. The car stays there now. I don't drive in Paris any more.' Francis, remembering some fearsome Paris near-misses, replied wryly 'I'm glad to hear it.'

Beckett asked how Walter Starkie was. He used to go to Starkie's lectures in Trinity College, Dublin, and remembers him playing his violin at a Modern Languages meeting. Starkie had been to stay with Francis in Oxford, and talked to his pupils; and Francis had recently stayed with Starkie in Los Angeles – which Walter always pronounced with a hard 'g'. Other Dublin gossip included Stephen, Joyce's grandson, 'only Stephen left now,' and Giorgio.

I asked to be excused for a moment. He looked up anxiously as though I wanted to leave. I explained it was to go to the Ladies'. He graciously stood up and showed me the way and took me there.

When I came back we told him we had been to the bookshop 'Shakespeare and Co.' It was not the original one, he said. Sylvia Beach's original one had been near the Odéon. Adrienne Monnier had been oppo-site. 'I've been there many times.' Francis spoke of what we owe to that shop for publishing *Ulysses,* and the enormous cost. 'They've taken the name but it's quite different now,' Beckett replied.

Francis gave him a copy of the James Joyce book that Beckett had written a Foreword to at his request: *James Joyce: an International Perspective,* edited by Suheil Bushrui and Bernard Benstock (Colin Smythe 1982). The talk led on to Beirut, where Suheil Bushrui had been a Professor, and Francis's visits there before and during the Lebanese war;

how we had been about to go, only to receive a telephone call on the morning of departure that the airport had been bombed. Beckett spoke of the killing of two of the ex-Shah's men by the Khomeni men in Paris. 'Assassins just melt away afterwards. On both sides of the Iraq/Iran war there are fighters of ten years old! We hadn't seen that; even with the Nazis in the Second World War!'

'After the war, in the summer of 1945, the Irish Red Cross tried to set up a temporary hospital at St-Lô [Normandy]. I was an interpreter and store keeper . . . You can imagine what the stores were like!' He chuckled. 'The supplies came from Dublin. This hospital was a free hospital so nobody paid anything for treatment. They just turned up and we treated them. The French surgeons did not like it. They were losing patients. (He gave a little chuckle again.) The Americans had bombed St-Lô flat in the pre-invasion bombardment of '44'.

Finally, Beckett sorted out the bill as we were his guests. He smiled a lot with his eyes, with great gentleness. He was not afraid of eye contact, and wanted to hold it. He spoke of his wife at some length – maybe because Francis had re-married. There was no sense of hurry. He was enjoying this reunion after so long. His face did not seem as lined and severe as in photographs, but he was relaxed, and happy to be with Francis.

It was farewell. After Beckett had paid the bill, Francis fetched the coats. Beckett walked out and we followed him. At the entrance we stood to say 'Goodbye'. He came forward to kiss me on both cheeks, and then did the same to Francis; then turned and disappeared into the hotel as we left through the revolving doors, out into the open, with a warm, happy feeling in our hearts. It had been a perfect meeting; one I shall never forget.

Penelope Warner

Francis Warner as a Musician in the 1950s, by Bernard Martin

From the booklet for Compact Disc OxRecs Digital, OXCD-94, AAD, 2003

KING DAVID

BY ARTHUR HONEGGER

CONDUCTED BY FRANCIS WARNER

in King's College Chapel, Cambridge
on 28 February and 1 March 1958

Reviewing other CDs in this Landmark Recordings series, in May 2001, *Friends of Cathedral Music* confirmed:

> 'There can be no doubt that this was the golden age of sacred
> choral performances in Oxford and Cambridge.'

During the 1950s in Cambridge, Boris Ord at King's College and George Guest at St John's College, and Bernard Rose (from St Catharine's College, Cambridge) at Magdalen College, Oxford, set new standards of musical excellence that are still acknowledged today.

In addition to these choirmasters, there were many outstanding musicians – choristers, choral and organ scholars – who worked with them to enrich this flowering, one of whom was Francis Warner, Choral Exhibitioner at St Catharine's College, Cambridge, founder (with Boris Ord as patron) of the Elgar Centenary Choir and Orchestra, and conductor of the two performances of Honegger's *King David* in King's College Chapel on 28 February and 1 March 1958.

Roger Martin, his Narrator (heard here on this CD), was also an undergraduate, a Mediaeval History Scholar at King's, who had already played Thomas Becket in two different productions by Francis Warner of T. S. Eliot's

Murder in the Cathedral – one in 1954/1955
on tour performing in Southwark Cathedral
and in churches along the Pilgrims' Way,
and the other in Great St Mary's, the
University Church, Cambridge, in February
1957.

   That year Francis Warner also produced
Mozart's *Magic Flute* for the Cambridge
University Opera Group (May 1957), and
in November Elgar's *Dream of Gerontius*
in Ely Cathedral to an audience of over
600. Before going up to Cambridge he had
studied conducting and composition at
the London College of Music, attending
Sir Thomas Beecham's Wednesday morning rehearsals of the Royal Philharmonic
Orchestra in the Royal Festival Hall. Only
six London music students were permit-

Roger Martin as Narrator in King
David

ted to observe (one from each music college), and then only provided they
were silent and Beecham did not have to speak to them.

   While at school at Christ's Hospital, Warner had, in 1954 aged 16, won
the School's Traer Harris Prize for Instrumental Music (playing 'cello, trumpet and organ), as well as his Cambridge Choral Award. He and Martin had

*Francis Warner
playing the spinet*

been trained by the school's legendary Director of Music, Cecil Cochrane: Rev. W. C. M. Cochrane, M.A., Mus. B.. Cochrane in his time had been both a chorister and a Choral Scholar in the King's College Choir, and at Christ's Hospital prepared many, in addition to Warner, for choral scholarships: at King's College, Cambridge, Donald Gowring, John Walker, John Marvin, Christopher Scott, Peter Bingham, Brian Head, and Brian Etheridge; at St John's College, Cambridge, Robert Beers; and at Oxford, Martin Priestly and David Howard at Queen's College, Ronald Tidmarsh at Exeter College, and John Steen at Magdalen. It is to Cecil Cochrane's memory that this recording is dedicated.

Dr Warner writes:

> Arthur Honegger (1892–1955) wrote *King David* in 1921. Many years later he was to recall that the first performances of *Le Roi David* had to be limited to an orchestra of no more than seventeen musicians:
>
>> 'Talking about this to Stravinsky, I told him of my perplexity, and he gave me a very good piece of advice: "Imagine that it was you who wanted this formation of 17 musicians." I followed his advice.'
>
> We know now that this original scoring was for 2 flutes (1st doubling piccolo), oboe (doubling cor anglais), 2 clarinets (2nd doubling bass clarinet), bassoon, horn, 2 trumpets, trombone, timpani, percussion (cymbals, side drum, bass drum, gong and tambourine), celesta, harmonium, piano, double bass (and 'cello *ad lib.*).
>
> Honegger later re-scored the work for full orchestra. As I was unable, in 1958 as an undergraduate, to obtain the earlier scoring, I re-scored the work from the full score to something like the original small orchestra for these performances.
>
> St Catharine's College, Cambridge
1 March 2003

REVIEW

A fine performance of such a work as Honegger's *King David* is
a joy to hear in any surroundings, but last Saturday's concert
in King's College Chapel was an exhilarating experience. Set
under the organ screen in the ante-chapel, the choir sang to a
near capacity audience which from the opening bars to the
final chorale preserved complete silence . . .

    King David was the first concert this year in King's Chapel,
and Francis Warner, who arranged the score and conducted
the performance, is to be congratulated for setting so high a
standard for 1958, and for a truly memorable evening.

Cambridge Daily News, 4 March 1958

Fifty-three years later in a similar work: Francis Warner, not as conductor but as soloist
(Narrator), *in Vaughan Williams's* An Oxford Elegy, *conducted by Roger Allen,*
19 November 2011. The concert celebrated the fiftieth anniversary of St Peter's becoming
a full college of Oxford University

Compact Disc: Francis Warner as Musician in Performance

OxRecs Digital, OXCD–113, Beauty for Ashes, 2012

Track 1.   Arthur Honegger, *King David*, re-scored and conducted by Francis Warner. Live concert recording, King's College Chapel, Cambridge, 28 February and 1 March 1958. A Landmark Recording from OxRecs Digital, issued 2003 (OXCD 94). Two extracts: Part Two in full; close of Part Three. Soprano soloist Anne Keynes, Narrator Roger Martin.

Track 2.   *Variations on a Theme by Francis Warner*, composed by David Goode, and here played by David Goode on the organ of King's College, Cambridge.

Track 3.   R. Vaughan Williams, *An Oxford Elegy*, conducted by Roger Allen. Live recording from the concert celebrating 50th Anniversary of the Royal Charter for St Peter's College, Oxford, 19 November 2011, St Peter's College Chapel. Soloist: Francis Warner, Narrator.

Track 4.   *Anthem for Christ the King*, music by David Goode, text, Francis Warner. Stephen Cleobury conducting the Choir of King's College, Cambridge, accompanied by members of *Prime Brass*, King's College Chapel, Evensong, 21 November 2009, the Eve of the Feast of Christ the King. Organist: Peter Stevens.

Tracks 1, 2 and 4 by kind permission of the Provost and Fellows of King's College, Cambridge. Track 3 by kind permission of the Master and Fellows of St Peter's College, Oxford.

King David, conclusion. Soprano and mixed chorus.

And God said: the day shall dawn
To bring a flower, newly born,
From thy stem in fullness growing;
In fragrance sweet, night and morn,
All my people shall adorn,
    With breath of life bestowing.

Alleluia.

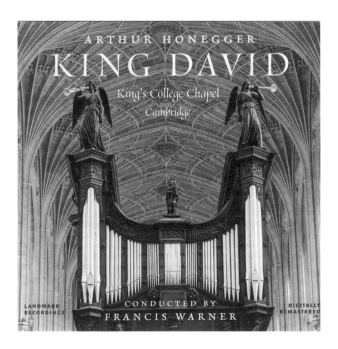

ANTHEM FOR CHRIST THE KING

Not in a crown of gold but with the stars,
With oceans as his coronation drums,
Not in a crown of thorns but lightning's wars
The maker of the universe, Christ comes.
Yet to the heart of suffering he plumbs.
The past torments us, what's to come dismays.
His understanding pity draws our praise.

The resurrected Christ, King of Creation,
Whose flags are branches, coach a donkey's trot,
Who fills relationships with love's elation,
Who chose straw in a stable for his cot,
Answers our anguish as our bodies rot:
'Lord, in your kingdom reach us through our vice!'
'Today you'll be with me in Paradise.'

He turns our royal pageants upside-down,
Subverts earth's power structures into dust.
Blest bride and bridegroom close the General's frown,
For dew of youth lasts not by laws but trust,
And open homes dissolve the beggar's crust.
The margin is the centre. Losing all,
We find grace comes back like a waterfall.

Magnificence, ruler of seas and shores,
Music and joy of life, whose flaming force
Turned timid men into world conquerors,
Your spirit's light reflects back to its source,
Praying within us, healing our remorse.
Come Holy Trinity, your kingdom won:
Lover, belov'd, and love itself, in one.

Notes

Frontispiece. Francis Warner, M.A.(Cantab), D.Litt.(Oxon) Hon. D. Mus. (William Jewell College, U.S.A.) as Pro-Proctor. He was elected as one of Oxford University's two Pro-Proctors three times: 1989–90, 1996–97, and 1999–2000.

Page 7: Dedication. Sonnet, line 1. See p. 14. Published together with *For Molly Linn* p.70, *Epsom* p.70, and *For Miles Hursthouse* p.71, as *Four War Sonnets* in ACUMEN, A Literary Journal, No. 74 ed. Patricia Oxley, September 2012, pp.70–72 ISSN 0964-0304

Friday, 27 September 1940

It was about to get worse in the London area, where Kesselring launched one of his last great daylight offensives on the capital. At 8.00 am the first raid appeared on the plotting tables, and soon the radar screens along the southeast coast showed a number of aircraft approaching on a 50-mile front . . .

Just before midday another 300-strong German force approached London . . .

Patrick Bishop, *Battle of Britain*,
London, Quercus, 2009, pp. 359, 362.

On 27 September there was action all along the front. Groups of [Messerschmitt] Bf 100s and Bf 109s flew over Kent and Surrey to try to exhaust the defences . . .

Stephen Bungay, *The Most Dangerous Enemy*,
London, Aurum Press, 2000, p. 230.

Prime Minister Winston Churchill declared 'the heavy losses of the enemy . . . make 27 September rank with 15 September and 15 August as the third great and victorious day of the Fighter Command during the course of the Battle of Britain.'

D. Wood and D. Dempster, *The Narrow Margin*,
London, Hutchinson, 1961, p. 366.

Page 11: *Armageddon and Faith: a survivor's meditation on the Blitz, 1940–45.* Madingley Lecture, University of Cambridge, 19 February 2011, published by the University of Cambridge Institute of Continuing Education, Madingley Hall, Cambridge, CB23 8AQ, 2011. ISBN 978-0-9564157-1-4.

On 22 October 2011 Warner gave the same lecture in St Martin's Parish Church, Epsom, from his father's old pulpit, but replacing the Cambridge details with Epsom ones. As at Madingley, David Goode followed the lecture with a piano recital in homage to musicians of the Blitz.

> Dr Francis Warner said: The invitation to recall these events has compelled me to turn and face experiences I have spent a lifetime trying to forget: the nights, for instance, when we were bombed out across the road in Church Street, and had to bring our pillows and sleep between these pews where you are now sitting, while Nazi bombers deafened us overhead, and a moving searchlight beam lit up these cold but protecting walls.
>
> *Epsom Guardian*, 24 November 2011, p. 20.

Page 49: *On a Ferry Boat, Summer 1944*, ACUMEN, A Literary Journal, No 76, ed. Patricia Oxley, May 2013, p.58. ISSN 0964-0304.

The intensity of the Nazi onslaught during the summer and autumn of 1944, with rockets by day and bombers by night, can be glimpsed as experienced by Lambeth Palace in a letter from William Temple, Archbishop of Canterbury, to the Archbishop of York on 26 July.

> 'On no night was it possible to look forward to undisturbed rest, and Temple took to sleeping on a sofa in the ground floor passage of the palace . . . He wrote:

> "The flying bombs have been falling rather near here lately: there was one at the end of the garden which broke all our windows on that side of the house and some others . . . but last Friday morning there was one just across Lambeth Road . . . which blew in all the windows facing that way as well as a good many others, and shook down several ceilings; it blasted the back door clean off its hinges on to the ground

and it jammed the front door and the big gates in Morton's Tower so they would not open (that is still true of the big gates) . . ."'

F. A. Iremonger, William Temple, O.U.P. 1948, p.619

My father, Temple's Personal Chaplain, and Vicar of Epsom, took me with him to Lambeth, where the Archbishop was ill, to give my mother respite from me after a near-miss had blasted the windows from our home, Epsom Vicarage. Though my two elder brothers had been evacuated, she still had my younger brother Martin and my baby sister to care for as well as me.

William Temple was my brother Andrew's Godfather, and his wife Frances Temple was my Godmother. In the event of my parents being killed they, who had no children of their own, had agreed to adopt us two. It was therefore an opportunity for Mrs Temple to come to know me a little better.

On the day this sonnet recalls, the only way messages could reach St Paul's Cathedral from the Archbishop was by the river bus. After what we had just been through, my father had hoped this boat-trip might have been my treat.

Page 60: *Blitz Requiem*, ACUMEN, A Literary Journal, No. 71, ed. Patricia Oxley, September 2011 pp.42–46. ISSN 0964-0304.

David Goode, composer and organist (Warner's collaborator for *Six Anthems and other Compositions*, Colin Smythe, 2013) has set *Blitz Requiem* to music for performance by The Bach Choir, conductor David Hill, and the Royal Philharmonic Orchestra in St Paul's Cathedral, London, on 26 September 2013.

Page 65: Remembrance Sunday Sermon, King's College Chapel, Cambridge, 2011.

Page 67: Kitty and Eric Brazier, aged 14 and 9, were also at Sandhurst Road School on that day. Eric relates that:

One block of masonry fell onto my left hand and the side of my head, pinning my hand to the floor, and knocking me unconscious. A moment later another fell onto my left ankle, smashing it.

Another block hit Kitty on the head. She was to die soon after she arrived at the hospital . . . Kitty had been found on top of me, shielding my right side and that was why that part of me was uninjured. That Kitty had given her life for me.

The fighter-bomber, having dropped his [1,100 lb] bomb, immediately began machine-gunning the streets . . .

So why were schools attacked at all – my mother told me six were – when it was obvious they were schools by the children running around in the playgrounds at the time of the attacks?

The next day in a radio broadcast from occupied France, Hauptmann Heinz Schumann of the Luftwaffe, the leader of the [28 Fockewulfe 19DA-4UZ fighter bombers'] raid, described it as a 'merry party', and that 'we dropped our bombs where they were to be dropped'. [*Evening Standard*, 21 January 1943. Also *Daily Mail*, 31 March 2006, 'Questions' page, letter from F. J. Newby of Hexham, Northumberland.]
Eric R Brady [pen-name of Eric Brazier], *Class War*, Chippenham, Wiltshire, Pipers' Ash World Wide, [no date]. ISBN 978-1-904494-84-3.

Schumann was shot down and killed near Charleroi by the RAF seven months later.

Pages 70–71: *Four War Sonnets*, ACUMEN, A Literary Journal, No 74, ed. Patricia Oxley, September 2012, pp.70–72. ISSN 0964-0304. See p.315.

Page 71: Letter to Warner from Miles and Jillian Hursthouse, 2 January 2011. These events are not recorded in Dr Hursthouse's autobiography: Miles Hursthouse, M.B., Ch.B., F.A.C.D., *Vintage Doctor*, Christchurch, N.Z., Shoal Bay Press 2011.

I was interested in your remarks re. W. Churchill – a mighty man – and also note your remarks re. the atomic bombs which ended the war. Those of us who had years of war service (five and a bit for me), especially in the Pacific area, and those who had friends, relatives or comrades killed, tortured or imprisoned, were all more than delighted to get the news. I had a cousin who was a doctor in the NZ Navy and in charge of the Singapore hospital. When invaded, he moved out to the advancing Japanese, surrendered to the head officer, and said he would work to their command and look after the hospital for them. The Officer just had him bayoneted to death on the spot and then did the same to all the patients. I guess there would have been more lives lost if the war had continued until Japan was invaded, and I guess that the US wanted to make sure by dropping the second bomb.

I had a number of mates killed in various world areas, some of them as observers in small Pacific islets were beheaded. Forgive and forget is sometimes difficult! But I make sure that I am always courteous and welcoming to any Japanese I meet.

Page 73: 'Christ's Hospital Three-and-Sixty Years Ago', *The Charles Lamb Bulletin*, New Series No. 150, April 2010. ISSN 0308-0951.

Page 90: Footnote 19. CD: *The Cranmer Legacy 1662–2012: A Celebration of the 350th Anniversary of the Book of Common Prayer*. Choir of St Michael at the North Gate, the City Church of Oxford, Benjamin Bloor Organ, Tom Hammond- Davies Director of Music. Booklet, pp. 16–17, Regent REGCD 389 2012:

'*A Personal Note*, contributed by Francis Warner.

I sang in the Christ's Hospital Chapel Choir for five years, and Vaughan Williams was a familiar sight to us. Even in later life he would enjoy mimicking 'the aloof, faintly adenoidal and precise voice' of his old Headmaster at Charterhouse, Dr Haig Brown; so his ghost will not mind if I tell that when, looking like an over-used back cushion of a sofa, he slumped in Chapel beside our tall, straight-backed Headmaster, whose chin when at rest stayed above the horizontal, we could overhear *our* Headmaster's equally precise, adenoidal, and now proprietorial stage-whisper to incoming teachers filing past his stall hissing: 'Maayeee Composer.'

Vaughan Williams took an interest in our feeble exercises in harmony and counterpoint – 'Your compositions', as he startled us by calling them. We had to reply into his large wooden ear trumpet as, his face turned away, he bent its bowl to us.

He also took a particular interest in the music for our daily services in the huge chapel; so much so that he sent a furious letter to our Director of Music, C. S. Lang's successor, Rev. Cecil Cochrane (or 'Corks') in 1950 when I was a treble. Corks was much loved by us. He trained many of us for the Choral and Organ Scholarships that gave us our Cambridge education. We felt he did not deserve this; and as a result I still have a copy:

```
                                  The White Gates,
                                     Dorking,   SURREY.
                                  20th December, 1950.
        Telephone: Dorking 3055.



        Dear Mr. Cochrane,

                  I was much shocked to see the programme of
        your so-called "Carol Service" on Sunday.

                  There were very few carols in it and only one
        traditional English song which is not really a carol.
        Do you really believe that those English carol tunes
        and words are not worth singing, and that it is better
        to give the boys poor translations of German and French
        originals to sing?

                  It seems to me you have a great responsibility;
        and if you believe, as I cannot help thinking you do,
        that many English carols are beautiful, both in words
        and music, is not it rather dreadful to think that all
        these young boys under your care are growing up without
        a knowledge of them?

                  Yours sincerely,



                  (R. Vaughan Williams).


        The Rev. Cecil Cochrane,
        Christ Hospital,
        HORSHAM.
```

It is not surprising, then, that our interested visitor wrote for us these three glorious compositions, all in D minor, to include the whole school, choir and non-choir alike – 840 boys, and the large teaching staff – in a Morning, an Evening, and a Communion Service.

The non-choir members sang in unison, a melodic line that integrated with the full harmony of the choir. This was not new. Clement Spurling, the Director of Music at Oundle, had led the way; but C. S. Lang built up a large repertory of arrangements to develop the inclusion of everyone, the majority in mass unison, even in some choruses of performed oratorios.

Vaughan Williams published each of these services with the generous caption above the title: 'Written for and dedicated to Dr C. S. Lang and his singers at Christ's Hospital'. As we whole-heartedly responded to them – even if for some boys it was only to join in the colossal noise – he felt they vindicated his belief that the average English boy was musical at heart, if only given the chance to learn to sing.'

Page 95: Footnote 22. Plaque on outside wall of the Music School at Christ's Hospital, inscribed in stone by Lida Lopes Cardozo Kindersley. The words are lines 319 and 320 from Warner's poem 'Oxford', in Francis Warner, *By the Cam and the Isis 1954–2000*, Colin Smythe 2005. The plaque was presented to the school by Madison and Suzanne Murphy, who with Lida Kindersley unveiled it before the Beating of The Retreat, on 30 June 2012.

Page 96: Memorial Service Address: 'Henry the Musician': The Very Revd. Professor Henry Chadwick, K.B.E., D.D., Mus.B., 23 June 1920 – 17 June 2008; Great St Mary's, Cambridge, 22 November 2008. *Peterhouse Annual Record*, 2008, Cambridge.

Page 99: Richard White, b 18 August 1943, possessed what was probably the finest King's treble voice in the twentieth century. He was a treble in the choir from January 1953 – July 1957 (Head Chorister 1956-1957), and sang the treble solo in Mendelssohn's 'Hear my prayer – O for the wings of a dove' with the choir on 4 March 1956, and on 26 May 1957.

Other solos sung by White during his last two years as a chorister were Handel's 'I know that my Redeemer liveth' (*Messiah*), Brahms's 'Ye now are sorrowful' (*Requiem*); and the solo in Stanford's 'Magnificat in G', paired with John Walker, 24 July 1931 – 3 November 1995 (see notes to ll. 204-206), as soloist for the 'Nunc Dimittis'. This performance of Stanford's settings has been re-issued on compact disc: '*Evensong* (1956) Choir of King's College, Cambridge, conducted by Boris Ord,' Decca/Belart 1997, 461 4532 10.

Francis Warner, *By the Cam and the Isis*, Gerrards Cross, Colin Smythe, 2005, *note* to 'Cambridge', l.51.

Page 105 'The Song that is Christmas', *Western Mail*, 4 December 1965.

Page 111: Published in *Lighting a Candle*, ed. J. Carey and S. Overy, London, Temenos Academy, 2008, pp. 201–207. ISBN 978-0-9551934-1-5.

Page 120: 'Lewis and the Revision of the Psalter', *C. S. Lewis and the Church: Essays in Honour of Walter Hooper*, ed. J. and B. N. Wolfe, London, T. and T. Clark International, 2011, pp. 52–63. ISBN 10: 0-567-04736-9. Letter to Francis Warner from C. S. Lewis 6 December 1961:

> The Kilns,
> Headington Quarry
> Oxford
>
> 6 Dec 61
>
> Dear Warner
>
> I've written to the Master of Christ's and sent a copy of my letter to Tom Henn, and I wish you good luck.
>
> Since you ask about myself, the position is that they won't operate on my prostate till they've got my heart and kidneys right, and it begins to look as if they can't get my heart & kidneys right till they operate on my prostate. So we're in what an executive, by a happy slip of the pen, called "a viscous circle." Still, it is not quite closed. Meanwhile, I have no pain and am neither depressed nor bored.
>
> Who is supervising you now? I told them to put someone else on in my place.
>
> yours
> C. S. Lewis

Page 133: *C. S. Lewis Remembered*, ed. H. L. Poe and R. H. Poe, Grand Rapids, Michigan, USA, Zondervan, 2006, pp. 230–234. ISBN 10: 0-310-26509-6.

Page 139: Hugh Wybrew, *Risen with Christ: Eastertide in the Orthodox Church*, London, SPCK, 2001, pp. vii–viii. ISBN 0-281-05343-x.

As in the previous two books, the texts have been freshly translated from the Greek into modern English. Once again I am indebted to Francis Warner, Lord White Fellow and Tutor in English Literature at

St Peter's College, Oxford, now Emeritus, for checking and improving my translations, and encouraging me in undertaking the work.

Hugh Wybrew, *Risen with Christ*, p.3.

Page 141: The Ashmolean Museum, Oxford, will be holding an exhibition of the art of Henry Moore and Francis Bacon for sixteen weeks, 12 September 2013 – 5 January 2014. The exhibition will then travel to Toronto, Canada, to the Art Gallery of Ontario.

Footnote 3. Warner gave Bacon Kathleen Raine's lavishly illustrated *Blake and Tradition*, 2 vols., Princeton University Press 1968 (a boxed set), a work on which Warner had spent much editorial time. See pp. 111–112.

Footnote 21. Melinda Camber, later Camber Porter, 18 September 1953 – 9 October 2008; British-born American artist and writer. See her *Through Parisian Eyes: Reflections on Contemporary French Art and Culture*, O.U.P. 1987, ISBN 10.019504–1046 and 13.973–019504–1040 and the Video Film (VHS) *The Art of Love: The Paintings and Writings of Melinda Camber Porter*, music by Carman Moore. Directed by Michael Camarini, Blake Productions, New York, NY 1993. IBSN 0–9637552–1–8.

Footnote 47. Bacon also asked Warner to invite 'your ascetic archbishop'. Samuel (not Thomas) Beckett, Warner's Paris host, politely declined adding to Warner: 'It's not that I don't know he's a great painter. I had enough of mutilation in the war.'

Page 185: 'The Sorceress', *Temenos 13*, London, Temenos Academy, 1992, pp. 157–173 and 296. ISSN 0262-4524.

The discovery by Warner of the archive of Palmer letters was announced and described in the *Oxford Mail* 8 July 1966, *The Daily Telegraph* and *The Guardian* 9 July 1966.

Page 206: 'The Poetry of James Joyce', *James Joyce: An International Perspective*, ed. S.B. Bushrui and B. Benstock, Gerrards Cross, Colin Smythe, 1982, pp. 115–127. ISBN 0-389-20290-8 (Barnes and Noble) AACR2.

Page 220: 'A Note on the Poems of J. M. Synge', *Sunshine and the Moon's*

Delight: A Centenary Tribute to John Millington Synge, ed. S.B. Bushrui, Gerrards Cross, Colin Smythe, 1972, pp. 141–152. SBN: 900675-55-1.

Page 236: 'Blunden's Pastoral Poetry', *In Honour of Edmund Blunden: The Centennial Celebrations, Christ's Hospital, 8 November 1996*, ed. J.E. Morpurgo, Christ's Hospital, 1997, pp. 22–26. ISBN 0-9507843-5-4.

Page 241: *Andrew Marvell's* Hortus *Translated* was published in *Eleven Poems by Edmund Blunden*, ed. Francis Warner, Cambridge, Golden Head Press 1965, pp.19–20

Page 242: 'Richard Wall: *In Aliquot Parts* — A Rondeau Cycle, Sceptre Press, 1976', *Cross Keys 1977*, ed. D. Nicholls and A. Kennedy, Oxford, St Peter's College, pp. 26–28.

Page 248: 'Japanese Noh Plays and English Drama', *Discourse on Multi-cultural Cultures: Popular Cultures, Societies and Art*, ed. Yuichi Midzunoe, Tokyo, Japan, Taga Shuppan, 1999, pp. 3–17. ISBN 4-8115-5351-9 C-1095. Lectured under the sponsorship of the Japan Foundation at Chiba University on 21 September 1995.

Page 263: Manuscript of Beckett's *Breath*. See p. 261. T.V. Broadcast 14 March 1970, B.B.C.2, 'Review' 9.50 p.m.

Page 264: 'The absence of nationalism in the work of Samuel Beckett', *Theatre and Nationalism in twentieth century Ireland*, ed. R. O'Driscoll, University of Toronto Press and Oxford University Press 1971, pp. 179–204 and 216. ISBN 0-19-690390-4.

Page 264: Footnote 3. Beckett, knowing Warner's poetry, encouraged him as a playwright, e.g. offering to provide the words 'Very interesting and effective – Samuel Beckett' for the poster of *Maquettes*, and also helping discreetly without Warner's knowledge:

> 'Warner wrote heartened by Hobson's article. I hope you'll be able to help [Warner in directing his own plays] in Edinburgh and Toronto. He has it in him I feel.'

Maurice Harman, ed., *No author better served: the correspondence of Samuel Beckett and Alan Schneider*, Harvard University Press 1998, p. 236.

Page 291: Manuscript of Beckett's covering letter for *Sans*.

Samuel Beckett to Francis Warner; Paris, 16 February 1970.

Line 12   O.C. = *Oh! Calcutta!*

22   M.S. Lourenço's Portuguese translation of Samuel Beckett's *Imagination Dead Imagine (Imaginação Morta Imagina)* was published in *O tempo e o modo* (magazine), Lisbon, issue number 71/72, May/June 1969.

Manuel Lourenço, b. 13 May 1936, also worked with Warner translating the opening three paragraphs of James Joyce's *Finnegans Wake* into Portuguese. The fragment was published in *O tempo e o modo*, Lisbon, No: 57/58, February/March 1968, pp 243–244.

Manuel Lourenço's own volume of poems, *arte combinatória*, Moraes Editores (CIRCULO DE POESIA), Lisbon 1971, is dedicated to Francis Warner with the added sentence: 'de quem nunca deixei de aprender Poesia desde que foi meu professor em 1965.'

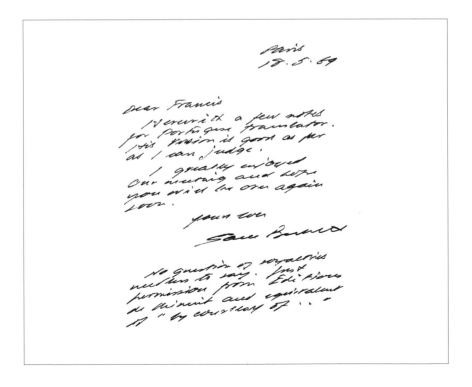

Page 1. Line 3   céu — delete if possible

" 6   pi — " "

" 17   entra — volta a entrar

" 18   morre — baixa, i.e.
Same word as line 20.
Cf. also Page 2 line 20.

Page 2   line 1   a mesma — delete a if possible

" 3   "colonne chaleur" Image
suggested by the column
of mercury that shows
temperature. In the rotunda
the synchronised light and
heat columns rising & falling.
Sense simply "du côté de la
chaleur" "in the case of the
heat". "Perhaps "o che lado
+ temperatura.."

" 5   a experiência mostra-o } throughout
mostra-o a experiência } one or other of these word-orders,
not now one now the other.
Cf P. 1 l. 27 & P.2. l.19

" 20   cf. P. 1 l. 18

" 23   a mesma. Cf. Page 2 l. 1

" 31   negro } one or the other throughout
preto } not now one now the other
Cf. P.4 l. 13
bastante   too mild : far
beyond

Page 3   line 26   "Pour peu que les 2 versants se vaillent"
only the left side (versant) of each
face is visible, the right being against
the ground. If the hidden sides are
up to the standard of the exposed,
then it may be said that the faces
seem to want nothing. English
translation: "assuming the 2 sides
of a piece" "of a piece" meaning
"uniform, consistent with each other".

" 32   Don't understand what difficulty here.
"faites seulement ah; "faith" in the
sense of "utter". Say only a tiny ah be
uttered and the bodies shaken by a shudder.

Page 4   lines 5/6

23   'as I did that of *Imagination*': see manuscript letter from
Beckett to Warner; Paris, 18 May 1969, with Beckett's accompanying
manuscript page of 'a few notes', pp.325–326.

31   Budgen. Frank Budgen's oil portrait of James Joyce. See page
208.

37   Sir Alexander Cairncross, Economist, 11 February 1911–21
October 1998. Master of St Peter's College, Oxford, 1969–78.
Warner had introduced Sir Alec to Beckett in Paris in 1969.
See Alec Cairncross (autobiography), *Living with the Century*,
Fife, Lynx, ISBN 0–9535413–0–4.

Pages 292–298: Manuscript of Beckett's *Sans* (*Lessness*). *Lessness* was first
performed at the Oxford Playhouse 17–20 February 1982, directed and designed
by Lucy Bailey, then an undergraduate pupil of Warner's at St Peter's College.
Warner was a member of her cast.

Page 299: 'A Cup of Coffee in Paris', Penelope Warner, *Oxford Magazine, No.*
308, Second Week, Hilary Term, O.U.P. 2011, pp. 17–19. An abridged version
was published in ACUMEN: A Literary Journal, No. 68, ed. Patricia Oxley,
September 2010, pp. 58–62. ISSN 0964 0304.

Page 307: Arthur Honegger, *King David*, conducted by Francis Warner, Compact
Disc OxRecs Digital OXCD-94, AAD, 2003, pp. 1–4 and 23 of accompanying
booklet.

Index

POETRY
Collected Poems 1960–1984
Nightingales: Poems 1985–1996
By the Cam and the Isis 1954–2000

Six Anthems and other Compositions,
  by David Goode and Francis Warner,
  with compact disc.

PLAYS
Agora – A Dramatic Epic; sixteen plays in fourteen volumes,
in chronological order of action consisting of:

Healing Nature – The Athens of Pericles
Virgil and Caesar
Moving Reflections   } Roman Trilogy
Light Shadows
Byzantium
Living Creation – Medici Florence
King Francis I   } Europa Tetralogy
Rembrandt's Mirror
Goethe's Weimar
A Conception of Love
Maquettes for the Requiem   Trilogy of one-act plays
Lying Figures
Killing Time   } Requiem Trilogy
Meeting Ends